The Sociology of Consumption

The Sociology of Consumption

An Introduction

Peter Corrigan

SAGE Publications
London · Thousand Oaks · New Delhi

SAGE Publications Ltd
6 Bonhill Street
London EC2A 4PU

SAGE Publications Inc
2455 Teller Road
Thousand Oaks, California 91320

SAGE Publications India Pvt Ltd
32, M-Block Market
Greater Kailash-I
New Delhi 110 048

British Library Cataloguing in Publication data

A catalogue record for this book is available
from the British Library

ISBN 0 7619 5010 9
ISBN 0 7619 5011 7 (pbk)

Library of Congress Catalog record available

Typeset by Type Study, Scarborough
Printed in Great Britain at the University Press, Cambridge

To the memory of BW-H

Contents

Acknowledgements

I would like to thank the following for permission to reproduce visual material:

Australian Consolidated Press for the illustrations from feature articles from *The Australian Women's Weekly*, May, 1993, reproduced in Chapter 6.

Continental Brand Soups for the advertisements reproduced in Chapter 5.

RC Roberts Pty Ltd of Bayswater, Victoria, for the tag reproduced in Chapter 3.

1
Introduction:
Advents of the Consuming Society

O, wonder!
How many worldly goods are there here!
How beauteous commodities are! O brave new world
That has such consumers in't!

           – Miranda Postmodern

Although consumption takes place in all human cultures, it is only in the present century that consumption on a truly mass scale has begun to appear as a foundational, rather than merely epiphenomenal, characteristic of society. Where there is subsistence production, there will be subsistence consumption: all that is produced is consumed without remainder, and such items as food and clothing appear entirely plain and functional. It is unlikely, however, that such a minimalist society could exist under anything other than extreme conditions. Production generally implies more than subsistence, and the question of a surplus to be distributed has been rather a contentious one in class societies. Production here becomes subsistence for some but the source of consumptionist pleasures for others, and the reader may recall Marx's outrage at this fact in his writings on alienation (Marx, 1975 [1844]). But now the majority of the populace have access to the ever-growing consumerist fruits of the productivist tree, and so perhaps it is time to stand Marx on his head and claim that consumption, and not production, is the central motor of contemporary society. Competition among status groups, which, according to Weber (1948), are organized around modes of consumption, now seems of more import than struggle among classes, which, according to Marx, are organized around modes of production.

This book begins with a look at the rise of consumption over the last few centuries and its development into an increasingly important component of the ways in which we live our daily lives. The second chapter switches attention away from historical developments towards the more abstract sociological approaches which have tried to make theoretical sense of consumption and consumer practices. The remaining chapters take a detailed look at various specific areas of consumption.

Students of sociology will be familiar with the notion of the Great Transformation, which refers to the large number of economic, political and social changes that accompanied the process of capitalist industrialization in nineteenth-century Europe (Lee and Newby, 1983: 26–39). So if one asks sociologists to locate the beginnings of industrial society, they will probably have no real difficulty in assigning them to the first part of the nineteenth century, or possibly slightly earlier. But if one asks sociologists to locate the beginnings of consumer society, one may get a few puzzled looks. Many may be tempted to go no further back than the aftermath of the Second World War, when the Marshall Plan helped rebuild Europe and an economic boom lasting a quarter of a century ensured that social classes that previously could never have hoped to accumulate much suddenly began to have access to all sorts of goods their parents never could have imagined. The key period here, then, would be the 1950s. But it would be a mistake to assume that consumption had no important role to play before then. Grant McCracken (1988) maintains that the first Elizabeth's insistence that nobles attend at court led inevitably to competition among them to be noticed, and modes of consumption were an ideal way of catching attention. As nobles jostled for position, the consumptionist weapons they used became increasingly subtle and complex, and a class of people began to form that wanted goods different in kind, and not merely in measure, to those desired by subordinate classes. Distinctions could now be indicated through the types of goods consumed. By the eighteenth century, more than just courtiers were engaged in social competition, and so there was a ready market for the great expansion in the availability of consumer goods: ' "luxuries" came to be seen as mere "decencies", and "decencies" came to be seen as "necessities" ' (McKendrick et al., 1982: 1).

Campbell (1983, 1987) provocatively argues that the industrial revolution necessarily entailed a *simultaneous* revolution in production and consumption: just as making money came to be seen as an end in itself, so consumption of goods came to be seen as an end in itself, and both of these represent breaks from tradition. In traditional societies, particular patterns of 'proper' consumption could be learned, but in modern societies a general orientation to consuming is acquired. Campbell contends that, just as the Protestant ethic provided the spirit of production, Romanticism, with its cult of the expressive individual, was central in providing the spirit of consumption. If the working classes were fundamental to the development of production, readers of novels were fundamental to the development of consumption.

Consumption springs from politics: the court of Elizabeth I

Grant McCracken (1988) notes two particularly important moments in the expansion of consumerism in Europe: a consumer boom in Elizabethan England, and an eighteenth-century explosion in the fashionable use of consumer objects such as pottery (Josiah Wedgwood is an important figure here).

Why was there a consumer boom in England in the last quarter of the sixteenth century? Where did this desire to consume come from? McCracken locates it squarely in the attempt by Elizabeth I to centralize her realm. Consumption here flows from the political sphere and not from the desires of the isolated individuals familiar to economic theory. It may seem a little strange to claim that consumption was an instrument of Elizabethan rule – how could this work? Firstly, argues McCracken, the court was to become a splendid theatre of ceremonial and spectacle which would show the world that Elizabeth's rule was indeed splendid. But splendour for its own sake was not the point, for splendour is perhaps the theatrical form of political legitimacy. It is also very expensive, and Elizabeth managed rather cleverly to get the nobility to foot part of the bill. In order to do this, she had first to get them to come to court. Up to this time, the nobility could quite happily spend their days in their country seats, receiving their share of royal goods and favours through various intermediaries. Elizabeth put an end to this, and insisted that everything come directly from her and not through go-betweens. As a result, the nobility had to come down to London and press their case directly before the queen – and if they wanted to get what they desired, they had to take part in the ceremony and theatre of the court. This, of course, was enormously expensive, and thus the nobility became even more dependent upon royal largesse. So Elizabeth not only managed to proclaim her power through the magnificence of ceremony, but she also managed to get the nobles to pay for part of this (McCracken, G., 1988: 11–12).

The second factor is closely related to the first, and concerns the new position of the nobleman. At home in the country, he was indisputably at the top of the local hierarchy and was duly treated as such. At court, however, he was just one nobleman among others. One can easily see the problem these poor fellows faced: how to get the queen to notice them, how to stand out in a crowd. They were driven to further expenditure above and beyond what the queen expected for her ceremonies of royal power, as they wore more magnificent clothes than the next, gave better feasts and more gifts, perhaps built better town houses. In McCracken's words, the nobleman was 'drawn into a riot of consumption' (1988: 12).

Now none of this might matter very much if it had no consequences beyond the immediate bounds of the court – but McCracken shows that it did have broader consequences, consequences on both the form of the family and the form of local communities. Family consumption at this period was not limited to the nuclear core, as would generally be the case today. Rather, goods were purchased with a view to establishing the honour and prestige of the family across a number of generations. One used the goods of an earlier generation to capture and continue their honour, and one bought new goods with a view to increasing the honour both of one's present family and of one's descendants. But the nobleman newly decamped to London was, as we have seen, forced to spend vast sums of money in order merely to survive, let alone prosper, in the competitive consumer hothouse of the court. As a result, he began to spend less for the generation-spanning family and more on himself for the necessities of the here-and-now: instead of the family as basic unit of consumption, the individual became the consuming unit. This notion of the here-and-now is also important, for it marks a break with older valuations of time and the rise to prominence of a new temporal principle. Under the old system where goods were bought for transgenerational family honour, the longer the goods remained in the family the more honourable they became (McCracken, G., 1988: 13). Under the new system of social competition at court, no one had the time to hang around and wait for goods to get older and thus accrue honour and prestige. The old system was turned upside down: it was not the family heirloom with its accumulation of ancient honours that counted, but the new, the up-to-date, and the different. We see here the birth of one of the most important phenomena in all of consumerdom: fashion.

What of the consequences for the local community? It was mentioned above that the nobleman was at the top of the hierarchy in his local area and this meant, among other things, that he was the main channel through which outside resources came into the community. It was through his offices, good or otherwise, that wealth was spread about a little more widely (McCracken, G., 1988: 14). We should not think that the nobleman kept everything for himself and his family, for the concept of *noblesse oblige* meant that he also had duties and responsibilities towards others. But now he was down in London, trying to catch Elizabeth's eye through spending money as if it was going out of fashion – although, of course, spending money was what allowed him to remain *in* fashion in the first place. Clearly, a lot less money was going to find its way back to the local community under these circumstances. Before Elizabeth's clever plan, the nobleman's subordinates would expect that goods would eventually trickle their way down towards them, but this particular warbling brook of wealth was now blocked. If the nobles and their subordinates once lived in much the same conceptual universe of consumption (that is, they more or less agreed on the sorts of goods that were relevant and valuable), they now began to live in quite different conceptual universes – what the noble got up to at court must have seemed very odd indeed to the folks back home. Here, then, we find the beginnings of the division of the world into different consuming universes, a division that has multiplied many times in our own world. As the noble was at home much less often, there was also a growing social distance between the two worlds (McCracken, G., 1988: 14–15).

Despite all of this, McCracken maintains that the nobles still influenced the consumption patterns of their subordinates, although to perhaps a lesser degree than earlier. After all, society was still very hierarchical in the sixteenth century and ruling royal heads had not yet begun to be axed, so the idea that different and more frequently changing modes of consumption were possible began to spread over the social spectrum, preparing various strata, mentally at least, for a new way of living in the world.

From the old to the new: McCracken's account of the end of patina

Consider the following: Rich person A – 'I'm fed up having all this money, it causes more problems than it's worth. I'd like to give it all away.' Rich person B – 'But you've had it for such a short time!' Now most of us would probably interpret B's utterance as a put-down: old money sneering at the pretensions of the new. But surely, you might argue, money is just money: anyone's money is the same as anybody else's – $10 million of old money is worth the same as $10 million of newly acquired wealth. At the risk of offending economists, logicians and mathematicians, we may say that no, X dollars is not the same as X dollars. Why do we make a distinction between old and new money? Old money proves that a family has been successful over several generations, that it has known how to live in a properly rich manner over time and has not lost its wealth. It is secure in itself, and derives high social status from being considered almost naturally rich. These people just *are* rich – it seems to be in the nature of things. Nobody questions their wealth, for their claims to high status appear perfectly legitimate. For the Elizabethans, it took five generations of riches before a wealthy family could be considered 'gentle' (McCracken, G., 1988: 38). New money, however, lacks a track record: it could be gone in six months or a year and could simply be a freakish occurrence. One could put no long-term trust in these people, and the ways they made their money may still be highly visible. They have not yet acquired the fixity of apparent laws of nature and thus their claims to high social status may be built upon shifting sands.

This contrast between old wealth and new wealth is perhaps one of the few surviving forms of a more general process of old/new distinctions that governed social status claims in the period before fashion became dominant. Instead of talking in terms of money, McCracken (1988: 32) talks in terms of the objects of material culture – furniture, cutlery, buildings and the like. These functioned as a means of claiming that social status was legitimate, and they did this by showing signs of age. The more bashed about they looked, the higher in social value they became. They took on a new surface thanks to the knocks they experienced as part of long-term existence, and this new surface was known as patina. Patina showed that the family had owned these objects over a long period and so, as McCracken (1988: 32) puts it, served as a kind of visual proof of status. An expensive plate with no signs of age may prove that one has money, but it says nothing about how good one's family is. Patina was proof against those who wanted to pass as legitimate members of the upper classes without any of the 'proper' claims – it was a defence against money that was new and lacked proper 'breeding'. Patina protected against pretenders.

McCracken considers several ways in which these pretenders to social status could be unmasked and kept at bay, but they all have disadvantages compared to patina. A rather crude approach can be seen in the case of sumptuary laws. These prescribed the proper attire for persons of different social strata, and it was an offence to dress above one's station. For example, only a knight might be allowed to wear fur, or members of different strata might have rights to wear different numbers of colours or different amounts of material. Sumptuary laws were to be found all over Europe, and here are two instances from my own country. An old Irish law used colour in an attempt to make an exact correspondence between social rank position and external appearance:

> The Peasantry and Soldiers were to wear garments of one colour; – military officers and private Gentlemen, of two; – Commanders of battalions, of three; – Beatachs, Buighnibbs, or Keepers of houses of hospitality, of four; the principal Nobility and Knights, of five; the Ollamhs and dignified Bards, of six; and the Kings and Princes of the blood, of seven. (Walker, 1788: 16)

According to an Act of Parliament at Dublin in 1541, noblemen, vassals, grooms and labourers could wear shirts containing respectively 20, 18, 12 and 10 cubits of linen cloth (McClintock, 1943: 67). These laws were hard to enforce, however, and few paid attention to them. Nobody could really be sure whether somebody was dressing above their station or not if external appearance was all they could go on – unless of course they knew the person in the first place. If anything, sumptuary laws might make deception easier, because they were very explicit about what each rank was entitled to wear.

Another way of rapidly detecting pretenders to status is through what McCracken calls the 'invisible ink' strategy. Here, groups make knowledge of certain things central to belonging to that group. So if you want to join a gang but say you like the 'wrong' singer, or painter or novelist, or wear the 'wrong' make of shoes, then you simply cannot belong. This strategy is particularly effective if you do not know what the 'correct' singer, painter or novelist would be in the first place. This sort of knowledge must remain secret to the in-group if it is to function properly as a rampart against unsuitable outsiders who want to become insiders. McCracken maintains that this really only works for closely organized groups with a steady membership, and so is not entirely suitable to a rapidly changing world. Nevertheless, I think many of us in situations such as a job interview would worry about saying the 'right' sorts of things that show we really are 'one of them' and would fit in, but job applicants often do not really know what an interview panel requires beyond the obvious things like qualifications. I recall a long job interview that included candidates taking lunch with the panel. One of the latter remarked to me afterwards that that part of the day was known as 'trial by knife and fork'. He was more than half serious, as table manners seemed to join academic qualifications as a way of selecting a candidate. So the 'invisible ink' strategy may not be as outmoded as McCracken seems to think.

Status may also derive from particular sorts of honours or coats of arms and the like (McCracken, G., 1988: 34). Here such honours are granted by a particular authority, but that authority may find it hard to take such honours back. The disadvantage here, then, is that such honours may not accurately reflect the current state of play in the great game of social status.

Patina overcomes the problems in the above approaches while retaining many of their advantages, which is why it was so important in pre-fashion societies. Patina immediately shows that wealth is old; lack of patina shows that it is new. Where sumptuary legislation depended upon the state to enforce the law, here the local social actor can detect fraud. The 'invisible ink' strategy may also be retained, for those with wealth of long standing may have quite a sophisticated understanding of the nuances of patina, nuances that remain hidden to more recent gainers of riches (McCracken, 1988: 35). Patina may also be quite an up-to-date indicator of status, for previously rich families may be forced to sell their valuable items – it is not the loss of the items themselves that matters so much as the loss of the legitimizing patina that has accrued over the years. With less and less patina-based proof of social status, claims become less and less legitimate (McCracken, G., 1988: 35).

The advent of fashion displaced patina from the central status-control function it fulfilled for so long. Out with the old, in with the new. This, according to McCracken, had several consequences. Firstly, it meant that old wealth could no longer be distinguished from new in many areas of consumption – if you could afford it, you could have it. Secondly, lower classes could imitate upper classes much more closely now that signs of newness rather than signs of age were what mattered – we get what McCracken calls 'an explosion of imitative behaviour on the part of low-standing consumers' (1988: 40). Thirdly, to reiterate a point made above, lower-class imitation led the upper classes to differentiate themselves again, only to be imitated again, and then differentiate themselves once more, then be imitated again, then yet again differentiate themselves – and so on without any apparent limit. Patina today, argues McCracken (1988: 42), is important only to the super-rich. The rest of us are caught up in the status competition based

Table 1.1   *Patina versus fashion*

Patina	Fashion
Favours 'old' money	Favours 'new' money
Proves that wealth stretches across generations, hence: establishes historically grounded legitimacy and prestige beyond current moment	Shows that wealth at least exists here and now, hence: establishes 'punctual' legitimacy and prestige valid only for the moment
Is difficult for competing classes to emulate	Is easier for competing classes to emulate
Provides relatively low impulse to the expansion of consumerism across social classes	Provides relatively high impulse to the expansion of consumerism across social classes
Today is a strategy for demonstrating social prestige suited only to the super-rich	Today is a strategy for demonstrating social prestige suited to all except the super-rich

Source: based on McCracken, G., 1988

around the fashion process. The relations between patina and fashion are summarized in Table 1.1.

Consumption springs from economics: eighteenth-century England

The economic prosperity of England in the eighteenth century opened up the world of fashionable goods to ever more social classes, and it is at this historical point that McKendrick et al. (1982) locate the beginnings of consumer society. The springs of consumption appear to be quite different to the political ones of Elizabeth, and are to be found in economics. As McKendrick suggests, 'the consumer revolution was the necessary analogue to the industrial revolution, the necessary convulsion on the demand side of the equation to match the convulsion on the supply side' (1982: 9). Here we have the beginnings of *mass* consumption as opposed to the *elite* consumption of McCracken's sixteenth century. It took until the late eighteenth century for the idea of consumption as a motor force of the economy to be accepted: 'as the growth of new wants stimulated increased effort and output, improved consumption by all ranks of society would further stimulate economic progress' (McKendrick et al., 1982: 19).

Compared to other European societies of the time, England was unusual because of the relative closeness of social ranks, a closeness that made transitions between ranks easier to achieve than elsewhere (McKendrick et al., 1982: 20). The goods at one's disposal were a convenient index of one's social standing, and of course obtaining the goods associated with a higher stratum was a convenient way of publicly (pro)claiming rank. This appears to have been a realizable goal for many in the England of the period, if not elsewhere in Europe, and so the closeness of the ranks and the possibility of mobility may have facilitated the growth of emulative consumer expenditure. With entire families employed in certain growth sectors, even parts of the working class were propelled into the class of consumers at this period. McKendrick et al. (1982: 23) point out that with many women employed there was also bound to be a demand for those goods that women would once have produced in the home but that could now be supplied by manufacturers. Furthermore, 'With women having command of earnings of their own and access to a greater total family income, one would expect a greater demand for goods dominated by female consumer choice – clothes, curtains, linens, pottery, cutlery, furniture, brass and copper for the home; buckles, buttons and fashion accessories for the person' (McKendrick et al., 1982: 23). Sociological analysis may have had a tendency to ignore the importance of such apparently 'small' things in the past, but we can see that they loom large in both the economy and everyday life: huge fortunes could be made from such small things, and women had more opportunity to create home and personal surroundings suiting their own designs. It may be that female consumer demand played a considerably more important role in the advent of industrial society than has hitherto been suspected, but further research would be required to establish this.

If having the socially 'correct' goods would grant one social status, and if 'correctness' was still set by the upper classes, then classes lower in the hierarchy would imitate as best they could the consumption patterns of the higher classes who, of course, would then change just to make sure a difference was retained. The upper classes made fashion for themselves or followed the court – but what if the tastes of the upper classes could be influenced by something outside of this? Here is where marketing and advertising begin to enter the consumptionist picture. Josiah Wedgwood, owner of Wedgwood potteries in north Staffordshire, deliberately tried to direct upper-class taste through these means, hoping that success here would mean that lower social classes would also begin scrambling for his pottery to prove their good breeding and refinement. In his own words, 'do in this as we have done in other things – begin at the *Head* first, & then proceed to the inferior members'; 'Few ladies, you know, dare venture at anything out of the common stile [*sic*] 'till authoris'd by their betters – by the Ladies of superior spirit who set the ton' (quoted in McKendrick et al., 1982: 110, 112). McKendrick et al. (1982: 100–45) show just how spectacularly successful Wedgwood's approach was.

Other items were also subject to these new attempts to mould taste through the spread of advertising and marketing. The important point to note here is that the hold of local and traditional ways of consuming was being loosened by the extra-local and new ways that were being promoted by all sorts of magazines and salespeople that found their way across the English provinces. Fashion began to draw more and more goods into its mighty maw, and the use-value of an object began to become less important than its fashion value: if it ain't broke, throw it out anyway – we would not be seen dead using it now, for we would lose the social status fashionable goods give us. This, historically, is a new way of looking at goods. Fashion meant repeated purchases of goods, a very desirable state of affairs indeed from the point of view of manufacturers. So fashion affected both more and more goods and more and more social classes: the eighteenth century, then, saw the beginnings of *mass* consumption, as opposed to the elite consumption characterizing Elizabeth's court.

Consumption springs from the heart: Romanticism and the consumer ethic

As interesting and convincing as McCracken's account of the rise of consumption is, he does not really try to get under the skin of the consumer. He remains at the level of political life and status competition. Colin Campbell, however, tries to understand why consumers actually consume in the way they do in a more 'idealist' way. Just as Weber tried to complement Marxist approaches to production by studying developments at the level of ideas (certain forms of Protestantism) rather than at the level of historical materialism, so Campbell tries to approach consumption by exploring the possibility that there might be an ethic of consumption based on particular sorts of ideas of the person. Weber, in *The Protestant Ethic and the Spirit of Capitalism* (1976 [1904]), provided powerful evidence of the role of ascetic Protestantism in the development of an ethic that led to ever more production and accumulation as a duty to God, as an end in itself. He did not discuss consumption in this context. Campbell wants to know if it is possible to argue that consumption also became an ethic, an end in itself, and if so, how? If Weber found an ethic leading to the accumulation of capital for the greater glory of God, can Campbell discover an ethic leading to consumption for the greater glory of . . . what exactly? The individual human person, as it turns out.

A point common to modern production and consumption lies in the fact that they both represent breaks with tradition. What sort of tradition does consumption break with? Traditional consumption is quite fixed: there is a finite number of needs to be filled, and the only wants and desires anyone might have would relate quite directly to this rather narrow sphere. Just as Weber's traditional peasants would regard anyone who worked for more than normal fixed subsistence as rather strange and possibly dangerous to their whole way of life (and they were right), so the traditional consumer would regard with alarm anyone who consumed outside the boundaries sanctified by tradition. Today, of course, matters seem to be reversed – the modern consumer considers with alarm anyone who does not want to consume more and more, who does not seem to be interested in new wants and desires. We've come a long way.

Let us deepen the contrast between traditional and modern consumption. Campbell (1983: 281) argues that the fixity of traditional societies meant that one could learn the actual patterns of consumption – there was quite a limited number of things that entered into the consumer consciousness, and so one could learn the proper modes of consuming relatively easily. But in modern societies a general orientation to consuming is required – what may be consumed is not fixed in number or kind, and may be undergoing rapid change. It is not so much that we desire very particular things, although of course we might sometimes, it is rather that we want to want, we desire to desire, and we want new and different things in an endless pattern of discontent (Campbell, 1983: 282). This wanting and desiring is a process separate from the actual concrete things that might be desired, and is, in fact, a generalized mode of being. As Campbell (1983: 282) puts it, 'The crucial feature of the role of the modern consumer is the primary obligation to want to want under all circumstances and at all times irrespective of what goods and services are actually acquired or consumed.' He further points out that this has nothing to do with human psychology as such (that is, there is no innate disposition to want to want), but has to do with a particular form of civilization. This form of civilization is industrial civilization, which split production and consumption apart in a way unknown to societies marked by traditional ways of both producing and consuming. Consumption in industrial societies is not merely a matter of rational calculation, as an economist might imagine, nor is it a matter of an irrational impulse, as some psychologists might fantasize. Campbell sees it rather as based upon a strong sense of duty, 'an obligation to engage in "want satisfaction" as an end in itself' (1983: 284). There is, then, an ethic underlying consumption just as, for Weber, there was an ethic underlying production. If production can be linked to the Protestant ethic, consumption can be linked to the Romantic ethic. But what did Romanticism bring to the world that made it so important to consumption?

In one of those ironies that history seems to indulge in from time to time, Romanticism actually began as a reaction against industrial society and all it stood for, including materialist and rationalist philosophies and the reason and science that were so important during the period of the Enlightenment. So it preferred feeling to knowing, imagination to the intellect, and the inner world to the outer one. More importantly for present purposes, it replaced the old idea of the individual with a new one (Campbell, 1983: 284–5). The pre-Romantic individual, to quote Campbell (1983: 285), 'emphasized the commonality of mankind, the sense in which all men shared a common status leading to possession of common rights'.

The use of 'man' is not accidental here, for women would not normally have been included in this view of the individual. Although Campbell does not mention this, it is possible that the Romantic view of the individual left some more space for non-male human beings to become, precisely, individuals. The Romantics saw the individual as a distinct and autonomous being – the uniqueness rather than the generalizable side of the individual came to dominate views of what it was to be a person (Campbell, 1983: 285–6). If in pre-Romantic times the individual was seen as linked to society in formal ways and perhaps was an individual only through these links, the Romantics saw an opposition, rather than a continuity, between the two: self and the nasty society outside came to be understood as opposing, rather than complementary, concepts. The individual becomes understood as something divorced from society, and its job comes to be the development of its own uniqueness – this, indeed, becomes a duty. One major way in which it can do this is through the cultivation of more and more diverse experiences, and this generally meant going outside the constraints of society that tried to limit experiential possibilities. The Romantic was duty-bound to rebel against constraints, for only without constraints could individuals freely experience all the world had to offer. This, of course, included all sorts of pleasurable experiences. As Campbell remarks,

What the romantics did was to redefine the doctrine of individualism and the associated idea of improvement or advancement. Instead of individuals improving themselves in this world through hard work, discipline and self-denial they substituted the idea of individuals 'expressing' or 'realizing' themselves through exposure to powerful feelings and by means of many and varied intense experiences. (Campbell, 1983: 287)

The idea was to seek out newer and more diverse forms of gratification, and this was clearly behaviour of an anti-traditional kind. It may also be a little easier now to see links between this Romantic ethic of the experiencing individual and the practices of consumption.

Central to these links is the idea of the self. Notions of self-expression and self-development seem to us now so obviously good things that it is perhaps hard to realize that they are relatively recent concepts. Campbell considers the case of what he calls 'that "specialist of the self", the modern artist' (1983: 288). Artists were happy enough at the overthrow of traditional society, because it meant that they could escape the ties of patronage and experiment on their own. But once these ties were broken, they quickly found that they faced the choice of either producing commercial art for the public taste, thus becoming a slave to public fickleness, or persisting with their experiments and starving interestingly in a garret. They got around this unpleasant choice by coming up with what Campbell (1983: 288) calls the 'expressive' theory of art: artists were not merely engaging in a craft producing work to order, but geniuses whose works expressed their superior sensibilities. The artistic genius did not really exist before the Romantics.

We can see the power this image still has when we are slightly shocked by the fact that painters of an earlier era, like Michelangelo or Rembrandt, routinely used pupils and helpers to do bits of 'their' paintings. We somehow feel cheated of the authentic outpourings of artistic genius because we are so tied to the romantic notion of the artist. How would you feel if, say, Picasso had farmed out bits of his paintings to various pupils: 'Here, you do the red bits, you take care of the greys, you can draw so do a few squiggly bits down here for me, will you please'? The fact that this sort of thing would have been quite normal and accepted before the romantics shows that we really do have quite a different view of what art is for now: the expression of individual genius. The cult of the genius can be seen as a reaction to the dilemmas of industrial society – a genius is about as 'natural' an occurrence as a microwave oven.

But enough genius-bashing. What about this romantic art from the point of view of the consumer? If the consumer of pre-Romantic art was supposed to draw moral lessons from the work (that is, something not really tied to the person of the artist but to more general social meaning), Campbell's romantic consumer was supposed to try to re-create the experiences and feelings of artists as expressed through the work. So one way of attending to the duty of experiencing widely and deeply as an essential element of the cultivation of the self was to consume cultural products in this sort of way. Campbell writes:

> Hence, romantic doctrines provided a new set of motivations and justifications for consuming cultural products, ones which emphasized the value of the subjectively-apprehended experience of consumption itself. When this is coupled with the powerful insistence which the romantics placed upon the freedom of the artist to create without hindrance from any traditional, moral, or religious taboos and

restrictions, one can see how a natural consequence of these new doctrines would be the freedom of the consumer to experience all and any form of artistically mediated experience. In effect, therefore, one of the consequences of the romantic teachings on art and the artist was to provide powerful cultural support for the principle of consumer sovereignty in relation to cultural products; a consequence, which in reality, few of them would probably have approved. (1983: 289)

But cultural products are not just expensive paintings appreciated by an elite audience. Novelists were also artists, and their works were perfectly accessible to the vast 'uncultured' hordes of the rising middle classes. Romanticism, then, could also provide a new way of experiencing the world for the masses. Campbell (1983: 289–90) points out that the novel, because of its form and wide distribution, was one of the most important means by which romantic values and ideas were disseminated. It did not really matter whether the novels passed as high literature or as low literature such as the Gothic novels that were the most popular form in the late eighteenth and early nineteenth centuries: the romantic attitude could be taken to both. He maintains that young middle-class women were the great consumers of novels, and so it was through this group that the romantic ethic was most influentially carried. The pre-Romantic reader read for instruction or improvement, and writings had an uplifting moral purpose, while the romantic reader wanted experiences and more experiences of the novelist-genius, and so novels could logically become quite sensationalist. People were now reading for amusement and entertainment rather than instruction or morals, and this was considered by many to be quite a shocking development (Campbell, 1983: 290). Apart from being accused of spreading immorality and notions of romantic love (which was quite serious, as romantic love based on ideas of the individual was bound to undermine a marriage system based on transfers of property), the novel was accused of creating dissatisfaction in the reader. She was plunged into an imaginative world of apparently infinite possibility, a world which showed up the constraints of her own life and experiences and made her rather unhappy with her lot. As the nineteenth century wore on and literacy spread to the working classes, more and more groups of people picked up the habit of reading fiction and so more and more social classes became discontented with their station and experiences in life. People wanted more and more in order to fulfil themselves, and traditional constraints on behaviour began to seem intolerable. From paintings and novels we can work outwards to all sorts of other cultural products, and thus to consumption of such products on a great scale. Table 1.2 summarizes consumption in England in the historical perspective explored in this chapter.

If for Weber the development of capitalism was tied to inner-worldly asceticism and self-*denying* activity, for Campbell the development of consumerism was tied to consistent self-*gratificatory* activity. Such ethics may appear to be contradictory, but one seems to account for production and the other for consumption: they seem to work hand in hand to produce consumer capitalism as a way of life. Indeed, in his later work of 1987 Campbell

Table 1.2 *Consumption in England in historical perspective*

Motor of consumption	Historical period	Key consuming classes	Key consuming gender	How consumption spread	Author
Politics	16th century	Aristocratic elite	Men	Competitive emulation at court	McCracken
Economics	18th century	Middle classes	Women	Advertising and marketing – emulation of upper-class taste	McKendrick
Romanticism	Late 18th–19th centuries	Middle classes, increasingly working classes	Women	Novels and increasing literacy	Campbell

shows how the Puritan ethic is in fact intimately tied to the new pleasure-seeking activities of the consuming actor. How can this be? We shall now look at his argument. The key concept here is *autonomous control.*

We commonly make a distinction between necessities and luxuries. From necessities we derive satisfaction, but from luxuries we derive pleasure. Necessities may provide what we need for existence and relieve discomfort, but luxuries are the way to pleasure rather than mere comfort. Campbell (1987: 60) remarks that these are in fact two contrasting models of human action: satisfying needs and pursuing pleasures are not at all the same thing. The first relates to a lack that needs to be filled so that some sort of imbalance can be righted, while the second aims to experience greater stimulation. Pleasure is tied to our capacity to evaluate stimuli, so that for example we may gain all sorts of pleasures from thinking about certain foods, but we can only gain satisfaction from actually eating the food. For pleasure, we do not actually have to eat it, although of course we may. So how does pleasure-seeking operate? Campbell contrasts traditional with modern forms of hedonism. In traditional societies, the search for pleasure is the search for sensations. This search applied only to the wealthy elite group whose general satisfactions could be guaranteed – they were not going to go hungry or lack shelter. The scarce commodity under these circumstances is not bread but pleasure dissociated from the guaranteed needs, pleasure as an end in itself. Satisfaction may be obtained from eating a meal, but pleasure comes through the old Roman habit of making oneself sick so that one can eat over and over again. A tidier solution lies in an ever more varied art of cookery (or other relevant arts). But even this has severe limits: 'The sense of taste (which is also the sense of smell), for example, is only capable of distinguishing the four categories of salt, sweet, bitter and sour. Clearly, any moderately powerful figure may soon exhaust the potential for fresh stimulative pleasures which these can afford' (Campbell, 1987: 66–7).

In general, traditional hedonism is characterized by the search for pleasures that are tied to quite specific practices, such as eating, drinking, sex, and so on. A different, more modern, strategy is to look for pleasurable aspects in all experiences. Pleasure in traditional hedonism will be found in very particular experiences, pleasure in modern hedonism can be found in any or all experiences: experience of life itself seems to become the seat of pleasure. But how do we move from traditional to modern modes? The central change, argues Campbell (1987: 69), appears to be the shift from seeking pleasure in *sensations* to seeking pleasure in *emotions* – he sees the advantage here in the capacity of emotion to provide prolonged stimulation that can be coupled with a significant degree of autonomous control. Of course one of our first reactions even to ourselves when we are 'tired and emotional' is to think that control is the last thing we seem to have. Are emotions and control not in contradiction? We tend to see emotions as taking control of us, rather than ourselves as taking control of emotions. Before we can talk of enjoying an emotion, maintains Campbell, it must become 'subject to willed control, adjustable in its intensity, and separated from its association with involuntary overt behaviour . . . it is precisely in the degree to which an individual comes to possess the ability to decide the nature and strength of his own feelings that the secret of modern hedonism lies' (Campbell, 1987: 70).

So we must be able to take a distance from our emotions in order to enjoy them. But how can this come about? Campbell sees the advent of Puritanism as a key event in this context. Although Puritans may have managed to suppress the evidence of unwanted emotion, it would be misleading to think that that was all they did – the capacity they had to suppress emotion could also be used to *express* emotion in a *controlled* way (Campbell, 1987: 74). The Puritan ethic worked against the expression of 'natural' emotion, emotion of the kind that takes us over and controls us, and so it left the door open to the expression of what we might call 'artificial' emotion: we could now express emotions, emotions no longer expressed us. As Campbell puts it, Puritanism 'contributed greatly to the development of an individualistic ability to manipulate the meaning of objects and events, and hence toward the self-determination of emotional experience' (1987: 74). We now had the capacity to take what meanings we liked from various symbols: we enjoy being frightened by horror films because we knew that we had voluntarily chosen to suspend disbelief for a particular period of time. The horror is under our control in the end, so we can be amused by it. So a big difference between traditional and modern hedonism lies in the fact that the former tried to control objects and events in the world in order to gain pleasure from them, while the latter finds pleasure in control over the meaning of things. The modern pleasure seeker, then, can find pleasure in almost anything. This would seem to be necessary in order for the world of consumer goods to appear as the hedonistic playground we take it to be today. The differences between traditional and modern hedonism are summarized in Table 1.3.

In this opening chapter we have looked at the historical rise of consumerism both from the point of view of political and economic developments and from the standpoint of an ethic that produced a peculiarly new kind of individual. In the next chapter we consider some more directly sociological approaches to consumer societies.

Table 1.3   *Traditional versus modern hedonism*

Traditional hedonism	Modern hedonism
Search for pleasure tied to specific practices	Search for pleasure in any or all experiences
Pleasure tied to sensations	Pleasure tied to emotions
Emotions not under control of subject	Emotions controlled by subject
Pleasure derived from control of objects and events	Pleasure derived from control of the meanings of objects and events

Source: based on Campbell, 1987

2
Theoretical Approaches to Consumption

After the historical approach of the introductory chapter, we now take a look at some of the theories that have been influential in the development of sociological accounts of consumption. An important common theme in the texts considered here is the idea that consumers and their objects communicate positions in the social world, and that this is more fundamental than any idea of simply fulfilling a particular concrete need. We begin with Douglas and Isherwood's (1979) argument that consumers use goods to construct an intelligible universe and to make and maintain social relationships. Then we consider Baudrillard's (1988 [1970]) perspective that consumption is something that is tightly linked not to the individual consumer but to the overall economic system as a whole – consumption here becomes part of a communication system, but not one tied to individuals. Next, we concentrate on a specific area of communication, namely the effort to indicate social distinction through the uses of goods. This is central to the work both of the nineteenth-century Norwegian-American economist Thorstein Veblen (1975 [1899]) and the contemporary French writer Pierre Bourdieu (1984 [1979]).

In Veblen's rather cynical view of the world, the basis of one's good repute in society lies in one's pecuniary strength. In other words, one is esteemed in direct proportion to one's wealth, and one is esteemed even more if that wealth was untainted by the dirtied hands of work. Hence inherited wealth has a distinctly more impressive cachet than the millions one may have earned from the fruits of one's own labour. There are two possible ways of indicating one's pecuniary standing, according to Veblen: conspicuous leisure and conspicuous consumption. The latter holds an advantage over the former in situations such as that of the big city and, indeed, anywhere that the cosy *Gemeinschaft*, where everybody knows everybody else, has been replaced by the alienated *Gesellschaft*, where nobody knows anybody else in the whirl of ever-circulating strangers. Conspicuous consumption of goods is an ideal way of displaying one's pecuniary strength to those who know nothing of one apart from what they see. Bourdieu (1984 [1979]) also sees goods as expressive, and he is especially interested in the ways in which different classes use different goods to (pro)claim their places in the social structure. Classes are in competition and goods are the weapons of this competition, so there is a permanent tension between 'distinguished' goods and the popularization which threatens their distinguished status. Goods, then, are involved in endless definitions and redefinitions of social status.

The uses of goods: Mary Douglas and Baron Isherwood

Douglas and Isherwood take a generally anthropological approach to consumption when asking the question: what are the uses of goods? They propose two main functions. Firstly, goods 'are needed for making visible and stable the categories of culture' (1979: 59). This seems directed against the model of the consumer generally adopted in economic thought. For the economist, the consumer is an individual and that individual exercises sovereign choice in fulfilling needs. The economic model remains locked within the individual. Douglas and Isherwood move beyond this to the much more general level of culture. So goods here not only show us what particular social categories are relevant in a given culture, but they stabilize these categories in quite concrete ways. As they put it, 'It is standard ethnographic practice to assume that all material possessions carry social meanings and to concentrate a main part of cultural analysis upon their use as communicators' (Douglas and Isherwood, 1979: 59) – indeed, this is a theme that will recur throughout the course of this book. But goods have another use that is also important: they 'make and maintain social relationships' (1979: 60). Again, this takes us beyond the individual consumer of the economist to a whole web of kinship and friendship – and no doubt enemyship as well, were we to pursue the matter further. In the example given by Douglas and Isherwood, cattle among the Nuer act very directly to link people. They quote Evans-Pritchard:

> The union of marriage is brought about by the payment of cattle and every phase of the ritual is marked by their transference or slaughter. The legal status of the partners is defined by cattle rights and obligations . . . movements of cattle from kraal to kraal are equivalent to lines in a genealogical chart . . . Nuer tend to define all social processes and relationships in terms of cattle. Their social idiom is a bovine idiom. (Evans-Pritchard, 1940: 17–19, quoted in Douglas and Isherwood, 1979: 60)

For Douglas and Isherwood, the essential function of consumption is not to fulfil needs in any prosaically useful way, such as food for eating, but rather its capacity to make sense (1979: 62): it is not so much that food is good for eating, but that it is good for thinking. Indeed, we might say that food of any sort might be able to fulfil our bodily needs, but we know that we do not think about food like this: we do not normally eat human flesh because it lacks nutritional value but because of what it means to us. Some people will not eat kangaroo, again, because of what it means (see Chapter 8). Indeed, Douglas and Isherwood go so far as to claim that

> The main problem of social life is to pin down meanings so that they stay still for a little time. Without some conventional ways of selecting and fixing agreed meanings, the minimum consensual basis of society is missing. As for tribal society, so too for us: rituals serve to contain the drift of meanings . . . Goods, in this perspective, are ritual adjuncts; consumption is a ritual process whose primary function is to make sense of the inchoate flux of events . . . The most general objective of the consumer can only be to construct an intelligible universe with the goods he chooses. (Douglas and Isherwood, 1979: 65)

Different classes, of course, have different goods at their disposal to make their own classed sense of the world, a theme which crops up again with particular force in the discussion of Pierre Bourdieu below.

The system of objects: Jean Baudrillard

Baudrillard (1988 [1970]) is interested in the systematic aspects of consumption, but he does not see consumers as having much hand in shaping their practices nor does he pay very much attention to the empirical level. His main claim is that the explanation of needs with respect to an individual's relation to an object is not appropriate to the understanding of present-day consumption. Instead, needs are related to a *system* of objects: they have nothing to do with particular concrete objects as such, nor with particular individual desires for particular individual objects. How can he argue this, and what sort of picture of consumption arises from his account?

He begins by considering the explanation of needs in terms of the relationship between an individual and an object. Where do needs come from? The *homo economicus* of classical economic theory is somehow ' "endowed" with needs which "direct" him towards objects that "give" him satisfaction' (Baudrillard, 1988 [1970]: 35). Douglas and Isherwood (1979), as we have seen, criticize this because it locks needs into the individual and fails to grasp the social dimension of consumption. Baudrillard's objection seems to be that there is no reliable way of ever being able to specify what these needs might be, although this has not stopped anybody from making up their own lists. Needs seem to be present in a magic sort of way: they just are. If these needs are innate then there is no reason for them to expand. But it should be clear to everyone that what we consider 'needs' today are vastly more complex than what they would have been a couple of centuries ago. Therefore needs must be located somewhere other than in the individual person. Where? In the practices of marketing and advertising, unsurprisingly. It is not a question of the market reacting to the expressed desires – the sovereign needs – of the consumer, it is rather that manufacturers deliberately attempt to shape consumer behaviour through advertising. This topic will be dealt with in more detail in later chapters. As Baudrillard remarks, 'In its tendencies at least, this is a total dictatorship by the sector of production' (1988 [1970]: 38). It undermines 'the fundamental myth of the classical relation, which assumes that it is the individual who exercises power in the economic system' (1988 [1970]: 38). Baudrillard argues that we should not interpret needs simply as the generation of needs by manufacturers for *specific* products. For example, a television manufacturer might want to 'create' the need in consumers for a new television set but this, for Baudrillard, is not the point:

> The truth is not that 'needs are the fruits of production', but that the *system of needs* is *the product of the system of production*, which is quite a different matter. By a system of needs we mean to imply that needs are not produced one at a time,

in relation to their respective objects. Needs are produced as a *force of consumption*, and as a general potential reserve within the larger framework of productive forces. (Baudrillard, 1988 [1970]: 42)

Putting it slightly differently, what happens is not that needs for specific objects are created but rather the need to need, the desire to desire: this is something much more general that can be attached to *any* objects. We become consumers in a very broad sense, not merely consumers of a very particular set of objects: in Baudrillard's words, needs 'are produced *as elements of a system* and not *as a relation between an individual and an object* . . .* needs and consumption are in fact an *organized extension of productive forces*' (1988 [1970]: 42–3). In this perspective, needs have nothing much to do with pleasure and satisfaction – instead, consumption seems to stabilize capitalism.

Implicit in the above is the suggestion that we do not purchase an object because it can accomplish certain things tied to its own concrete nature. Certainly, we do not normally buy a washing machine in order to cook fish. At a different level, however, we may buy washing machines or microwave ovens in order to purchase a certain degree of comfort or prestige. In this light, there is indeed an equivalence between a washing machine and a microwave oven. Here we find ourselves not in the realm of objects so much as in the realm of signs: so consumers consume not so much specific objects to accomplish specific concrete ends, but signs in general for general social ends. Social differentiation becomes the name of the game, and here there is no way to limit needs in any rational-utilitarian manner. As with Douglas and Isherwood (1979), the purpose of commodities for Baudrillard is to communicate: 'commodities and objects, like words and once like women, constitute a global, arbitrary, and coherent system of signs, a *cultural* system which substitutes a social order of values and classifications for a contingent world of needs and pleasures, the natural and biological order' (Baudrillard, 1988 [1970]: 47).

Baudrillard sees consumption as another logical step in the development of capitalism. Consumption deepens labour discipline: under subsistence conditions, one cannot be manipulated by ever-increasing consumptionist demands and so cannot be exploited as a force of consumption. Beyond subsistence, however, consumption forces people into an economizing and controlled labour force if they want to be able to live as proper consumers. So exploitation and control now take place not only in the area of production, but also in the area of consumption. Rather than seeing consumption as the free play of consumer desires, Baudrillard here sees it as yet another area of life to be controlled by the productive system: not the site of freedom, but the locus of deepened dependence. He maintains that what is happening with consumption is just the next logical step after what happened in the nineteenth century. Then, rural populations had to be brought into the conditions of industrial labour, which meant that they had to be socialized into completely new and differently disciplined ways of acting and thinking:

The same process of rationalization of productive forces, which took place in the nineteenth century in the sector of *production*, is accomplished, in the twentieth century, in the sector of *consumption*. Having socialized the masses into a labour force, the industrial system had to go further in order to fulfil itself and to socialize the masses (that is, to control them) into a force of consumption. (Baudrillard, 1988 [1970]: 50, italics in original)

That is, 'Production and Consumption are *one and the same grand logical process in the expanded reproduction of the productive forces and of their control*' (ibid., italics in original). So not only do you serve the system by producing, you also serve it by consuming.

Now that we have established the notion that consumption is essentially communication, let us look at how it communicates social distinction.

Establishing distinction 1: Veblen

Thorstein Veblen's *Theory of the Leisure Class* of 1899 is the first major contribution to the literature on consumption. One Veblenian question that could be asked is: what lies at the basis of social honour, social prestige, social status? (I use these terms interchangeably in this context.) Veblen's simple, if rather cynical, answer is: wealth. In other words, the possession of wealth can grant us social currency of a more important kind than mere dollars. The reader may think this superficial as well as cynical, and of course there are many moral tales that seem to say that there are more important things than material wealth. Veblen might say that such tales exist only to make the unwealthy feel a little better about themselves in a world where social prestige comes gift-wrapped in $100 bills. But let us persist with this cynical approach, and see if it allows us to understand anything about society.

If one possesses wealth and desires social honour, it follows that one must *demonstrate* that one is wealthy. Think of the odium heaped upon the figure of the miser: why do we react so negatively to such a person? One reason might be that the miser does not re-invest wealth in a productive manner, and is thus acting irresponsibly with the wealth given into his or her charge. That could be a puritan objection. But it might also be possible to think ill of misers because they do not spend on consumption either: no nice new clothes, no extravagant meals, no exotic holidays – and it's never their turn to buy a drink. There seems to be little honour in being mean either to oneself or to others. So whether we look at the matter from the point of view of production or consumption, the miser still cuts a poor figure. From a Veblenian point of view, the miser fails to demonstrate wealth and therefore fails to attain social honour. The miser is undoubtedly an ignoble character in this perspective. The question then becomes, rather obviously: how does one demonstrate that one has wealth so that all can see and, consequently, admire? Veblen identifies two main ways in which this aim can be accomplished. The first refers to conspicuous leisure and the second to conspicuous consumption.

Conspicuous leisure should not be confused with enforced leisure, a fact recognized ironically by the man on the dole queue who described himself as a 'gentleman of leisure'. Veblen writes that, in the period before industrialization came to dominate almost everyone's lives, 'a life of leisure is the readiest and most conclusive evidence of pecuniary strength, and therefore of superior force; provided always that the gentleman of leisure can live in manifest ease and comfort' (Veblen, 1975 [1899]: 38). In particular circumstances conspicuous leisure is the most efficient way of demonstrating wealth and thereby claiming status. A central question to ask, then, is: given many different social systems, what is the most efficient way of demonstrating wealth in a particular system? This indicates that while wealth-demonstration is the fundamental phenomenon for Veblen, the actual form that wealth-demonstration takes is likely to vary across social systems. In the early period of which he is writing here, he remarks that 'Conspicuous abstention from labour ... becomes the conventional mark of superior pecuniary achievement and the conventional index of reputability' (Veblen, 1975 [1899]: 38). Non-abstention from labour has the reverse effect. He goes even further: 'Abstention from labour is not only a honorific or meritorious act, but it presently comes to be a requisite of decency' (1975 [1899]: 41). Labour is dishonourable and indicates social indecency. Honourable occupations include 'government, wars, sports, and devout observances' (1975 [1899]: 40) – these may have involved great effort, but they were not intended to further productive labour. A trace of this sort of distinction can still be seen in the realms of sport: it is not so long since the 'players versus gentlemen' distinction in tennis and cricket divided the world into the amateur and hence honourable gentleman and the professional but therefore dishonourable player. For the former, sport was a leisure pursuit; for the latter, it was a way of earning a living. Socially speaking, then, participating in the same sport – indeed, in exactly the same game and on the same team – could mean very different things. Of course, participating in different sports is another way of accomplishing the same sort of distinction: the working class may be able to play soccer, but polo may be financially beyond their means.

Veblen's leisure class would avoid anything to do with productive labour, and so occupied themselves with things that did not produce anything intrinsically useful. The leisure time they did not spend in front of others proving that they did not have to work was still put to good use by being devoted to pursuits that could later clearly demonstrate that they did not have to work. Knowledge of good manners and etiquette is important here, and a breach of decorum can lead one to be judged an unworthy human being, definitely not someone who can use time in a gloriously unproductive manner. If you spent your time learning dead languages and dabbled in the occult sciences then you could fairly clearly show that you did not spend your time in industrial employment. It is thus not at all strange to learn dead languages, for from the point of view of social honour the dead are far more valuable than the living. Learning economically important modern languages might show evidence of vocational, and therefore disreputable, inclinations, so learning ancient Greek is a much safer thing to do. Before you think that I have become just as cynical as Veblen, try to apply these distinctions to, say, the difference between education and training. Is there a difference between describing someone as 'a well-educated person' (non-vocational) and a 'well-trained person' (vocational)? Is this the same as the distinction between those who think and those who do, between conception and execution? Can these not be mapped on to social honour in different ways?

One can expand one's prestige by being able to support more and more people who produce nothing – so if one has lots of servants with no productive tasks to accomplish, then one will be very honoured indeed. These sorts of servants will be kept close to the body of the master the better to set off his superior status, while servants who do the dirty productive work will be kept out of sight. Veblen argues that this tendency begins with the exemption from productive labour of the wife, or the chief wife, and spreads outwards. All of these people display the ability of the master to pay – that appears to be their main function. They waste time conspicuously on his behalf. They may actually be very busy indeed, but not with types of work considered demeaning labour. So Veblen can quite sensibly claim that 'the labour spent in these services is to be classed as leisure; and when performed by others than the economically free and self-directing head of the establishment, they are to be classed as vicarious leisure' (Veblen, 1975 [1899]: 59). The leisure of the servant is not the servant's, but belongs to the master. An unskilled servant is not much good here either – more time and money should be seen to have been spent in training the servant in all the niceties of the job, because a master's pecuniary standing can clearly be read from the skills (or lack of them) of the servant. This resembles the patina discussed in Chapter 1 in that it provides evidence of time – perhaps it could be called 'temporal capital'.

Conspicuous leisure is not the only way in which one's ability to pay may be declared to the world. One may attain the same goal through the conspicuous consumption of goods, and this has its advantages in a society such as our own where pretty much everybody has to work for a living and a leisure class such as we have just been considering seems to have shrunk to the realms of the super-rich. Just as the unproductive consumption of time is honourable, so too is the unproductive consumption of goods. In Veblen's model, consumption of goods by the lower classes is supposed to be merely for their continued reproduction, while only the upper classes can consume for reasons that go far beyond subsistence, consuming conspicuously in order to indicate their qualities to the world. Certain sorts of activities, foods, clothes or drink are reserved for the conspicuously consuming classes. Indeed, as Veblen writes,

> Drunkenness and the other pathological consequences of the free use of stimulants therefore tend in their turn to become honorific, as being a mark, at the second remove, of the superior status of those who are able to afford the

indulgence. Infirmities induced by over-indulgence are among some peoples freely recognized as manly attributes. (Veblen, 1975 [1899]: 70)

Gout was worn (or borne) as a badge of honour. These 'symptoms of expensive vice' (1975 [1899]: 71) may be less prestigious than they once were when only the rich could afford them, but Veblen maintains that there is a continued tendency to look relatively indulgently upon wealthy men who engage with such things and relatively indulgently upon 'women, minors, and inferiors' (ibid.) who do the same.

The more society enriched itself, the less simple consumption alone could indicate one's pecuniary standing. As more and more classes could actually engage in consumption, it became essential to be able to show that one consumed in a manner that left no doubt about one's ability to pay. Here, one had to be able to afford to spend the time in learning how to consume in a conspicuously impressive way. Veblen writes that the

> cultivation of the aesthetic faculty requires time and application, and the demands made upon the gentleman in this direction therefore tend to change his life of leisure into a more or less arduous application to the business of learning how to live a life of ostensible leisure in a becoming way. Closely related to the requirement that the gentleman must consume freely and of the right kind of goods, there is the requirement that he know how to consume them in a seemly manner. (Veblen, 1975 [1899]: 74–5)

So to consume correctly in this perspective is to demonstrate that one has had the leisure to learn the appropriate ways.

Just as conspicuous leisure can be used to gain greater prestige by extending it to other persons, such as wife or servants, who then vicariously consume time in an unproductive manner for the glory of the master, so is it also possible to extend the consumption of goods from the master himself to these others. Servants, for example, might be clothed in expensive liveries and wives and daughters dressed even more expensively – we shall return to this last point in Chapter 11. But one can also throw a party, at which the guests consume vicariously of the host's wealth in the shape of, principally, food and drink, or give presents. The party or the ball demonstrates quite clearly the person's ability to pay to those who might be rivals for prestige. It is easy to see how such things as parties and balls can be used as weapons against others in the effort to show that one is more honourable than the next. This is not to say that they do not fulfil other social functions, such as solidarity and recreation, but they can also serve an invidious purpose.

Even in Veblen's day, the time of the domestic servant was drawing to an end as more and more attractive employment opportunities were opening up to working-class people, and the growing middle class was not really rich enough to sustain servants. In these circumstances, says Veblen, 'the duties of vicarious leisure and consumption devolve upon the wife alone' (1975 [1899]: 80–1). Here we come across what he is pleased to call a 'curious inversion'. The head of the household cannot pretend to leisure, being forced to engage in labour that brings in money. But vicarious leisure and vicarious consumption still continue, and that is the job of the wife: 'It is by no means an uncommon spectacle to find a man applying himself to work with the utmost assiduity, in order that his wife may in due form render for him that degree of vicarious leisure which the common sense of the time demands' (Veblen, 1975 [1899]: 81). Face and honour are saved in this way. Those who proudly claim that 'my wife does not have to work' mean that she works at displaying the wealth of the husband through consuming time and goods on his behalf. That is not at all the same as consuming them on her own behalf. The same may be said of children – and maybe of the dog, for those who dress it up in the latest canine fashions. The principle of demonstrating unproductive use still continues.

As feudal society with its rigid separation of classes gave way to the more fluid model of bourgeois society, the upper classes could be seen as setting the standards to which the rest of society aspired. So consumption patterns in general became increasingly pale imitations of upper-class ways of doing things as one descended the social scale. The lower one goes the less likely that one can use leisure as a way of attaining honour, and so the consumption of goods becomes the principal way in which people display their wealth and hence their honour. As Veblen writes:

> No class of society, not even the most abjectly poor, forgoes all customary conspicuous consumption. The last items of this category of consumption are not given up except under stress of the direst necessity. Very much of squalor and discomfort will be endured before the last trinket or the last pretence of pecuniary decency is put away. (Veblen, 1975 [1899]: 85)

To be a social being, then, appears to entail conspicuous consumption of some kind: all societies must provide what a strict moralist might consider waste – waste of time and/or waste of goods, for that is how one attains social honour. A similar point is made in *King Lear* (II, iv):

> O, reason not the need: our basest beggars
> Are in the poorest thing superfluous:
> Allow not nature more than nature needs,
> Man's life is cheap as beast's

This implies that only a bestial life can be led by those who cannot have more than the minimum necessary for existence. It will be interesting to see if ecological myths of living in harmony with nature eventually come to grief on this principle of necessary waste, or if the problem might be solved by a shift from conspicuous consumption of goods back to conspicuous consumption of leisure.

But let us return to the more familiar territory of complex industrial societies. Consumption eventually becomes more important than leisure for the display of one's pecuniary standing. Why is this? Leisure works as a way of attaining honour in small societies where everyone knows everyone else, but conspicuous consumption comes into its own in large societies of strangers, where it is a much more efficient communicator of pecuniary standing. It is not difficult to see that those living in cities will need to

Table 2.1   *Methods of demonstrating wealth and claiming status*

Conspicuous leisure	Conspicuous consumption
Unproductive consumption of time	Unproductive consumption of goods
Suited to smaller, less developed societies of non-strangers	Suited to larger, more developed societies of strangers
Upper-class strategy	Middle- and lower-class strategy
Feudalism [and future 'green' society?]	Capitalism

Source: based on Veblen, 1975 [1899]

consume more conspicuously than those in the country, for they have far more strangers to impress. The differences between conspicuous leisure and conspicuous consumption are summarized in Table 2.1.

Veblen provides a subsidiary explanation for the decline of leisure and the rise of consumption as the royal road to social honour, namely what he calls 'the instinct of workmanship' (Veblen, 1975 [1899]: 93). This is contradictory to the law of conspicuous waste, and refers to a tendency to look positively on productive efficiency and use. It then becomes shameful to be doing absolutely nothing. This may, however, be restricted to classes that see it as in their interest to replace one principle of social honour with another, and indeed Veblen admits that 'Ostensibly purposeless leisure has come to be deprecated, especially among that large proportion of the leisure class [of] plebeian origin' (Veblen, 1975 [1899]: 95). The only real effect of this principle seems to have been to force people of the leisure class to pretend that they are engaged in useful employment, even if they are not. But if Veblen had pushed this point a bit more he might have been in a position to sketch a struggle over the very grounds of reputability. Instead, he tends to assume that all classes want to emulate higher classes, rather than that they might live according to different and competing principles. The model of society at work here is clearly consensual: all agree that reputability rests upon some sort of wasteful expenditure. The work of Pierre Bourdieu, to which we now turn, is distinctly more sophisticated, but still in the broad Veblenian tradition.

Establishing distinction 2: Bourdieu

Where much of Veblen's work remains at the level of plausible and interesting theory, Bourdieu (1984 [1979]) examines the links between social class and the practices of consumption in a detailed and empirical way. In this chapter, however, we intend to remain at an essentially theoretical level. One of Bourdieu's most useful innovations is perhaps the distinction he draws between two types of capital. Normally when we think of capital we think of economic capital only – but Bourdieu argues that there is another sort of capital, a capital that itself can sometimes be converted into economic capital and at other times act in opposition to it. This second kind of capital is known as cultural capital. Cultural capital can be likened to something that we have already met in Veblen: the idea that it is not enough merely to consume, but one must consume in a proper and seemly manner, this manner having been attained through an expenditure of time and money on such unproductive matters.

For Bourdieu, time and money are also involved in cultural capital, and a key concept here is that of education. The longer one has attended educational institutions and the more elite these institutions are considered to be, the higher one's store of cultural capital. It is possible to combine these two different sorts of capital, so that, to mention the four main possibilities, certain social groups will be (1) high in both economic and cultural capital; (2) high in economic but low in cultural capital; (3) low in economic capital but high in cultural capital; (4) low in both economic and cultural capital. Groups can also combine all sorts of intermediary amounts, and so it is possible to place social groups in a map of social space according to their peculiar combinations of the two types of capital. Bourdieu (1984 [1979]: 128–9) does just that for the various groups one finds in French society. Indeed, he takes two different things – the space of social positions that we have just been discussing and the space of lifestyles – and superimposes the map of one on the map of the other. This enables us to see how particular sorts of lifestyle characterize particular social groups. We probably know that in an intuitive way already, but Bourdieu provides the details. It is not simply that preferred drinks move from ordinary red wine, to beer, to sparkling white wine, to mineral water, to whisky and finally up to cocktails as one ascends from low to high economic capital, or that preferred composers move from Bizet and Tchaikovsky to Ravel and Stravinsky as we move from low cultural to high cultural capital while keeping economic capital steady, or to Xenakis, Webern and Boulez where both forms of capital are high, but rather that each social position has a whole combination of specific cultural practices associated with it. So for example those high in cultural and fairly high in economic capital will prefer paintings by Warhol, *and* music by the above-mentioned Xenakis, Boulez and Webern, *and* they will frequent Left Bank art galleries *and* avant-garde festivals, *and* eat in Chinese restaurants *and* listen to France-Musique (the French equivalent of BBC Radio 3) *and* like to read political or philosophical essays, *and* take *Le Monde* as their newspaper; while those lowish in both capital forms might like the idea of going on a picnic, listening to the popular station Radio Luxembourg, playing music by Charles Aznavour or Johnny Hallyday, reading love stories, and taking *Le Parisien Libéré* (a tabloid newspaper).

One thing that might be becoming clear now is that different social groups appear to live in different but consistent worlds of specific combinations of cultural practices – they can all be mapped according to Bourdieu's concepts, but they also strike one as almost self-contained worlds that continually create a particular sense of reality through particular combinations of things to consume and, presumably, ways of consuming them. Let me give an example of the feeling that a particular social world is created by reading a particular newspaper. Before I moved to Australia I worked at Keele University in the northern part of the English Midlands. I and everybody I knew there read the *Guardian* or the *Independent* newspaper on a more or less daily basis – if someone did not, I probably would have considered them strange and to be avoided. But any time I took the train to London I would be surrounded by readers of the *Daily Telegraph*, and would actually be slightly shocked that such people could exist and, worse, share the same train carriage. A certain newspaper was so much a part of the construction of my social world that I had great difficulty in coming to terms with the fact that other newspapers could construct other social worlds. Now if you add in all the other things that would be consumed in different ways as parts of the world of *Guardian* readers and *Daily Telegraph* readers, then you will see that many different practices conspire together to produce worlds that appear perfectly real and consistent and apparently the only legitimate world to the people involved. These worlds that actually depend upon highly specific combinations of cultural and economic capitals appear perfectly natural to those who belong to them. Different social groups are at ease within different economico-cultural combinations, and will feel very awkward outside them. A new acquaintance who asks you a question such as 'So what sorts of music do you like, then?' is probably looking for the key to unlock your position in social space. If you know the sort of music someone likes then you may well be in a position to know about their other cultural practices, because, as we have seen, such practices do not occur as isolated events but fit into more or less coherent combinations of practices. The reader may wish to reflect on their own techniques for placing new people in social space – what exactly do you draw upon in order to do this?

These combinations, as Bourdieu writes, 'allow the most fundamental social differences to be expressed' (1984 [1979]: 226) through the ways in which they differ from each other. In other words, each act of consumption reproduces social difference. So why is the consumption of some goods considered a sign of distinction and the consumption of others a sign of a lack of social distinction? Why is it that, given the choice between Bach's *Well-Tempered Clavier*, Gershwin's *Rhapsody in Blue*, and Strauss's *Beautiful Blue Danube*, not a single worker will choose the Bach, 20.5 per cent will choose the Gershwin and 50.5 per cent will choose the Strauss, while 33.5 per cent of the higher professions and artistic producers prefer to be well-tempered, 12 per cent rhapsodic, and not one wants to splash about in the river? (Bourdieu, 1984 [1979]: 17). Indeed as one goes up the social class ladder one finds quite an even climb in the percentage of Bach-fanciers and a generally even descent in the percentage of Straussians. Gershwin scored best in the middle classes, tapering off in the lower- and upper-class ranges. The profit in distinction, as Bourdieu calls it, is 'proportionate to the rarity of the means required to appropriate' (1984 [1979]: 228) various cultural products. He writes that 'Cultural objects, with their subtle hierarchy, are predisposed to mark the stages and degrees of the initiatory progress which defines the enterprise of culture ... it leads from the "illiterate" to the "literate", via the "non-literate" and "semi-literate", or the "common-reader" . . . to the truly cultivated reader' (Bourdieu, 1984 [1979]: 229). The cultivated reader is the only one with the means to appropriate 'difficult' art, the one who can claim to appreciate refinements and subtleties. In this way, certain sorts of art are constructed as 'high', others as 'low', and others as 'middle' by those whose claim to legitimacy rests on the years of education (formal and informal) that they have spent in obtaining this knowledge. Education grants one aestheticizing capabilities, so that one learns to take a contemplative, evaluative distance from things. Bourdieu sees this as the Kantian aesthetic, if we may launch into philosophy for a moment. What is the Kantian aesthetic? Daniel Miller puts matters very clearly:

> The Kantian aesthetic is one of refusal, a forgoing of the immediate pleasure of the sensual and the evident in favour of a cultivated and abstracted appropriation through an achieved understanding. It therefore tends towards a rejection of representation of the signified or naturalistic, in favour of the principles of convention, the esoteric and formal. The overt display of wealth and consumption by Veblen's leisure class is challenged by a more subtle, detached and inconspicuous form to be appreciated only by those sufficiently cultivated or civilized. It is an aesthetic clearly expressed in the cool, detached and 'difficult' forms of modern art. (Miller, D., 1987: 149)

And if there is a Kantian aesthetic, there must be an anti-Kantian aesthetic. But what is this exactly? Miller again:

> [The anti-Kantian aesthetic] is the aesthetic of popular culture, a preference for immediate entertainment, pleasure, the gut feeling, a regard for the sensual and the representational. Here, it is the substance and the signified which are of importance. A telling illustration resulted from questions concerning suitable subjects for photography. The Kantian perspective prefers cabbages and a car crash, the anti-Kantian favours sunset and first communion (Bourdieu, 1984 [1979]: 34–41). For the former, beauty is created through the mode of representation; for the latter it is inherent in the subject. (Miller, D., 1987: 150)

So an increase in cultural capital is likely to foster a Kantian approach to objects in the world, while those low in such capital will tend to opt for the

Table 2.2   *Kantian and anti-Kantian aesthetics*

Kantian aesthetic	Anti-Kantian aesthetic
Higher cultural capital	Lower cultural capital
Elite culture	Popular culture
Cultivated, abstracted appropriation	Immediate pleasure
Mind-centred (understanding)	Body-centred (sensuality)
Representation as convention, esoteric, formal	Representation as naturalistic
Subtle, detached, inconspicuous form of display readable only by those sufficiently cultivated or civilized	Overt display of wealth and consumption readable by anyone
Preferred photos: cabbages and car crash	Preferred photos: sunset and first communion

Source: based on Miller, D., 1987

anti-Kantian aesthetic of the immediate, the sensual and the representational. Clearly, these opposed aesthetics mean that goods and cultural matters generally will be consumed in quite different manners, manners which will class the consumers in an unambiguous way. Table 2.2 presents a summary of the characteristics of Kantian and anti-Kantian aesthetics.

High cultural capital is relatively rare, and this rarity needs to be protected. The argument here will be familiar: if a group's exclusive objects, qualifications and cultural practices begin to become accessible to other groups (through, say, increased opportunities for education, more money, or the drop in price of hitherto expensive goods) then they will have to be changed in order to retain the distinguishing distance. There is also, of course, the struggle over which is the more appropriate basis for distinction: cultural capital or economic capital. This characterizes struggles within the dominant class, which Bourdieu sees as divided into the dominant fraction of the dominant class, which is based upon economic capital, and the dominated fraction of the dominant class, which is based upon cultural capital. So it should be clear why academics, artists and intellectuals like to despise the taste of those who have merely money: it is part of the struggle to establish the legitimacy of one's claims to distinction. In mid-position in the social game are the new petty bourgeoisie, a class Featherstone (1991a) discusses in a Bourdieu-esque manner. They both popularize ideas developed by intellectuals and the avant-garde, and also, as Featherstone puts it,

> act as cultural entrepreneurs in their own right in seeking to legitimate the intellectualization of new areas of expertise such as popular music, fashion, design, holidays, sport, popular culture, etc. which increasingly are subjected to serious analysis. Here it is not a question of the new petite bourgeoisie promoting a particular style, but rather catering for and promoting a general interest in style itself, the nostalgia for past styles, the interest in the latest style. (Featherstone, 1991a: 91)

Colonizing new areas for intellectual work is a way of claiming distinction that hitherto could be attained only by becoming an expert in high culture, so this is one way the petty bourgeoisie could gain cultural capital that might otherwise be denied them. Perhaps we could say that they are trying to apply the Kantian aesthetic to areas that have hitherto not had this privilege. Of course, they will have a struggle to convince the world that what they are doing is indeed a legitimate pursuit, particularly those classes that see high culture as the only culture worthy of attention. Their interest in style means that they are likely to be avid consumers of the constantly changing.

But how is it that whole classes seem to go in droves for particular sorts of objects and practices and avoid others? How is it that particular sorts of objects become 'right' for particular groups without anyone actually having to think much about the matter? It is not that the whole world can be classed in a very simple manner into sophisticated Kantians and unsophisticated anti-Kantians – there are many different degrees of distinction. Even if we all shared a Kantian aesthetic, we would not all fall in love with exactly the same objects. Other social attributes come into play. Bourdieu argues that there is a homology between the fields of production and consumption which leads to an objective orchestration of the two. Similar divisions are at work within the field of production and social class generally, even if they are not *directly* connected (that is why he refers to homologies). He takes the example of fashion (Bourdieu, 1984 [1979]: 233), arguing that there is an objective orchestration of the logic of the struggles internal to the field of production with the logic of the struggles internal to the field of the dominant class. In fashion, these struggles are primarily organized around an opposition between the old and the new, which is in turn linked to the opposition between the old and the young, passing through other oppositions such as expensive/cheap, classical/practical. Similarly, struggles within the bourgeois class can also be understood in terms of an opposition between old and new, old and young (see Figure 2.1). Bourdieu accepts the equivalence of power and age here (especially economic power), that is, in general, the older one is the more power one has. One can of course be young biologically but proximity to power may grant one an older social age. So the same sorts of oppositions are at work in both fields:

> The couturiers who occupy a dominant position in the field of fashion only have to follow through the negative strategies of discretion and understatement that are forced on them by the aggressive competition of the challengers to find themselves directly attuned to the demands of the old bourgeoisie who are oriented towards the same refusal of emphasis by a homologous relation to the audacities of the new bourgeoisie; and, similarly, the newcomers to the field, young couturiers or designers endeavouring to win acceptance of their subversive ideas, are the 'objective allies' of the new fractions and the younger generation of the dominant fractions of the bourgeoisie. (Bourdieu, 1984 [1979]: 233)

So the fields share the same sets of oppositions, and that is why specific goods and specific classes or class fractions appear to choose each other in

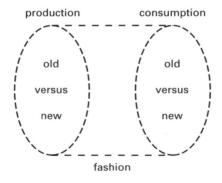

Divisions within the sphere of production match
divisions within the sphere of consumption

Figure 2.1   *Homologous relations (Bourdieu, 1984 [1979])*

an almost automatic manner. What is popularly called 'taste' is sociologic-
ally understood as that which 'brings together things and people that go
together' (Bourdieu, 1984 [1979]: 241). It is often said that there is no
accounting for taste – but accounting for taste is exactly what Bourdieu is
trying to do. Taste, writes Bourdieu,

> is a match-maker; it marries colours and also people, who make 'well-matched
> couples', initially in regard to taste . . . This spontaneous decoding of one habitus
> by another is the basis of the immediate affinities which orient social encounters,
> discouraging socially discordant relationships, encouraging well-matched
> relationships, without these operations ever having to be formulated other than
> in the socially innocent language of likes and dislikes. (Bourdieu, 1984 [1979]: 243)

So far from taste being something bizarrely individual, ineffable and innocent, it seems to lie at the very basis of social life, orchestrating it in a way
that should ensure harmony and social order, while at the same time reflect-
ing social struggles.

The main theme of this chapter can be summarized very simply: consumption communicates social meaning, and is the site of struggles over
social distinction. The fulfilling of more concrete needs arising from, say,
individual feelings of cold or hunger seems almost an accidental by-product.

3
Objects, Commodities, and Non-commodities

Perhaps the earliest and most influential sociological account of the social character of objects is to be found in Marx's discussion of the fetishism of commodities in the opening book of *Capital*. He sees commodities as fetishistic because they appear to relate exclusively to each other, hiding the fact that they are in actuality products of human labour and thus bring human beings into particular relations with each other. Where personal relations in feudalism were not disguised under the shape of the social relations between products of labour, such relations under capitalism take the form of a relation between things. These things can be exchanged on the market because they are all 'really' different manifestations of the same thing, namely human labour power. The 'reality' of an object for Marx, then, was to be found in its exchange-value, which in turn was based on labour power. Consequently, little attention was devoted to the use-value of an object, that is, to the sorts of things one could do with an object in its concrete form (as opposed to its abstract form of congealed human labour). From the point of view of consumption, however, it is precisely the peculiar use-value of an object that is of interest. It is likely, then, that the Marxist emphasis on the exchange-value of commodities has retarded the development of a sociology oriented to actual consumer practices.

Commodities may be commodities on the market, but once purchased they enter into quite different realms. Kopytoff (1986) argues that this is a common feature of commodities: because they can be exchanged they are therefore equivalent, but this undiscriminating homogenization, accompanied by despairing cries of 'Is nothing sacred?', is countered by attempts to singularize them through sacralization or restricting their spheres of exchange. McCracken (1988) gives an extreme example of the binding of the commodity to a highly restricted sphere of circulation in his account of one consumer, Lois Roget. Lois is the keeper of her family's things: every item of furniture seems to exist in her curatorial collection only through its link with family history. In other words, the history of her family through generations takes the form of items of furniture and the family stories attached to them. It is not abstract labour power that disappears into the objects, then, but the lives of family members. McCracken suggests that this is an example of consumption before the creation of the modern marketplace, and that families now buy goods on the market rather than inherit them.

Beyond exchange-value and use-value lies perhaps signifying value, or maybe signifying value is what we should call use-value when an object is seen to have 'uses' way beyond the obvious ones connected to its concrete form. The obvious use-value of a sweater, for example, may be to keep one warm in winter, but its signifying or symbolic use-value may be tied to the fact that it was a gift from a family member or friend. The symbolic use-value of a self-purchased Armani jacket may have little to do with family, but it also has little connection with keeping warm. The value collectors find in their objects also seems to lie beyond exchange-value or the simple use-value of the things gathered together. These topics are explored through McCracken's theory of displaced meaning and Baudrillard's (1990 [1968]) account of the system of objects.

Marx and the fetishism of commodities

Objects for Karl Marx (1974 [1867]) have two dimensions. The first is called use-value, and refers to the actual concrete uses to which an object may be put. For example, one may use a frying pan to cook food and a computer to write a lecture, but it might be difficult to write a lecture using a frying pan. Viewed from the point of view of use-value, then, objects are incompatible with each other – they are useful for different purposes. Of course it may be possible to state some equivalences between a frying pan, a wok and a stewpot or, less easily, a computer, a fountain pen, a pencil, and a feather dipped in ink. These equivalences remain at the level of use-value. But it also makes sense to say that one computer is the same as 50 frying pans or that one frying pan is the same as 100 pencils, or that a Calvin Klein shirt and a bottle of Grange Hermitage are quite equal. Under capitalism, indeed, practically any object X can be made equivalent to particular proportions of practically any object Y: $X = nY$, where n is a number. As these objects are all destined for different uses it clearly is not on the level of use-value that they may be compared. This brings us to the second dimension of the object in the Marxian view: an object has not only use-value but also exchange-value, and this is what makes it a commodity exchangeable on the market. Indeed exchange-value, far more than use-value, is what is essential to capitalism. As Marx puts it in his slightly fanciful way,

> Could commodities themselves speak, they would say: Our use-value may be a thing that interests men. It is no part of us as objects. What, however, does belong to us as objects, is our value. Our natural intercourse as commodities proves it. In the eyes of each other we are nothing but exchange-values. (Marx, 1974 [1867]: 87)

So in the Marxist tradition, objects appear not as things to be analysed according to use but rather as things to be analysed according to exchange. But what is it that composes exchange-value in the first place? For Marx, the secret of the commodity was labour power: when commodity X is exchanged for n amounts of commodity Y, equivalent amounts of labour power are being exchanged. This is the one thing the different commodities share, and it is what makes them exchangeable in the first place. This labour theory of value is, of course, controversial, but for the purposes of this chapter the controversy is not relevant – here we are simply trying to understand how the world of objects has appeared to Marx and later writers in this tradition. What interested Marx was the fact that a social relation between people became transformed into a relation between things: the things became the reality as labour power disappeared into them, and so objects began to rule our relations with each other. As he puts it:

> A commodity is therefore a mysterious thing, simply because in it the social character of men's labour appears to them as an objective character stamped upon the product of that labour; because the relation of the producers to the sum total of their own labour is presented to them as a social relation, existing not between themselves, but between the products of their labour. (Marx, 1974 [1867]: 77)

So we can understand commodities as an example of alienated relations between people. This becomes intensified when, as is the inevitable development of expanding capitalism, things are no longer produced with use-value in mind but are deliberately produced for exchange-value. Use-value does not disappear, of course, but it becomes subordinate to exchange-value and to the shifting of goods on the market. Exchange-value may no longer even need the excuse of use-value, as we now tend to buy less for use than for signifying-value. But Marx did not have a concept of signifying-value, and we shall return to this notion below.

Objects for Marx covered over the real relations between people once they became commodities with exchange-value, and Marx saw the reality of relations as referring to relations between producers – not, note, relations between consumers. So while Marx's approach can show us how it is possible for commodities to be exchanged and that exchange-value in capitalism covers over the relations between producers, his approach does not tell us anything about what happens to commodities once they are obtained and removed, temporarily or permanently, from the sphere of exchange. It should be clear that his approach would tend to exclude the understanding of objects from the point of view of consumers. Let us now look more closely at commodities and how they are decommodified, recommodified or sacralized.

The cultural biography of things

An extreme view of capitalism might propose that every object is a commodity that can be exchanged with any other commodity, and that objects are commodities at all times. Igor Kopytoff (1986) tries to show that this does not necessarily happen. In all societies, some objects are removed from the sphere of commodity exchange, some may never become commodities, and probably most objects are sometimes commodities and sometimes not. Somewhat provocatively, he approaches the notion of the commodity through an examination of what happens to people when they become commodities, bought and sold on the market. We refer here, of course, to slaves, and we do not like to think very much about the possibility that people and objects may be treated in the same manner. We usually see people and things as polar opposites, but that is both a recent view and culturally exceptional. So let us suspend for the moment any moral objections we may have to treating people as things and try to see what we can learn by looking at the traffic in persons.

Kopytoff (1986: 65) maintains that the slave's status as commodity is by no means permanent. A person is transformed into a commodity through, say, capture or defeat in war or whatever. The commodity is then purchased on the slave market, but at this moment a process of decommoditization begins – the slave is given a new sort of social identity (which could be anything from a worker on a plantation to Imperial Roman Admiral) which individualizes him or her and provides a role in the host society. For some time at least, slaves cease being a commodity. If they are resold, they become commodities again on the second-hand slave market, but once bought undergo yet again a process of decommodification and singularization. Kopytoff suggests that if we can see the career of the person-thing in shifting biographical terms like this, then it should be possible to apply the same approach to any commodity whatsoever. Any commodity may cease to be treated as a commodity once it is purchased because it becomes inserted into a particular world where it has its own place as an object with peculiar qualities (see Corrigan, 1989, for a demonstration of this in the case of items of clothing). Subsequently, of course, it may find its way back onto the market, but it may not if it becomes, say, a family heirloom. Objects have their own biographies and are often far more than mere commodities. Now a biography is not simply a unitary thing, for each of us could come up with a number of different partial biographies about ourselves: our professional and familial biographies may be very different or they may be closely implicated; we may also have our political biographies, our economic biographies and our psychological biographies. Depending on the emphasis, we will each have lived a number of different lives. Indeed, it is not the cat that has nine lives but we ourselves in our various biographies. Actually, the biography of a cat is a good example of the decommodification process. You may purchase a cat on the market (therefore a cat is a commodity), but once purchased it is given a place peculiar to itself in your life – it becomes singularized, and it is not likely that it will be recommodified at a later stage (see Figure 3.1).

We can imagine the world of goods in terms of two diametrically opposed possibilities: 'The perfect commodity would be one that is exchangeable with anything and everything else, as the perfectly commoditized world would be one in which everything is exchangeable or for sale. By the same token, the perfectly decommoditized world would be one in which everything is singular, unique, and unexchangeable' (Kopytoff, 1986: 69). Marx seemed to fear that capitalism had come very close to the first, where the cash nexus overthrew all feudal restraints on circulation and plunged everything into a dizzying whirl of commodities. In a totally commodified world

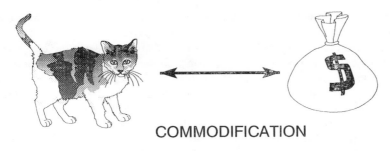

COMMODIFICATION

DECOMMODIFICATION

Figure 3.1   *Commodification and decommodification*
(Kopytoff, 1986)

there would be no sacred sites. We shall return to the problem of persons as commodities, but for the moment let us note that any given economy seems to lie somewhere between the polar opposites of complete commodification and complete decommodification: there are elements of both, in varying mixtures. It would seem as if any given society could be characterized in terms of which objects can become commodified and which cannot. The tension between the two can be seen in struggles over, say, whether a piece of land should be mined or serve as a protected area, between development and conservation, economic exploitation and sacred sites (or objects). A society may be characterized as the result of the tensions between commodification and decommodification processes that take place at many levels, not just in the example given. Most societies classify objects into categories that are closer to or further away from one or the other pole. Some objects will be classified and treated more like commodities and others will be classified and treated as more like non-commodities.

There may be several spheres of exchange-value. Not everything may be exchanged with anything: certain things may be exchanged only with certain other things, the common characteristic being not abstract human labour but an approximately equal distance between the commodified and decommodified poles. Kopytoff refers to Paul Bohannon's (1959) account of the Tiv of central Nigeria, which we can use as a relatively simple example allowing us to see how the notion of separate spheres of exchange operates. There are three spheres for the Tiv:

> (a) the sphere of subsistence items – yams, cereals, condiments, chickens, goats, utensils, tools, and the like; (b) the sphere of prestige items – mainly cattle, slaves, ritual offices, special cloth, medicines, and brass rods; and (c) the sphere of rights in people, which included rights in wives, wards, and offspring. The three spheres represent three separate universes of exchange-values, that is, three commodity spheres. Items within each were exchangeable, and each was ruled by its own kind of morality. Moreover, there was a moral hierarchy among the spheres: the subsistence sphere, with its untrammelled market morality, was the lowest, and the rights-in-people sphere, related to the world of kin and kin-group relations, was the highest. (Kopytoff, 1986: 71)

It was sometimes possible to move from sphere to sphere through the use of brass rods. So here we have a structure of three separate spheres of exchange arranged in a moral hierarchy and between which it is possible to move only in exceptional ways (see Figure 3.2). Normally the spheres are kept apart. Now this may seem rather complicated to us, but Kopytoff remarks, convincingly, I think, that this is in fact a great simplification. It places quite a neat order on the objects (including people, of course) that may circulate within Tiv society -- compare this to the social chaos that might result if anything was exchangeable for anything else. Our own system is much more confusing than that of the Tiv. The further a society is from commoditization, the greater the number of separate spheres of exchange it should have. At its limit, there should be as many spheres of exchange as there are objects. But this means that nothing could be exchanged for anything else and the notion of sphere of exchange would disappear, and probably the notion of human society along with it. The more commodified a society is, however, the fewer should be the spheres of exchange: everything becomes exchangeable with everything else without differentiation.

SPHERES OF EXCHANGE

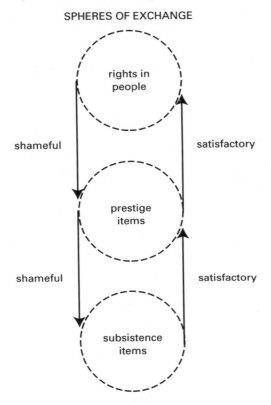

Figure 3.2   *Spheres of exchange among the Tiv of Nigeria (Bohannon, 1959)*

The drive to commoditization runs into its opposite: the drive to singularization – discrimination, separation and sacralization. Some things are held to be sacred and successfully resist commodification, other things are rescued from commodification and become sacralized. Examples of the former include monuments, national art collections, royal residences, and so on. One could hardly imagine the War Memorial in Canberra being sold to a fast food chain as the perfect site for the sale of their new line in Anzacburgers. It remains too sacred to Australians. But in January 1996 it was decided by the New South Wales government that the new State Governor (who represents the monarch) would be part-time and would no longer live at Government House (which would be used for other purposes), thus saving more than a million dollars a year (*The Australian*, 17 January 1996). A post connected to the monarchy has been downgraded at least partly through being translated into commodity terms, thereby removing it from the realm of the sacred. Once the process of commoditization touches the sacred, the latter is in serious danger of losing its reason for existence for it is no longer protected from the exigencies of the ordinary commodity world. So while the

War Memorial may remain sacred to Australians, it seems as if the monarchy may not.

Singularization can also be attained through restricted spheres of exchange, as we have seen with the Tiv. Here is a more familiar example:

Heritage Items
It is illegal to take or send out of Australia, without a permit, items identified as being of great importance to Australia's national heritage.
    These items include works of art, books, documents, maps, stamps, coins, furniture, Aboriginal artefacts and objects associated with our social, military and sporting history as well as our scientific and technological development. Also covered are items associated with the photographic, film and television industries and outstanding natural history items such as mineral specimens, ancient fossils and other archaeological finds. (Australian Customs Service, 1992: 9)

This passage says nothing about free or restricted exchange within Australia, but it is clear that once such items become candidates for export they become in some way sacred objects that cannot simply be bought and sold. They may well be bought or sold in the end, of course, but not without the permission of the Australian state. These objects are singularized and made special simply by being labelled heritage items, and one's heritage cannot be treated as just a commodity equivalent to X number of onions. Kopytoff suggests that the act of singularization is often a form of the exercise of power, and in the above example we can see the Australian state exercising its power over what counts as Australian culture – over what counts as essentially 'Australian', indeed.

If in simpler societies there is general agreement on the sorts of objects that are properly to be found within particular spheres of exchange (although this may be rather a simplification), in complex societies it is quite possible for there to be a tension between various views on the proper status of particular objects. Public culture may declare certain objects proper commodities, while certain groups and individuals may disagree. Indeed, one way in which groups may proclaim their identity is precisely through agreeing that certain sorts of objects must be singularized through restricted spheres of exchange. Kopytoff gives the example of the collection of African art among American Africanists. In the 1950s,

African art picked up randomly in the course of fieldwork was placed entirely in a closed sphere with a sacred cast. The objects created were greatly singularized; they were held to have for their collector a personal sentimental value, or a purely aesthetic one, or a scientific one, the last supported by the collector's supposed knowledge of the object's cultural context. It was not considered entirely proper to acquire an art object from African market traders or, worse, from European traders in Africa, or, worse still, from dealers in Europe or America. (Kopytoff, 1986: 78)

Such objects would have been contaminated, profaned by the commodity economy. Here we can see how a professional group, American Africanists, try to maintain a restricted and sacred sphere of circulation in opposition to those who would treat African art objects as commodities like any other (those who would buy from the unsacred class of dealers). The Africanists would exchange their art items only for other African or 'primitive' art objects – they could not be sold except to a museum at cost (museums, of course, being singular and sacred spaces in their own way) or in case of extreme need. On a rather more mundane level, the likes of beer cans or comic books are ideally exchanged only with other beer cans or comic books, and in this way they retain the charge of singularity so dear to their collectors. But, as Kopytoff points out, this leads to a paradox: 'as one makes them more singular and worthy of being collected, one makes them valuable; and if they are valuable, they acquire a price and become a commodity and their singularity is to that extent undermined' (1986: 81).

So there are many attempts to carve out singularized spheres protected from the ravages of the commodity world, but they seem often to be only partially successful in the case of private collectables. Deliberately producing things to be collected, indeed, can become an industry in itself. We can find another paradox in that most sacred and most profane of spheres, namely art. On the one hand, we see a painting by Leonardo or Rembrandt or Van Gogh or Picasso as priceless, but on the other hand it has to be insured for a certain sum by its owner or may even actually be sold on the market. So objects can be commodities or singularized but not really both at exactly the same moment. Paintings are only exceptionally commodities, spending most of their time singularized as sacred objects of Western art. The contrast between looking upon something as a commodity and looking upon it as a singularized object was well caught in Oscar Wilde's comment about cynics who know the price of everything but the value of nothing.

We can see now that objects are sometimes commodities and sometimes not, that they have careers of their own that go beyond the moment of exchange, and that even if they are commodities they may be exchangeable only with certain other commodities, not all other commodities. There seems to be a tension between commodification and decommodification tendencies in contemporary society, and each object is caught up in this tension. Let us now turn to a brief study of one particularly restricted sphere of exchange, Grant McCracken's (1988) account of the curatorial consumption of Lois Roget.

Restricted circulation: household goods as family objects

Where families once inherited a large portion of their worldly goods from parents and other relatives, there has been a tendency ever since the eighteenth century for the modern family to purchase its goods on the market. McCracken, in the course of his field research, came upon what he seems to see as a throwback example to the earlier form of relationship with the goods that one finds in family. 'Lois Roget is the keeper of her family's possessions' (McCracken, G., 1988: 44), as he puts it succinctly. The word 'keeper' may be interpreted here as someone who watches over things and knows their history, such as a keeper of antiquities in a museum. 'To keep' means much more here than merely to possess – one possesses, but relates goods to history, to family, and to the notion of preserving for posterity. McCracken's term 'curatorial' fits this quite well, for Lois stores, displays and conserves the objects in line with what she sees as her family duty. Her family draws some of its continuity from the fact that it has been in the same place for many generations, and this allows a regular accumulation of family objects. In a sense her family is more like the medieval family that would have remained in the same village over many centuries, and unlike the family more typical of modern industrial society which may have members scattered all over the country or, indeed, all over the globe. A nice steady accumulation of objects is rather more difficult in the circumstances of geo-graphical and social mobility that many of us have probably experienced at first hand. Now we tend to associate a sense of dynasty more with upper-class families in Europe who may have retained a 'family seat' for a long time and could thus devote time and energy to transforming themselves into objects in order to continue their existence after death – you can be rein-carnated as an expensive chair or art work in your own lifetime, while the house itself can come to be the object that sums up and distils the being of the family as a whole across generations. Items of furniture can stand for individuals, and the whole collection under one roof stands for the family as an entity that endures through time. The family here is like any major social institution such as a hospital, a prison or a university: although the individuals may die, the institution does not disappear. A university founded in 1592 is the 'same' institution today, but it does not contain the same people occupying the positions of student and academic. Lois Roget's family seems to occupy an analogous position to the upper-class family with a sense of history, if at a rather lower economic level. As McCracken reports:

> The relatives are so well represented I felt that she was reading me the family tree instead of showing me her living room. Each of the objects has its provenance. This includes the kinship term appropriate to the previous owner(s). An English aunt is recalled by some 'pretty little plates', Lois's great-grandmother by a chair in the hall. (McCracken, G., 1988: 46)

Any item in the house that was not connected with family history was dis-missed as being of no significance – that's 'just a chair'. One suspects that the chair will eventually become known as 'the chair Lois always used to dismiss', and so eventually find its way into the family story.

The non-Rogetian family (presumably the majority of families today) is free of both the crushing weight of history and the security that an enduring familyness of objects would bring. The modern family still constructs itself as a family through the consumption of objects, but the family that is thus constructed is a rather reduced thing: the family that creates itself is the nuclear family, not the extended family. The nuclear family uses goods more to produce itself as a family on its own, isolated both from the world and from kin, with no relation to ancestors or descendants. That is, I think, an

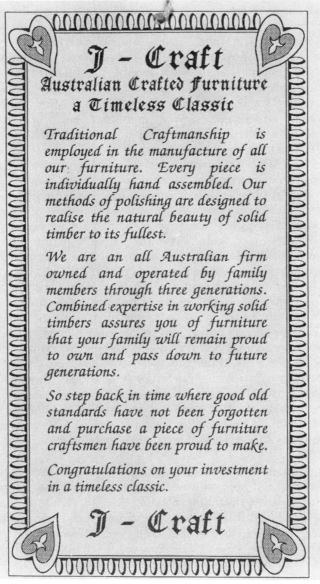

Figure 3.3   *J-Craft*

overstatement: the work by Csikszentmihalyi and Rochberg-Halton (1981) to be discussed in Chapter 7 shows a tendency to some continuities. I suspect that, while Lois Roget may be an extreme example, there is still an extended family history to be found in the objects in many people's homes, although more research needs to be done on this point if we want to make any sort of strong claims about the matter.

Certain items are *marketed* as if we did indeed take a Lois Roget approach to objects. Figure 3.3 reproduces a tag found on a piece of furniture made by R.C. Roberts of Bayswater, Victoria and purchased in 1993.

What are the key terms here from our point of view? 'Traditional', 'family members', 'three generations', 'your family', 'pass down to future generations', 'step back in time', 'good old standards', 'timeless classic'. There is some interesting treatment of time here. Take the term 'timeless' – this seems to claim an existence beyond time itself, but a rather less philosophical interpretation might see it as claiming simply that it is not bound to the particular time in which we are now living: it tries to set itself apart from the relatively brief timespan achieved by most consumer goods, which live for merely a season or two. 'Traditional', however, seems to want to re-insert a notion of time. Time's indifferent march is softened and captured into the non-indifferent meaning of tradition, so instead of being impervious to human concerns it now expresses their combined and age-sanctified activities. Time is on our side here. Family time in the old Lois Rogetian and medieval sense is deliberately evoked through the terms 'three generations' (which in this context encompasses past and present members of the J-Craft clan) and 'future generations' (of your clan). Time brings together the families of the maker and the purchaser: they share the notion of continuity through time, and there is a smooth continuation between the already-existing and past family and tradition of J-Craft and the already-existing and future family and tradition of the purchaser. All you need do is buy the piece of furniture and thereby inherit the J-Craft tradition, making it your own by leaving it to future generations. '[S]tep back in time' implies that J-Craft indeed provide something unusual in an object, something that can draw upon the solidity of past history – and there is always a tendency to think of the past as a golden age of higher standards and happier families, a topic we will come across below in a slightly different context.

The tag was found on an item of furniture that was far from traditional: a computer desk. So even with a very modern item, it is still possible to invoke tradition and generation-spanning. McCracken, then, may well be overstating the rarity of the Lois Roget approach to objects in the family. The reader may wish to look at their own family objects in the light of this discussion.

Objects, displaced meaning and desire for more objects

Why does the modern consumer want more and more goods, why does it appear impossible that 'enough' will ever be attained? McCracken understands this in terms of the concept of displaced meaning. In this perspective, objects represent bridges to meanings that cannot be attained easily in the here-and-now. But why should this happen in the first place? All societies seem to have ideal versions of the way the world should be even though the world never really is like this in actual practice. There always seems to be a gap between lived reality and some sort of ideal. So what happens to the ideals? They can be jettisoned completely, but that would lead to a world without hope where nothing could ever change, a world populated by bitter, disillusioned and permanently depressed cynics. A more common strategy perhaps is to displace the ideals to a place where they will be protected from the corrosive acid of reality and yet still appear attainable. Ideals, as McCracken (1988: 106) puts it, are removed 'from daily life and transport[ed] . . . to another cultural universe, there to be kept within reach but out of danger'. This is what he means by the strategy of displaced meaning. So what sorts of places can meaning be displaced to? One place is the past: a golden age is evoked where everything was perfect, or, at any rate, much more desirable than the present day. The reverse strategy is also possible: instead of a golden past, we put our faith in a golden future. McCracken (1988: 106–7) lists a number of possibilities: 'an anarchist's commune that has no law and no property, the perfect democracy in which all people are fully equal and free, the perfect socialist state that advances a common good over individual interest, the perfect laissez-faire society in which economic individualism decides all collective matters'. All will be perfect after the Revolution for the True Believers.

Ideals can be displaced across space as well as time. For several generations of Western Europeans, Russia appeared the actually existing model of the ideal society where everyone was equal, there were jobs for all, and nobody was in want. As it was difficult to check this out, the iron curtain could continue to foster the illusion. A similar displacement seemed to operate on the other side: this time, the capitalist countries of Western Europe seemed ideal places where everyone was rich, happy, and drove BMWs. This mutual displacement came to an end at the beginning of the 1990s, leaving many Europeans bereft of the protection and hope of traditional displaced meanings. Ideals once displaced to socialist-communist or capitalist societies now seem to have been displaced by some to exclusivist nationalism and Fascism.

This strategy of displaced meaning, which we have been discussing on a fairly macro level up to now, can also be applied on the level of individuals. This, as we shall see, takes on particular importance in consumer societies. We all have our ideals: if these are in the past, then maybe we saw perfection in our childhood; if they are in the future, then perhaps they take the form of 'when I get married', 'when I get divorced', 'when we own the house', 'when I get a new job', 'when I finally understand sociology', and so on. Goods for McCracken can act as bridges to these displaced ideals by being either something we desire but cannot quite attain, or something that we do indeed attain but that represents only a part of the displaced meaning. The problem of attaining everything we desire is that there may be nowhere left for meaning to be displaced to. When we cannot quite attain something, it can exist for us as a way of eventually attaining a whole ideal lifestyle that seems to be attached to it and so we are protected from losing our illusions.

This sort of bridge seems to operate mainly in the imagination. But one can take a concrete step along the way by purchasing an object that finds a place in the ideal lifestyle. Note that we understand lifestyle here as a whole combination of different objects and practices: the reader may recall from Bourdieu (1984 [1979]) that indeed different classes are characterized by particular collections or packages of specific goods and activities. So if you can get your hands on one of the objects associated with the lifestyle you desire, then this gives you a concrete bridge towards that lifestyle (see Figure 3.4). This still protects the desired lifestyle from the deceptions of reality by the fact that it is an isolated item: you can afford one thing, but not the whole package. For example, you might purchase a very expensive watch that would be totally out of place with the rest of your possessions but form an integral part of the desired lifestyle, or splash out on a Chanel suit when the rest of your wardrobe comes from K-Mart, or buy an ultra-expensive lipstick because you know that that is what you would do as a matter of course in the ideal lifestyle. In McCracken's words (1988: 111), 'These bridges serve as proof of the existence of this style of life and even as proof of the individual's ability to lay claim to it.' This is a risky game, of course. Once the bridge item is obtained it is part of the real and risks being subsumed into ordinary reality, and the Chanel suit is brought down into the K-Mart system simply by being made part of the same wardrobe. So in order to avoid this another object must be chosen as a bridge to displaced meaning, which then suffers the same fate – and so on and so forth as we begin our desperate relations with one object after another, as each stands for the ideal and is then drowned in the real. It is really only in consumer societies that this relation with objects is possible on a mass scale. But say you suddenly become very rich by winning the lottery: the distance between you and your ideal lifestyle may be instantly annulled, and there seems to be nowhere to place displaced meaning where it will be protected from the slings and arrows of outrageous reality. A solution to this is to collect what is rare and which great wealth alone will not obtain: 'Collectibles [sic], unique or very rare, must be hunted down, brought out of hiding, won away from other collectors. When goods have this special elusiveness, they can once again become bridges' (McCracken, G., 1988: 113). Most of us may never find ourselves in this position, and the world of consumer goods manages to offer us an alternative. There are always higher levels of consumption to which we can aspire, and so we keep our ideals safe, ever-displaced out of reach even as we can afford more and more. Indeed, as McCracken (1988: 115) puts it, 'The use of goods to recover displaced meaning is one of the engines of consumption in modern society.'

Let us now look at the ways in which objects may relate to each other as parts of systems, and consider Jean Baudrillard's (1990 [1968]) account of what he calls marginal objects and marginal systems. An example of the first is the bygone object, and an example of the second is the collection.

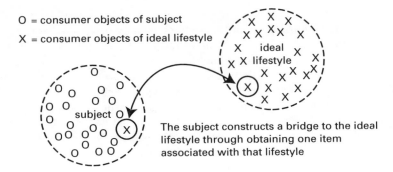

Figure 3.4 *Goods as bridges to displaced meaning*
(McCracken, 1988)

Baudrillard and the system of objects: the bygone object and the marginal object

When we spoke about Marx above we saw that objects that were com-modities could be understood in terms of exchange-value and use-value. Baudrillard contrasts use-value not so much with exchange-value as with what we might call signifying-value. Objects are not merely functional (that is, they do not exist only for their use-value), but signify certain things. This allows us to understand why we may possess many objects that have no obvious use-value: their value to us is signifying-value. He turns his attention first to the bygone object.

The bygone object, the old object, the ancient object – whatever you like to call it, Baudrillard's point is that this object is not an anomalous hangover from the past with no business or purpose in the present, but is an integral part of the present-day system of objects. Its value is for today, even if this value is not functional. Indeed, in Baudrillard's perspective, the only func-tion of the apparently functionless bygone object is to signify. And what does it signify? Time, of course – rather, the signs of time. Why is this important? Imagine a collection of objects all originating in the present day. They may well form a total system signifying the possessor's social class in the Bour-dieu manner we have evoked many times, but they lack any foundation in history. They just are: there is nothing to anchor them, to give them a reason for existing beyond the present moment. The bygone object placed among these present-day objects gives the collection precisely an enduring foun-dation in history, and so we are fascinated by antique furniture, period pieces, and so on. This sort of object serves as a myth of origin for Baudrillard, for we now have something in our collection that has existed before in other lives, that (ideally) dates from before the time we ourselves were born. There may well also be a touch of the golden age past that McCracken mentioned as one of the possible sites of displaced meaning, but Baudrillard seems to see it more in psychoanalytical terms as a regression to the mother. The bygone object also indicates authenticity, and Baudrillard sees this in terms of descent from the father – presumably because, in Western societies, property and legitimacy usually descended through the father. Fathers liked to be certain that their children really were theirs, and we can see this from the child's point of view in the case of those objects that carry certificates of authenticity. For example, in antique shops in my town one can find coffee tables that have certificates stating that they were made from wood rescued from a church that was demolished in 1902. The object has quite a precise history attached to it, and we can become the keepers of this sort of history: not family history in the Lois Roget sense, but community or religious or even national history – we are its authentic children and keepers, we assimilate history into ourselves. Perhaps we are even performing a civic and artistic duty by purchasing such bygone objects. Clearly, they give us an existence and a presence beyond the merely here-and-now. Baudrillard gives us another example of this in the case of building a home. Here, an old farmhouse is demolished but a few pieces kept to be incorporated into the new house. Three wooden beams and two stones of the old find their way into the new edifice, thereby giving it what Baudrillard calls a 'minute but sublime presence . . . testifying to past generations' (1990 [1968]: 38). In sum,

> Man is not 'at home' in the functional milieu. He needs, in order to make it livable, something like that splinter of the True Cross which sanctified a church, something like a talisman, like a fragment of absolute reality which would be at the heart of the real, and enshrined in the real. Such is the bygone object. (Baudrillard, 1990 [1968]: 39)

An object understood in terms of its functions has a very practical relationship to the world: a clock, for example, tells the time. But an object understood not in terms of its functions but in terms of possession can become quite a different thing. The clock may still tell the time, but the fact that it is *my* clock gives it a different dimension. Maybe it was a present from someone, or maybe I collect clocks. The point we are getting at here is that objects can be understood in terms of their relationship to a subject (Baudrillard, 1990 [1968]: 43).

This point becomes particularly clear in the case of the collection. Individuals collect, seeking out and arranging objects into particular forms: the clocks do not need to tell the time, but they do need to fall into certain patterns that depend on the collector. Perhaps all the clocks need to be French, for example, and date from before a certain period. In any case, the principle of unity of the collection depends on principles decided upon by the individual, whether one is talking about French clocks or beermats. There is a certain ambiguity at work here, of course. Once you are launched on the course of collecting French clocks, then French clocks seem to call out seductively, leading on your passion for these objects, dragging you to places where they might be found. It becomes hard to know whether you are collecting French clocks, or they are collecting you – there is a tight connection between the individual subject and the object. The ultimate aim is to have a complete set of something, but if this is actually accomplished then we face the same problem evoked by McCracken in the case of those who are

suddenly wealthy and can now attain everything that once held safe displaced meaning. The completion of a collection would mean the death of collecting, and another refuge for displaced meaning would need to be found.
Maybe then one can turn to collecting something else. Each object of a collection can be treated as both a unique piece (for example a drawing by a
particular artist) and as part of a series (such as the complete drawings and
sketches of artist *X*), so the collector can have the pleasures of the unique
and the serial at the same time. Baudrillard likens the collection of objects
to a harem,

> whose whole charm is that of a series of intimacies (always with a preferred object)
> and of intimacy with a series . . . In the field of human relations, which are unique
> and conflictual, this fusion of absolute singularity and an indefinite series is not per-
> mitted, which is why they are a source of continual anguish. Whereas the field of
> objects, made up of successive and homologous terms, is comforting . . . Objects
> are, in the plural, the only existing beings with whom coexistence is truly possible,
> since their differences do not set them one against the other as happens with living
> beings, but obediently converge around me, to be added together without difficulty
> in consciousness. (Baudrillard, 1990 [1968]: 45–6)

If the collection can be seen as a private domain, it can often be worth a lot
in terms of exchange-value. One can collect for investment purposes, but
even here the collecting will be driven by the logic of the objects and the
search for completeness, so there will be something of private passion even
in investors (unless they have no idea of the non-monetary logic that ties collections together, in which case they will merely accumulate objects rather
than collect them). The accumulation of objects is tied to exchange-value on
the market but collecting is tied to the subject, and will outlast that subject
even after death unless it is broken up: the break-up of the collection dis-
solves the material reality the subject has left behind, because this collection
would not exist at all without the prior existence of the collector.

Objects, then, are clearly not merely functional nor can their meanings be
exhausted by invoking exchange-value. They signify, and over the next few
chapters we consider a way in which objects can be infused systematically
and deliberately with meaning by, initially at least, agents other than their
purchasers. I refer, of course, to advertising.

4
Shops and Shopping:
the Department Store

One of the most important moments in the development of consumer culture was the advent of the department store in the middle of the nineteenth century. This came about, argues Richard Sennett (1978[1976]: 142), because of changes in the production system: the factory allowed more and more goods to be made more quickly than hand production ever could achieve, and thus more efficient outlets were required. Industrialization encouraged the existence of vast emporia in which practically anything could be purchased. Shopping became quite a different experience in the department stores: prices were fixed, there was free entry, and anybody's coin was as good as anybody else's. The fixed price meant there was none of the interminable haggling and bargaining that had characterized shopping, and free entry meant that one was not obliged to purchase anything – a necessary condition for the utterance of that most frequent phrase of the modern shopper: 'just looking!'. The great size and huge range of the new stores meant that it was possible to wander about for hours, fascinated by the inventive displays of this palace of fantasies. Shoppers changed from active hagglers, who would only go into a shop if they needed something, to passive accepters of fixed prices, who could freely circulate among commodities without being obliged to buy. They were often quite seduced by the goods which promised all manner of pleasures through their modes of display, and shoplifting became a serious problem among respectable middle-class women who would never dream of stealing in an ordinary shop. But department stores allowed one to exist in a dreamlike state, overcome by the alluring perfumes emanating from deliciously encircling commodities. Sensible shoppers slipped silkily into the gorgeous gowns of the entranced consumer. All classes of people could enter, and so each class in its own way could achieve a form of consumerhood through what has been called 'the democratization of luxury'. As we shall see, however, the department store provided the material means for the new middle classes in particular to stake out a cultural identity for themselves.

The department store affected more than just the buyer. Its very vastness entailed an increasingly bureaucratic form of internal organization, and it became an important public female space, an 'Adamless Eden' where many of the workers, as well as the shoppers, were women. Gail Reekie (1992, 1993) explores department stores in Australia, showing how both commodities and social space are gendered and genderizing. Rudi Laermans (1993) approaches the topic in a more general way.

Changes in shopping

One of the great pleasures, and sometimes great frustrations, of life in the modern big city is the activity of shopping: shopping for, shopping around, window shopping, just looking. It is probably not an exaggeration to say that shopping has become a cultural practice that can take up quite a bit of one's time. It has not always been like this, of course, and shopping underwent its own Great Transformation with the advent of the department store in the nineteenth century. So what sorts of before-and-after pictures do we get of shopping? We may find a hint in the definition of the verb 'to shop' found in the *Shorter Oxford Dictionary* (1973 revision of the 3rd edition): 'To visit a shop or shops for the purpose of making purchases or examining the contents.' Note the 'or' in this definition: the choice of examining the contents is quite a late development, and the earlier understanding of 'to shop' was indeed restricted to visiting a shop for the purpose of making purchases. There was no shopping around and no 'just looking'. Indeed, a trace of this can still be found in some shops in France that put a sign in their windows saying 'entrée libre', which means that one can enter without being obliged to make a purchase. So what we take for granted as one of the great fundamental rights of the contemporary shopper ('just looking') is perhaps not as self-evident as we imagine if it is still necessary for a shop to admit it explicitly.

So what was shopping like in the days before department stores? Firstly, shops were marked by ultra-specialization. They sold not a range of goods, but only one thing. But why was this? Michael Miller provides an explanation of the French instance, which we may take as a model of the European case generally:

> Before the Revolution, most retailing in France was governed by a guild system concerned primarily with maintaining established levels of craftsmanship and with assuring that no merchant or small producer (and most often these were one and the same) encroached on the trade of his neighbor. The guilds regulated and limited entry into the various trades. They insisted that each seller be confined to a single specialty and to a single shop; they set standards of work; and they set conditions for procuring supplies. At times they set a minimum selling price to prevent 'unfair' competition. (Miller, M., 1981: 21–2)

So this system seems to be governed by the guilds, which had the interests of their members at heart, rather than those of the shopper. We usually think of the guilds as important in controlling production, but here we see that they also had more than a hand in controlling distribution too. Clearly, there was no room for competition between guild members, and it was thus impossible for a supplier either to undercut somebody on price or to sell a range of goods outside what the guild considered their proper area.

The second point to be made about old-style shopping concerns the way in which the actual buying and selling was done once the customer arrived in the shop. Rudi Laermans describes it well:

> the customer implicitly engaged in a double contract with the merchant: one had to buy something at a price about which one had to bargain. Most of the time, the customer had no specific idea of the goods with which he or she would return home. The products were neither advertised nor displayed. Merchants dug goods out of big drawers or closed closets, recommended and praised them and, on being asked, mentioned a price about which one had to haggle. (Laermans, 1993: 85)

So if one goes into one of those stores, one is going to come out with something. The contract seems to work because both sides appear to accept that if the merchant invests a lot of time in singing the praises of the goods and generally persuading the customer, then this effort should be rewarded (Sennett, 1978 [1976]: 142). And if one is on the receiving end of the merchant's elegant (or otherwise) discourse, one feels that one has to reciprocate in some way unless one is happy taking someone's words without paying for them. Otherwise it would be a complete waste of time, and this way of buying and selling is certainly time consuming. The customer seems to purchase the performance almost as much as the good. Clearly, engaging in window shopping or shopping around generally is impossible under this system – the goods are even hidden away out of sight. To make matters worse, no exchanges or returns are allowed, so the buyer really does have to beware. The things a time-travelling shopper of today would find odd, then, include: no shops with a mixture of goods, no free entry but an obligation to buy, no fixed price and no marked prices even to act as a guide, no clear indication of what is in the shop in the first place, no exchange or return and thus no way of obtaining redress in case of trouble.

Some more recent forms of buying and selling partake of, or recently partook of, some of these elements: many markets in non-Western countries expect a process of haggling (although in markets at least one has the chance to look around), and it was not uncommon in the old Soviet Union to join a queue to buy something without actually knowing what was for sale at the other end – at least *something* was for sale, and it was likely to be of some use in a society where deficits in goods were common. State-socialist societies in general (such as the USSR and Eastern Europe until 1989) were not of the selling type, and indeed one may draw a parallel to the situation under the guilds: in both cases, the customer was not the most important element in the transaction, but rather the protection of, on the one hand, the interests of the guild members and, on the other, of the interests of the state-owned factories, the main purpose of which was to fill state-defined quotas. Distribution came as a bit of an afterthought. In both cases, then, the interests of the producers rather than the consumers were dominant.

The lack of interest of such societies in selling was brought home to me in a curious way one day in January 1989 when I found myself in the capital of what was then Czechoslovakia, Prague. I needed to go to a supermarket for some things, and headed for the one closest to my hotel. When I got there, I found a queue outside the supermarket, but very few people seemed to be inside shopping. Every few minutes a person would detach themselves from the head of the queue and enter the supermarket. As I shuffled closer and closer to the front in classical state-socialist queuing manner, I finally realized what was going on: the number of people in the supermarket at any one time could not exceed the limited number of shopping baskets available inside the doors. If they were all taken up, nobody else could enter. This system was not designed with the comfort of customers in mind, but was in the interest of the staff and, presumably, the factory that was fulfilling quotas for the production of supermarket baskets. I finally obtained the large bar of chocolate and larger bottle of vodka that I so desperately needed, and returned to the hotel, where I drank to my first meeting with an economic basket case.

So, shopping in Western societies before the nineteenth century, in some non-Western countries today, and in state-socialist Eastern Europe before 1990 is quite different to what we are used to: the customer is neither right nor first, and the interests served may be those of producers who are not actually in competition with each other (feudally based guilds or state-monopoly factories).

But why did things change as capitalism developed, what form did these changes take, and what were their effects on the shopper and on shopping as an experience? David Chaney proposes that urban development was one factor. Increasing rents led retailers 'to consider using space more economically – which meant in effect going upwards. The idea of a shop existing on several floors, and necessarily containing several departments, was in this respect a function of market forces' (Chaney, 1983: 23). Miller (1981: 33) maintains that mass production 'required a retail system far more efficient and far more expansive than anything small shopkeepers might be able to offer' and so, in Sennett's words (1978 [1976]: 142), 'The department store . . . is a response to the factory'. The old distribution system could not handle the deluge of mass-produced goods that was beginning to flood the market. These, then, appear to be the main reasons underlying changes in the form of shopping in capitalist societies.

A rather less direct influence was exercised by changes in transport and in the physical layout of cities (and indeed the mental layout of cities, as we shall see below in the case of London). The advent of railways made it much easier to bring materials to factories and products from factories to shops, and at the same time made it a lot easier for people to come into the big cities from suburbs and even from towns quite far away. The redesign of cities also had an impact: Sennett (1978 [1976]: 143) remarks that a journey in Paris which takes 15 minutes on foot today would have taken an hour and a half at the beginning of the nineteenth century. Clearly, one would have to have very good reasons for going outside one's own district. But the great boulevards cut through Paris in the 1860s, making much faster journeys possible, as did the creation of a public transport system in many other towns. Not only did this bring workers to work, it could also bring shoppers to shops. In Melbourne, for example, 'the Myers [department store owners] were greatly assisted by the pattern of Melbourne's transport, as all trains and trams converged on the few blocks of which Myers Store became the centre' (Kingston, 1994: 55). These infrastructural details made it possible to move great numbers of people and goods efficiently, and so it became quite feasible to shop in places far from one's own district. Obviously, this was essential if department stores were to flourish.

Department stores began to market themselves as being among the main sights of the big cities. In the case of the Paris Bon Marché store studied by Miller (1981), maps of the Paris region were produced showing various monuments so that, for example, Versailles had a drawing of the château beside it, St Denis was accompanied by a picture of its famous *Basilique*, Vincennes had its *Château-fort*, and Paris itself was represented by . . . an illustration of the Bon Marché, of course. The store was constructed as a monument to visit and be impressed by just as much as any famous château or basilica: a visit to Paris *meant* a visit to the Bon Marché.

The links between public transport systems and big stores can be seen clearly from Adrian Forty's account of London Transport (1986: 234–8). For example, posters with the slogan 'Winter sales are best reached by underground' promote the idea of travel and the idea of visiting the sales as one and the same activity. The equivalence between the big shops and other London attractions was made explicit by a whole series of posters which publicized theatres, cinemas, Hampton Court, Greenwich . . . and the West End shops. Like the Bon Marché maps, all of these became of equal value through featuring in the poster series.

A more subtle reworking of the city can be seen if we compare the old maps of the London underground with the current one that most people have probably seen (reproduced in Forty, 1986: 236–7). On the old map, stations are placed in their geographically correct positions so one can see the distance between them. The current maps, however, the first of which dates from 1931, are *schematic*: they give no indication of distance between stations and present the transport system as an abstract schema. This, of course, has the effect of abolishing notions of distance. As Forty writes:

> the new map . . . enlarged the distance between the stations in the central area, and reduced that between the stations in the outer area. The result was to make London look very much smaller than it actually is, as the outlying areas seem deceptively close to the centre . . . this . . . induced people to undertake journeys they might otherwise have hesitated to make . . . It is impossible to say to what extent London Transport's design policies excited people's appetite for travel, but there seems every reason to believe that by making travel seem easy, effortless and enjoyable, they contributed to the very substantial leisure traffic. (Forty, 1986: 237–8)

Again, this could only help in bringing people in to the big stores.

The department store, child of the revolutions in production and transport, did away with the restrictions imposed by guilds. Many goods were now sold under the same roof, prices were fixed, entry was free, return and exchange were allowed, and sales became a semi-regular feature (Miller, M., 1981: 27). The new industrial situation permitted the selling of low-cost goods at a high turnover, and the fixed prices indicated a reliable level of profit. Haggling was not possible now, and Sennett (1978 [1976]: 142) complains that the 'notion of free entrance made passivity into a norm'. The end of haggling transformed the shopper from an active participant in buying and selling to a passive participant ready to lap up whatever was displayed to them through either their eyes or their purse.

Although we can understand the development of the department store in relation to developments in capitalist industrialization, we still have not looked at how department stores go about shifting all these mass-produced goods into the hot and eager hands of the customers. What, in other words, gives the customers hot and eager hands in the first place? This brings us to the question of display.

Display

We may split our examination of the display elements in department stores into three different parts: presenting the stores themselves, presenting the goods, and presenting the sales staff.

Presenting the stores

A feature of the department stores that could not have failed to strike an observer was the sheer size of the buildings. This had several effects. Firstly, it seemed to indicate that shoppers really could find anything they wanted under the one roof, so they might gravitate to the department store for the convenience of this alone. The idea of providing everything, of course, may be linked to broader notions of power: rulers who really can provide everything will forever have the people in their debt, and a department store may well borrow some of the same effect. Suddenly finding a place with everything you could ever want almost magically abolishes all thought of deficits or shortages. Even those who cannot afford the goods can still have the pleasure of looking and touching. You will certainly be grateful to the gods that created such a wonderful thing. Secondly, size is a characteristic of many buildings that are designed to awe small human creatures. The designers of the great cathedrals knew this full well: the power of the Church and of God (possibly in that order) was made manifest in quite a material way. Certainly, the cathedrals of medieval Europe had little competition from other buildings and so imposed Church power on the faithful by the crushing weight of stone upon stone. In a similar manner, the palace or the château through its size imposed the power of the monarch or the noble as it dominated the landscape. Many of the early railway stations also represent the material embodiment of Victorian views of progress and industrialization, and indeed

London's St Pancras station actually looks like a cathedral – a clear demonstration that the Church and industry can draw upon the same awe-inspiring techniques. It is not an exaggeration to see department stores as similar to cathedrals: they attracted people to worship at the temple of consumerism.

The importance of size was realized by the stores: they made it a feature of their promotions. Miller describes the case of the Bon Marché, but his description could probably be adapted for other stores:

> Everything about the store was 'immense', 'vast', 'gigantic' . . . articles and pamphlets delighted in accounts of the size and scope of behind the scenes operations and projected an image of an incredible commercial machine that could impress the wildest of imaginations. Basements were a 'veritable labyrinth'. Giant electrical machines producing lights for thousands of lamps were described in meticulous detail. Statistics abounded on the hundreds of employees in various services or on the thousands of letters the store received daily. And always there were descriptions of the kitchens, of their enormous equipment that could roast 800 beefsteaks at a single time, or that could prepare more than 5,000 meals in a single day. (Miller, M., 1981: 174)

Huge galleries and staircases inside the building bolstered the impression of size even further, and the balconies along the upper tiers allowed floor wanderers to look right down into the vast and bustling throng, and drink in the awe of immensity.

But size is not *quite* everything, and this brings us to another element of the architecture, namely the impression of luxury it created. Why was this necessary? We remember that the department store depended upon the supply of cheap(ish) factory-made goods sold in high volume at a low mark-up – and cheap goods are, well, cheap. Cheapness does not lead to prestige, an observation that will hardly surprise after our discussion of Veblen (1975 [1899]) in Chapter 2. There is no pleasure to be found in cheapness for the sake of it either, except for those who think in strictly economic terms. So the dangers inherent in cheapness are overcome through the attention paid to turning the department store into a site – and a sight – of luxury. Laermans puts it like this:

> The abundant use of marble, carpets, ornaments, etc. and the refined, sophisticated 'styling' of balconies or lunch rooms all incarnated the idea of a luxurious, comfortable and fashionable way of life. The notion of luxury was also behind the concept of personal service. With their many free services for, and courteous treatment of, shoppers, the early department stores created an almost aristocratic ambience. The female customer was intended to feel like a real queen or at least a lady while she was shopping because she walked in a palace-like atmosphere that was thoroughly imbued with luxury. (Laermans, 1993: 93)

With the free entry policy, luxury was available as an experience to anybody who wanted it. It is not hard to see why the department stores must have looked extremely attractive to shoppers.

Presenting the goods

A task faced by the department stores was: now that we have dragged the public through the doors and treated them to luxurious and attractive surroundings, how do we get these people not only to look but actually to purchase the goods we need to shift? Remember that there was no obligation to buy under the new system, and sales talk was therefore less effective. How do you transform a mere commodity, the brute material reality of a thing, into something to be desired? First you prepare the ground by advertising: the department stores caused a huge upsurge in the use of newspapers, posters, leaflets, postcards and the like (Laermans, 1993: 90). The ads were also of a different type to the older ones, which were often just a rather dry list of what was available, an unadorned prosaic description (see Chapter 5). But through the use of catchphrases and slogans, the commodities became more than just objects for sale – they took on all sorts of other qualities. There is a big difference between, say, a one-line advertisement that says 'For sale: blankets' and a Sunbeam advertisement featuring a picture of blankets and the slogan 'Sweet Dreams in Comfort' (*Australian Women's Weekly*, May 1993: 120). The first is completely unexciting, but the second promises pleasures. The first step, then, is to turn commodities into desirable objects through advertising and thereby attract custom. People might not be too interested in coming into your store to buy a blanket, but they might be very interested if you are selling sweet dreams in comfort at the same time. Blankets here become symbolic objects as much as – or more than – material objects. The transformation of things from objects of need (old style) to objects of desire (new style) continues once one has crossed the threshold of the store. Shoppers are faced with 'dazzling decorations, architectural adornments, fairyland lighting and, first and foremost, a sophisticated display of mostly fashionable merchandise' (Laermans, 1993: 91).

The important goods to shift were the fashionable items, which were purchased cheaply and had, by definition, a short life. Attention could be drawn to these by elaborate window displays or by placing them in unexpected locations: if you are wandering around the furniture section and suddenly come across a display of the latest clothes you are very likely to be struck by the incongruity. This technique of making strange by the juxtaposition of different things is also commented upon by Sennett (1978 [1976]: 144), who argues that it suspends the use-value of an object: we forget about what the object might be for in a concrete way, and see it as something on display and therefore desirable. One can see something of the same effect in art galleries, where the two people over to the side are discussing the artistic merits of an object on display, and are then disappointed to find they cannot buy it because, in fact, they have been admiring the light switch. The light switch becomes desirable because of the context in which it is presented. Everything in the gallery is on display and exciting the senses, and it is the same in a department store: the most mundane of objects becomes desirable through display. The early department stores were theatres as much as art galleries, where everything was put in a magical context and everything was for sale – including, presumably, light switches. As Laermans (1993: 92) puts it, they 'transformed merchandise into a permanent spectacle, into a show-like theatre of commodities.' In the Bon Marché, for example, white sales were marked by the fact that 'the entire store was adorned in white: white sheets, white towels, white curtains, white flowers, *ad infinitum*, all forming a single [white] motif that covered even stairways and balconies' (Miller, M., 1981: 169).

It was also common to infuse objects with the exciting meanings of life in exotic places, and this was accomplished by presenting them against a background that spoke of, say, the Orient – a department store might be transformed into an Egyptian temple or a Japanese garden. In the US, of course, Europe is the exotic other, and stores would mimic Parisian streets or apartments. Exotically charged objects are probably among the most desirable of all, and the department stores went to elaborate lengths to stage objects in a way that promised exotic experiences.

This association of objects with meanings far beyond use-value lies at the base of consumer culture: we purchase the meanings of objects rather than the objects themselves. Laermans refers to this as the 'culturalization' of merchandise, and he summarizes well the main points I have been trying to make here: 'The early department stores pioneered the transformation of traditional customers into modern consumers and of "just merchandise" into spectacular "commodity signs" or "symbolic goods". Thus they laid the cornerstones of a culture we still inhabit' (Laermans, 1993: 94). We are all creations of the department store.

Presenting the sales staff

In the old style of buying and selling, salespeople were not necessarily objects pleasing to behold, and they had the reputation of being disorderly and untrustworthy (Miller, M., 1981: 171–2). A new sort of person was needed for the department store – and if the department store was all about presentation, this meant that the sales staff were part of the presentation too. They had to be disciplined, cultivated and pleasant. In a word, they had to be presentable. They became part of the general seduction machine that was the department store. The Bon Marché managed to convince the public that their sales staff was cultivated and disciplined through the institution of house concerts given by staff. Instead of promoting goods, the concerts aimed to promote the sales staff (Miller, M., 1981: 173). In later times it has perhaps been one of the roles of education generally to produce disciplined, cultivated and presentable personalities, so the department stores (and service industries generally) no longer have to do all the hard work of producing the proper salesperson from dubious material. Indeed, one of the functions of the higher levels of school certificates may be simply to prove not that one is intelligent or talented, but that one is disciplined and properly cultivated. In any case, the department stores needed to produce or obtain some sort of standard model of the salesperson that would fit in with the general atmosphere of the store. The bureaucratic nature of the store implies centralized control and no independent initiative on the part of the sales staff, so the latter have no choice but to act in ways set down for them by others. C. Wright Mills, in *White Collar*, sees this as an example of a new form of alienated labour: not only do you sell your labour power, but you also sell to the employer those of your own personal characteristics that make impressions on others:

> One knows the salesclerk not as a person but as a commercial mask, a stereotyped greeting and appreciation for patronage ... Kindness and friendliness become aspects of personalized service or of public relations of big firms, rationalized to further the sale of something. With anonymous insincerity the Successful Person thus makes an instrument of his own appearance and personality ... In the normal course of her work ... the salesgirl becomes self-alienated. In one large department store, a planted observer said of one girl: 'I have been watching her for three days now. She wears a fixed smile on her made-up face, and it never varies, no matter to whom she speaks. I never heard her laugh spontaneously or naturally. Either she is frowning or her face is devoid of any expression. When a customer approaches, she immediately assumes her hard, forced smile.' (Mills, 1956 [1951]: 182, 184)

So the department store needs a sales staff that is disciplined, cultivated, pleasant – and alienated from their own personality, for they have sold it to someone else.

Class

Where does class fit into the picture of the department store? A phrase that was often used in the early days of the stores was 'democratization of luxury'. This is a little misleading, for the upper classes would continue in their own luxurious way without needing the department stores. The working classes could certainly enter the big shops, but they might do rather more looking than buying. The intended market of the department stores consisted of the middle classes, and there were particular reasons that seemed to make the department store and the middle classes suit each other very well. Laermans (1993) points out that one reason why middle-class women found the stores so attractive was because they represented a *public* space that was female rather than male: they had been restricted to the female domestic sphere up to this. Working-class women had fewer difficulties in accessing public space because of course many of them worked anyway, and so the department store was of less import in that respect. We shall return to questions of gender below.

The big stores were founded at a moment when the urban middle class was growing very quickly in numbers. This middle class was new, created through the appearance of new institutions or the reorganization of old ones, so that, as Laermans (1993: 96–7) writes, 'The process of professionalization and the bureaucratization of public as well as private administrations created a steadily rising number of white-collar jobs (e.g. bookkeepers, school teachers, employees of large banks, insurance companies and railways).' Now new social classes tend to be very unsure of who they are and where they stand in society. They know they are not part of the old aristocracy or the great bourgeois classes, and they know they are also not members of the working class (although Marxists might disagree, but their account of class is derived from principles few of the new middle class would have accepted). So who are they, these new middle class people? They certainly did not want to be confused with the working class, and they could not really afford to live in the grand bourgeois style. Enter the department store with the perfect solution: goods they could afford, but goods that, as we have seen, were associated with luxury in all sorts of clever ways by new techniques. If, as Laermans (1993) maintains, the new middle class had not yet succeeded in forging its own cultural identity (and this seems very plausible), then it was the perfect target for a new form of store that could promise it identity – through consumption. Here, one could buy status off the shelf.

Because the new middle class was an *urban* phenomenon, appearance became a very important way of indicating status to strangers, a point also made in Chapter 2. So the new middle class became peculiarly attentive to appearance as a way of indicating class belonging, and again the big store could provide all they wanted. As Miller (1981: 184) puts it, 'Bon Marché goods were so interwoven with perceptions of the bourgeois way of life that a purchase of a Bon Marché tablecloth or a coat for the theatre became a purchase of bourgeois status too'. To be bourgeois now seemed to be a matter of appearance, an appearance defined by the models promoted by the department store and taken on by those who purchased them. The store became a sort of great book of etiquette where the proper objects for the proper people in the proper contexts were prescribed. They managed to impose an idea of what it was to be middle class. But as classes are in continual symbolic struggles, as we saw when we looked at Bourdieu's work in Chapter 2, new items need to be made available so that status may be maintained. It is not surprising, then, that the store managed a great turnover in fashionable goods and kept the customers coming back and back again. So the new middle class managed to find a cultural identity through the department stores, and for the first time we see the emergence of a class that was almost totally defined by consumption. Clearly, they were made for each other.

The changes wrought by the coming of the department store are summarized in Table 4.1.

Gender

It was mentioned above that the department stores provided a new female space in the public sphere, and indeed the department store could act as a perfect excuse for a woman to escape her immediately local area. Earlier, women would confine their shopping to the neighbourhood and meet lots of people they already knew. While this has its positive sides, it can also be

Table 4.1   *Changes in shopping*

Before the department store	After the department store
Purchase obligatory: 'just looking' impossible	Purchase optional: 'just looking' becomes possible
Ultra-specialization: each shop sells only one type of good	Ultra-generalization: each department store sells a vast range of goods
Retailing governed by guild system; restricted number of goods available in artisanal system	Retailing in the department store a response to the availability of mass quantities of goods produced by the factory
No competition between guild members	Competition between department stores
No fixed prices: bargaining obligatory	Fixed prices: bargaining impossible
Need-centred: goods neither displayed nor advertised	Desire-centred: display and advertising of goods becomes vital to successful retailing
'Shopping around' impossible	'Shopping around' possible
Selling mere merchandise	Selling fantasies
Exchange or return impossible	Exchange or return possible
Production-centred	Consumption-centred
Shopping restricted to one's local area	Department stores attract shoppers from all over city and beyond
Personal characteristics of seller relatively unimportant	Personal characteristics of sales clerk must match 'cultivated' image of store
Public space generally male	Creation of new female public space for both shoppers and workers
Could not provide cultural identity for new middle class	Cultural identity for new middle class can be bought off the shelf

a little constraining. The department store offered the possibility to escape not only the domestic sphere but also the neighbourhood, and swap the pleasures and restrictions of the known community for the quite different pleasures and restrictions of the community of strangers who thronged the city centres. Most people freed from the constraints of their home locality will probably feel a sense of freedom to experiment, and the department stores did encourage shoppers to try new things. There was also a certain freedom from men in these stores, and this must also have appeared attractive to women who felt nervous in public streets marked by masculine presences. One writer went so far as to maintain that 'the department store made the phenomenon of a feminine public possible'; 'the buying stage of shopping appeared as the most widely visible sign of female emancipation in the modern city' (Barth, 1980: 121, 137, quoted by Laermans, 1993: 87–8). Laermans (1993: 89) remarks that 'For more and more women, the stores became equivalents of male downtown clubs and cafés ... a number of stores even provided free meeting rooms for women's organizations.' In this sense, then, department stores played a role in eman-cipating women. As we see below, however, women (and men) were also shaped in definite ways by the stores.

Department stores not only provided new opportunities to women shoppers, they also provided new opportunities for women workers. Here was a highly respectable place for women to be – never mind that the work was hard, not well paid, and, as we have seen from Wright Mills (1956 [1951]) above, alienating in a way that factory work, for all its disadvantages, was not. Women were cheaper to employ than men, were less likely to be unionized, and had begun to have similar educational opportunities to most men. Coupled with the department store's emphasis on appearance, women were an ideal labour force for the stores. The clerks, it appears, were more likely to be lower middle-class than working-class. This is probably partly due to the fact that they were more presentable (given the middle class's fascination with appearance) and therefore more likely to be recruited, and partly because the work appeared very respectable and thus somehow 'right' for the middle class who wanted, at all costs, not to be confused with the working class.

We have already touched upon the notion of the genderization of space when talking about male and female public spheres. But space was also gen-dered within the department store itself, and this topic is addressed by Gail Reekie in her 1992 article 'Changes in the Adamless Eden'. She looks at how retail space was gendered in a Brisbane department store called McWhirters in the 1930s and contrasts this with the way space has in fact become degendered in the store's transformation into McWhirters Market-place in 1990. Why has this happened?

McWhirters opened a new building in August 1931, and from the very beginning constructed the store as a space primarily for women. Opening attractions included,

> daily mannequin parades attended by approximately 10,000 women over a four day period. More than a fashion show, these three-hour entertainments included a dancing demonstration by Phyl and Ray, Australia's leading adagio dancers, and a live revue promoting Berlei corsets. McWhirters secured the services of trained corsetière consultant Mrs Foster-Jones, who offered free advice on 'the art of correct corsetry' ... during the store's promotional week. Other promotions included children's parties and pantomimes, Max Factor make-up demon-strations, and a display of replicas of the English crown jewels. (Reekie, 1992: 174)

But perhaps more interesting than these promotional happenings was the *everyday* fact that store space was segregated. Goods for men and goods for women were in separate locations, and men's departments occupied less space and were placed in peripheral parts of the store. The separation was even translated into newspaper advertising, where 'Men's and women's goods were advertised on the front page of the *Courier Mail* on separate days' (Reekie, 1992: 177). Even in men's departments, however, the majority of the shoppers were probably women. Reekie (1992: 178) analy-ses the organization of retail space in McWhirters in the early 1930s according to whether it can be characterized as female, mixed or male. Female space could be found on all floors from basement to third, mixed space on all floors except the first, and exclusively male space only on the first. So men would seem to be quarantined in their own little corner. There were 30 female sections in the store, 8 mixed, and a mere 5 male sections. It seems strikingly clear not only that retail space is segregated according to gender, but also that female space easily dominates.

Let us now jump forward 60 years: 'On none of the four levels of the McWhirters Marketplace is the sexual segregation or the dominance of female space characteristic of the 1930s department store apparent' (Reekie, 1992: 186). In the 1930s goods were clearly gendered and such rigid separations easily translated into segregated spaces. But now:

> The consumption activities promoted by leisure retailing . . . constitute a form of creative self-expression in which the self is defined by the purchase of a variety of commodities, *few of which are clearly sexed*. The consumer of the 1990s, conceived of or promoted as genderless by the managers of consumption, purchases for him or her self an identity that can be assembled and reassembled from an apparently endless repertoire of 'unique' or non-standard components. (Reekie, 1992: 188, my emphasis)

It is not so much that gendered meanings have disappeared, but they have become confused: there is more available now than the standard sex kits of the 1930s. This is probably because men, too, have become consumers as more women enter the labour force and new markets, such as men, are courted by advertisers. Reekie maintains that there has been a reclassification of space: sites of family shopping (still mostly done by women) are to be found in the supermarket or suburban shopping centres, but sites of *leisure* retailing are less gender marked. The argument here is that mundane shopping is still a female space, but playful shopping has become mixed. Reekie (1992: 190) rather cynically remarks that 'Once certain kinds of shopping begin to lose their low-status denotations of feminine drudgery, consumption loses its unambiguously sexed associations.' Men are now consumers too, and to shop is no longer unmanly – at least, not when men are shopping for non-everyday goods for the family. The point of the postmodern McWhirters Marketplace is not the purchase of pre-gendered identities, but the playful purchase of goods to construct identities for oneself.

Although we have considered the role department stores have played in freeing women from certain kinds of restrictions, it ought not to be forgotten that the stores also tried to reshape women in an image that suited their own retailing purposes. It is this topic that we now address through Reekie's 1993 book *Temptations*. She looks at how department store advertising such as 'mail-order catalogues, newspapers and magazines, mannequin parades, store dummies and the promotion of beauty products sexualized consumerism and standardized gender between 1918 and 1930' (Reekie, 1993: 136). In the case of women, the general tendency seems to have been in the direction of the creation of a standard-model female body. This was accomplished through such techniques as drawing women with doll-like faces and emphasizing the lips, or even simply drawing exactly the same face on several models and stylizing the bodies in an angular way so that they resembled no real female body (illustrated in Reekie, 1993: 139). Why was this done? It neatly reversed what we might imagine as the 'natural' order of things in a way that entirely benefited the department store. By 'natural' order of things I mean the tendency to go to a shop to try and find clothes that fit one's body. Here, clothing is made subordinate to the demands of the body. But if the store manages to create a stylized image, an abstract model of a standard female body, then the body must be made to fit the clothes that the store makes available. Here, the body is made subordinate to an abstract model that stands outside it and is shaped by marketing. No longer does the store have to cope with the (for it) distressing irregularities of female bodies coming in all shapes and sizes, for now the projected image will appear as the only sort of body that women are supposed to have, and some will no doubt strive to attain that sort of standardized body, unreal though it may seem to women composed of flesh and blood rather than easily mouldable plastic. Standard sized and shaped bodies come to fit the standard sizes and shapes provided by mass manufacture – more profits can be made from these sorts of bodies than any other. Ready-made clothing demands ready-made bodies.

A similar tendency may be discerned in the use of shop dummies. Before the First World War, dressmakers' dummies had no heads and were relatively shapeless. This may sound unattractive to us, who have grown up with quite different experiences of shop dummies. But these headless and shapeless methods of display had definite advantages. In the words of the Champion Window-Dresser of 1924, this method

> leaves something to the imagination, so that the customer can easily visualize her own figure in the frock . . . the simple suggestion of a drape [leaves] the rest to the customer's imagination. She gets a real pleasure in fancying how she will look in this or that material etc. Don't deprive her of that pleasure. She can't imagine herself as the theatrical young lady with the pearly complexion and ruby lips of the wax model. (quoted by Reekie, 1993: 143)

So there was plenty of room for the woman to move to a fantasy constructed on the model of her own body. But when dummies are given heads and a definite shape, this possibility is removed. Here, the fantasy is based on the model of the dummy, and the woman is left with little choice but to conform to this – or be out of fashion with a body that has become anti-social. This model of the proper woman was even taken up by state agencies between 1918 and the mid-1920s. The period saw

> a series of state and commonwealth government enquiries into the basic wage and cost of living for adult women workers . . . In their attempts to specify the appropriate contents of the working-woman's wardrobe, arbitration court officials, male counsel and female expert witnesses drew on easily-accessible presentations of clothing advertised by the big drapery stores. (Reekie, 1993: 146–7)

Not only were women presented with ideal models by the stores, then, but the agencies of the state also took up these models and enshrined this standard-model female in wage agreements. So while department stores may have contributed to an increase in freedom for women in many ways, they also produced the standard-model female body, which would seem to restrict rather than empower.

Men did not play a major role as consumers in the high era of the department store. Their image in store catalogues and the like changed more slowly than women's and a greater range of ages seems to have been presented. Models of women tended to project a young image – again, a standardization that men seem to have escaped. One can be an ideal man at any age, while ideal women are much more restricted. Men tended to be represented as active in occupational roles, while women were presented as being at leisure. Men's bodies were also presented as taking up more space and being generally more assertive than female bodies (Reekie, 1993: 140).

The department store emerged to meet the distribution problems of rapidly industrializing economies and the identity problems of the new middle class. It gave women a new public social space, increased their employment opportunities, and created the standard-model female body familiar to us in the media of today. The shopping mall may now be taking over the role of the prime site of consumption from the department store, as the new middle class breaks down into ever more specific consumption-based groupings. That, however, is another story for another place.

5

Advertising

Readers of Max Weber (1976 [1904]) and Colin Campbell (1983, 1987) will recall that capitalism had to overcome traditional attitudes to work and accumulation in order to make any headway. For example:

> a man . . . who at the rate of 1 mark per acre mowed $2\frac{1}{2}$ acres per day and earned $2\frac{1}{2}$ marks when the rate was raised to 1.25 marks per acre mowed, not 3 acres, as he might easily have done, thus earning 3.75 marks, but only 2 acres, so that he could still earn the $2\frac{1}{2}$ marks to which he was accustomed. The opportunity of earning more was less attractive than that of working less. He did not ask: how much can I earn in a day if I work as much as possible? but: how much must I work in order to earn the wage, $2\frac{1}{2}$ marks, which I earned before and which takes care of my traditional needs? (Weber, 1976 [1904]: 59–60)

If consumers aspire to nothing more than traditional needs, then it is hard to see how anything beyond this would ever be required. For those not swayed by the Protestant ethic of accumulation, nothing here would encourage consumer-centred economic expansion. This is where advertising rides to the rescue. The new industrial situation with its hordes of cheap mass-produced goods needed what Stuart Ewen calls 'a continually responsive consumer market' (1976: 32): where once consumers looked for reliable goods, now goods manufacturers needed reliable consumers – a market needed to be created to handle all the new goods being produced, which meant that manufacturers had to fabricate not only goods but also the people to purchase these goods. Advertising aimed at the efficient creation of consumers, and one way it accomplished this was through presenting individuals as continually subject to the harsh social scrutiny of the surrounding world. Ewen (1976: 97) lists some of the terms advertisements used to create new inadequacies in their readers so that manufacturers might supply the solution: '"sneaker smell", "paralysed pores", "vacation knees", "spoon-food face", "office hips", "underarm offense", and "ashtray breath"'. If the department stores promised dreams, advertising of the early mass industrial period seemed to promise nightmares to which only manufacturers could supply the solution. Advertising today seems to combine the two, now offering pleasurable dreams, now social nightmares – the contemporary customer is the ever-shifting product of this ever-shifting dialectic.

In this chapter we look at the reasons for the rise of advertising, how readers are constructed by advertisements as massed and gendered consumers, how social movements such as feminism may be harnessed to sell more goods through what Goldman (1992) calls 'commodity feminism', how advertising actually accomplishes its aims in a technical sense, and how far the law may protect us from advertisements that may mislead.

The rise of advertising

It was stated above that a central aim of advertising was the creation of efficient consumers. But how does it do this? What sort of new social creature does advertising bring to the world? Early advertisements did not really attempt to create consumers in any serious way. If we look at the *St James Chronicle* of 17–19 January 1782, we find the following:

> *Morocco and Tambour Silk Pocket-Books.*
> A Very large Assortment of Morocco Pocket-Books, Letter-Cases, and Ladies Housewives, with Gold, Silver, Enamelled, or Metal Locks, red and black Writing-Cases for travelling, and Asses-Skin Memorandum-Books.
> Great Variety of Tortoise-Shell Smelling-Bottles and Tooth pick Cases, inlaid with Gold and Silver, Silver and Silk Purses and Cane Strings.
> A complete Set of Teeth Instruments, fit for Gentlemen to clean their own Teeth, in Fish-Skin case, 7s. single Instruments 1s. black Silk Bags for the Hair, 2s. 3d. Rosettes, 1s. 2d.
> Sold by R. Sangwine, at the Sign of the Rose, No. 38, opposite New Round Court-Strand. (quoted in Dyer, 1988 [1982]: 18)

This advertisement has very much a take-it-or-leave-it feel to it: this is what we have, these are the prices, and this is where you get them. There is little attempt to create a particular sort of consumer, although there is a hint of this in the phrase 'fit for Gentlemen to clean their own Teeth'. But even here it does not give any reason why the said gentlemen should want to do such a thing – the advertisement does nothing to create a desire to clean teeth, it just suggests that this is one thing that can be done. Contrast this with a more recent ad: 'Jordan denture brush – for sweeter kisses!' (*Australian Women's Weekly*, November 1993: 176). This seems rather more likely to create a desire to clean teeth, except perhaps among the more militant members of the anti-kissing party. More seriously, it suggests that kisses are evaluated according to sweetness and that yours might just not be up to the required level – it constructs you as possibly inadequate and proposes the Jordan brush as a solution. Here we find one of the essential characteristics of modern advertising: suggest to the consumer that they lack something in their relations with others, and propose the product as the answer. So it is not that advertising simply creates desires within individuals that begin and end with those individuals in an entirely self-contained way, but rather that desires have to do with relations with other people: modern advertising concentrates at those points where the individual and society meet, and claims to have ways of making the individual a more successful social being.

This approach can be traced to the influence on advertising of the psychologist Allport, who argued that 'our consciousness of ourselves is largely a reflection of the consciousness which others have of us . . . My idea of myself is rather my own idea of my neighbor's view of me' (Allport, 1924:

325, quoted in Ewen, 1976: 34). So my very idea of myself is not at all self-contained and individual in any classically bourgeois sense, but is dependent upon how others see me. Ewen remarks that 'This notion of the individual as the object of continual and harsh social scrutiny underscored the argument of much of the ad texts of the decade [1920s]' (1976: 34). We are always being scrutinized, we are always being evaluated, our very being is absorbed into the ways in which others look at us: at every moment and in every way we may fail the test of the scrutinizing world. One can see how it is entirely in the interests of manufacturers to espouse this approach to social life, for it permits them to market their products as solutions to problems that arise only if this particular theory of the social world is accepted. This is much more efficient at shifting goods than mere praising of the good itself, or appeals to entirely egocentric desires that do not include others.

The Allport approach allows the creation of the continually fearful social actor, an actor that can overcome fear only by continual recourse to the products specially designed for this purpose. The fear never goes away because we are always under scrutiny: a shaving cream advertisement reminds us that 'Critical eyes are sizing you up right now', and a blade manufacturer gives the slack shaver 'no way to escape those accusing eyes' (Marchand, 1985: 213, 216). Marchand (1985: 208) refers to this as the 'Parable of the First Impression', and indeed in the swift, swirling *Gesellschaft* of briefly interacting strangers the first impression may be all one has to go on. It becomes necessary to display one's desirable qualities in an easily recognizable manner, and to cover over the undesirable ones. Surface appearance becomes paramount, and the social actor would appear to have a single option: become a permanent consumer. If at an earlier period the consumer turned a critical eye upon the product, now the consumer turns a critical eye on him- or herself: it is no longer the product that is inadequate, but the person – and the person will only find adequacy with the help of the products available on the marketplace. To summarize in Ewen's words:

> ˎ The functional goal of national advertising [in the US] was the creation of desires and habits. In tune with the need for mass distribution that accompanied the development of mass production capabilities, advertising was trying to produce in readers personal needs which would dependently fluctuate with the expanding marketplace. (Ewen, 1976: 37)

One of the aims of advertising, as we have just seen, was the creation of a population composed of people consuming goods. Before marketing became more sophisticated and targeted narrow bands of consumers as well as a general consumer, advertising in the US, according to Ewen (1976: 41–4), was seen as a way of creating national homogeneity and thereby overcoming the tensions that seemed to spring up in countries marked by a great heterogeneity in population. Social solidarity was seen to be strengthened by the emergence of the person as consumer as opposed to the person as member of a specific ethnic group. Consumer goods claim to construct the nation as a culturally homogeneous entity, multiculturalism notwithstanding.

If we are all consumers of the same products, then we are all the same culturally, no matter where we originate from.

Putting the above points slightly differently, it appears that advertising in the US of the 1920s claimed to provide a 'universal' culture that would overcome social divisions. This was seen as part of the civilizing process, and ads were often designed 'to make people ashamed of their origins and, consequently, the habits and practices that betrayed them as alien' (Ewen, 1976: 43). One could become a proper American by drinking Coca-Cola and consuming other appropriate goods: this was seen as a universal, civilized instinct, when in fact it was simply something that grew out of a particular stage of capitalism. Nevertheless, it must be admitted that consumerism is indeed a possible way of constructing a form of social solidarity. It might, however, be more like Durkheim's (1984 [1893]) mechanical solidarity rather than the organic form. Students of sociology will recall that mechanical solidarity characterized societies with low differentiation among their component elements. Here, solidarity would come from the fact that all consumers consumed in more or less the same way (they do not in practice, but sameness seemed to be the aim of advertising at this period) and all would aspire to the same models of consumption. The problem of mechanical solidarity of course is that it precludes development precisely because of the sameness involved. Organic solidarity, with its high level of differentiation, made much more complex societies possible. Recent advertising targeting particular groups in particular ways may be constructing a more organic model of solidarity in a more complex consuming society, unless it simply fragments and thereby undermines solidarity. But this is not something that has been researched yet as far as I can tell. It may be argued, at any rate, that an earlier phase of advertising constructing a homogeneous market is followed by a later phase of advertising that constructs market segments. The later phase is possible because the first has succeeded very well in turning us all into consumers, so it is then quite safe to divide us up again once our identity as consumers has irreversibly been achieved.

The other main social division that advertising attempted to overcome was class, and it did this by creating the notion of the mass consumer. Ewen writes: 'By transforming the notion of "class" into "mass", business hoped to create an "individual" who could locate his needs and frustrations in terms of the consumption of goods rather than the quality and content of his life (work)' (1976: 43). The problems of life in capitalist industrial societies were turned to advantage by advertising: rather than considering them as problems of capitalist industrialism as a system, they interpreted them as individual problems to be overcome by the uses of particular products. The problem lies not in the system, but in ourselves. Ewen provides an extract from an advertisement for Listerine, which claims to offer a solution to halitosis, that shows this very well: 'He was conscious that something stood between him and greater business success – between him and greater popularity. Some subtle something he couldn't lay his hands on . . . Finally, one day, it dawned on him . . . the truth that his friends had been too delicate to mention' (1976: 46). The foulness of his breath is the only thing that keeps this man from succeeding in business, and Listerine will of course promise to solve the problem. Success has nothing to do with inequalities of access or the like, but seems to depend only upon a bodily problem. The self becomes transformed into the commodity self: the body is constructed as having all sorts of problems (bad breath, enlarged pores, or whatever) and it therefore absolutely requires the aid of commodities in order to be a properly social body.

The properly social body may, of course, refer not only to the classed or massed body, but also to the gendered body. In the next section, we consider some of the ways in which advertising has constructed notions of the properly gendered.

Gender in advertising

Here we look at Erving Goffman's (1979 [1976]) account of gender relations in advertising and Robert Goldman's (1992) analysis of how feminism has been used by advertisers to sell goods.

There is an excellent collection of no fewer than 508 advertising images of the 1970s in Goffman's book *Gender Advertisements* (1979 [1976]). Here we look at five of the main themes he extracted from his sample: relative size, the feminine touch, function ranking, the family, and the ritualization of subordination.

Relative size

We tend to assume that when two people are represented in art or drawings, the taller will be the one with more authority. Relative size, in this sense, is an index of power. Generally, men in advertisements are made to appear taller than women, and this can be perhaps best seen when the reverse is true: in Goffman's illustrations 'the men seem almost always to be not only subordinated in social class status, but also thoroughly costumed as craft-bound servitors who – it might appear – can be safely treated totally in the circumscribed terms of their modest trade' (Goffman, 1979 [1976]: 28). So women appear taller than men when it is a question of representing social class rather than gender differences, where the woman is the one who comes from the higher social class.

The feminine touch

Goffman notes that women are represented as cradling or caressing an object but not grasping, holding or manipulating it in a utilitarian way. His illustrations show a clear gender difference in the use of touch: a man holds firmly a bottle of Jägermeister, a glass filled with alcohol (two instances of this), a cigarette, and a steering wheel – in each case, the woman merely caresses the man's hand and/or the object in a delicate way. This would seem to indicate that women and men have different relationships both to objects in the world and to each other. It is as if women do not want to impose themselves on the objects, but treat them as precious and to be admired in an aesthetic way. Men, by contrast, show the objects who's boss, treating them as means to a particular end rather than as objects of beauty to be admired. There seems to be a contrast between aesthetic and instrumentalist approaches to objects, a contrast that constructs gender differences and relations in a specific way: men act with clear purpose, women just look on admiringly.

Function ranking

Where women and men are depicted as collaborating face to face in an undertaking, who gets to perform the executive role? In almost all of Goffman's illustrations, it is the man who does this. For example: male doctor examines patient while female nurse looks on, man pumps water while woman delicately holds bucket to receive with pleasure the spewing liquid, man kicks football while woman holds it delicately in place, man adjusts sail while woman in bikini stands on display, two instances of men taking photos while the women merely pose, several instances of men pointing to buildings and the like and the women looking towards the object in question.

The family

The images Goffman chooses construct boys and their fathers as different and sometimes in conflict, while girls and their mothers are shown as merely younger and older versions of each other. The boys are seen as having to *do* something to achieve manhood, and the fathers here are generally doing something different to the sons: one lights a cigar while the other sits in a toy car, another smokes a cigar and stands behind his son, who seems to be sitting on a swing. The girls and their mothers are generally engaged in the same activity or are posed in similar positions or in similar clothes. In other advertisements, 'Often the father (or in his absence, a son) stands a little outside the physical circle of the other members of the family, as if to express a relationship whose protectiveness is linked with, perhaps even requires, distance' (Goffman, 1979 [1976]: 39). The images here clearly say that men protect (and often survey), and that women and children are protected (and are often surveyed). The theme of the family will be treated again in Chapter 6.

Ritualization of subordination

Goffman's fifth theme is of special interest as it concerns the power relations between men and women as constructed through advertising. One of the ways in which display of an inferior position is demonstrated is through the less powerful one lying on the bed or the floor: Goffman remarks that such positions make it difficult to physically defend oneself, so one is very dependent on the surroundings being benign. In his sample, 'it appears that children and women are pictured on floors and beds more than are men' (Goffman, 1979 [1976]: 41). For Goffman, 'high physical place symboliz[es] high social place' (1979 [1976]: 43), and in the majority of cases the men in adverts occupy a higher physical place than the women. Even in the exceptions the man is generally looking at the woman while the latter's head is turned demurely away, so the power of being the one who surveys an object still rests with him. There are other body postures, such as the 'bashful knee bend' (1979 [1976]: 45), that indicate a less powerful position. This 'can be read as forgoing of full effort to be prepared and on the ready in the current social situation, for the position adds a moment to any effort to fight or flee' (ibid.). Women are frequently posed in this position, men rarely. One finds a similar pattern in the case of lowering the head relative to others for women again are the ones portrayed in this way. For Goffman, 'The resulting configurations can be read as an acceptance of subordination, an expression of ingratiation, submissiveness, and appeasement' (1979 [1976]: 46).

Commodity feminism

Given the above, it is not difficult to see why there has been much popular feminist criticism of the ways in which women were portrayed in advertisements. This could have posed problems for advertisers, so they took the obvious way out by trying to incorporate feminist ideas and thus remove the critical power of feminism with respect to advertising. The general principle is simple: take a social movement or an idea that looks as if it is in opposition to the capitalist world as currently constructed, use it to sell more capitalist goods, and thus strengthen the system the social movement or idea was supposed to subvert. For example, one can see everywhere how advertisers took over the message of green movements, which could be interpreted as very anti-capitalist and anti-consumption, and used the notion of 'green commodities' all the better to sell their own goods. In the case of feminism, we find what Goldman (1992) calls 'commodity feminism'. This is, of course, a pun on the phrase 'commodity fetishism' that will be familiar from the discussion of Marx's account of the commodity form that we considered in the chapter devoted to objects. Goldman writes that this pun

> is a reminder that commodity relations turn the relations of acting subjects into the relations between objects. The process of turning feminism into sign values *fetishizes* feminism into an iconography of things. When advertisers appropriate feminism, they cook it to distil out a residue – an object: a look, a style. Women's discourses are thus relocated and respoken by named objects like *Hanes* hose, *Nike* shoes, *Esprit* jeans. Sign-objects are thus made to stand for, and made equivalent to, feminist goals of independence and professional success. Personality can be represented, relationships achieved and resources acquired through personal consumer choices. (Goldman, 1992: 131)

Putting this another way, we may suggest that, from the point of view of advertisers, feminism is something that is not so much a social movement with a particular politics and ideology and a desire to change the world, but a state that can be attained by consuming the right goods: certain objects will signify 'feminist lifestyle', and that is all that is required. 'The feminist' is constructed as just another consumer category amongst others.

How, then, is feminism signified by advertisements? They 'assemble signs which connote independence, participation in the work force, individual freedom and self control' (Goldman, 1992: 133). Some readers may remember the launch by Revlon in 1973 of Charlie perfume, which showed a young, active woman who did not need a man to give her a meaningful existence (Goldman, 1987: 699). This seems to be one of the earliest attempts to handle the rise of feminism: you too could become an independent woman by simply purchasing the Charlie line from Revlon. A more recent example is an advertisement for the magazine *Self* reproduced by Goldman (1992: 134–5). The fact that the modern woman has more than one role in life is constructed visually in quite a striking manner. The woman here is split into three parts: the bottom third shows her clad in hiking boots and jeans, the middle third of her body wears an evening dress, and the top part is apparelled in a business suit. So she is sporty *and* sexy *and* businesslike, not limited to just one of these roles. The accompanying text is also a good example of how advertisers have taken feminism and used it for their own purposes. It begins 'Today's women are tuned into more than their bodies.' So it is making a point that feminists could hardly disagree with: women are more than their bodies. The advertisement, indeed, seems to be claiming feminist credentials. These people, it continues, 'are successful career women, used to making decisions' – again, a construction feminists would find it hard to object to. What does the magazine *Self* give them? 'An edge' in their roles as successful career women. More specifically, 'Timely articles on medical breakthroughs. In-depth fitness and nutrition coverage. New fashion and beauty ideas. Advice on finance, careers, relationships.' So the new career woman needs knowledge of health, keeping the body fit, food (here under its scientific guise of 'nutrition', but it may well mean 'recipes'), fashion, beauty, finance, career and relationships – the 'self' of this woman is composed of these component parts, and her success is constructed as dependent upon the purchase of the one commodity that will give her the edge she requires, namely the magazine *Self*. Career woman or not, she still takes part in those areas more associated with the traditional interests of women: the body, food, fashion, beauty and relationships. The ad seems to claim that you can be a successful career woman, but the traditional areas are still a part of this: you are not allowed to be 'only' a career woman, with no interest in your body, the food you eat, the clothes you put on and the make-up you wear – all standard consumer areas. It is as if the career is just one more thing to be added to one's identity as a consumer self.

The idea of the modern successful woman as a consumer of commodities is continued in Goldman's comparison (1992: 138–9) of ads for the magazines *Ms*, which would certainly claim feminist credentials, and *Cosmopolitan*, which may have fewer reasons to claim such a thing. Both construct women as in powerful positions: the *Ms* ad asks 'What do you call a woman who's made it to the top? Ms', while *Cosmopolitan* uses the headline 'The power behind the pretty face'. And how do we know that one woman has made it to the top and the other is powerful as well as pretty? By the collection of objects they are seen as possessing. The *Ms* woman has 'a passport; Tictac breath mints; a child's drawing; calculator; keys; American Express Card [a sure sign of belonging to the consumer society]; perfume atomizer; gold charm bracelet; a crumpled $100 bill; Anacin; and a business card' (Goldman, 1992: 137). The *Cosmopolitan* woman has a set of objects which partly overlaps with the *Ms* woman, but they are more obviously consumer objects: 'American Express gold card [obviously a very serious consumer!]; make-up brushes; Pan Am World air travel card; Hertz Rent-a-Car card; compact disk (Mozart); portable Sharp calculator; motorcycle helmet; scuba diving mask' (Goldman, 1992: 137, 140). Being at the top or being powerful is translated into a particular set of objects.

To be the sort of woman feminists approve of, it seems, is to be a consumer of particular goods and services. This is easily recuperable within capitalism. The main point should be clear: advertisers have handled the challenges of feminism by constructing women as independent and in control, but only thanks to particular commodities. Instead of posing a threat to the world of consumption, feminist concerns are simply used as fuel to further its reach. Consumption absorbs politics, and re-emerges strengthened.

The effects of advertising in the twentieth century are summarized in Table 5.1.

How advertising works

Up to this, we have been considering the relations between advertising and such important social concepts as class, mass, and gender in a relatively broad way. Let us now look a little more closely at the technicalities of how

Table 5.1 *Effects of advertising in the twentieth century*

Produces reliable consumers

Promises to remedy a 'lack' in the consumer that advertising itself has created: it is not the product but the person who is inadequate

Focuses on the consumer not as individual but as social being

Transforms 'class' society into 'mass' society

Turns the 'self' into a 'commodity self'

Matches goods to persons

Reduces social movements to the display of appropriate commodities through promoting products that provide visible evidence that one is living the 'feminist' or 'green' lifestyle advertisements work. There are two main ways we could go about finding this out. One would be to see how people perceived and acted upon advertisements in everyday life, but lack of space forbids me from addressing that topic here. Or we could look at the advertisements themselves. Here, we treat advertisements as cultural artefacts among others and seek to understand what they are trying to do *as* cultural artefacts. This is a bit like looking at how a poem or a novel is constructed as a way of understanding what it is trying to accomplish, and a number of people who have written on advertising do indeed come out of a language and literature tradition rather than a sociological background. So the focus here will be on formal analysis: if we want to think of advertisements as machines that produce certain types of meaning, then what we are trying to do here is to understand what makes the machines tick. The account below can only be a brief introduction to this sort of analysis, and readers interested in knowing more should consult Judith Williamson's by now classic book of 1978. Here we can touch upon only a few of the more important points.

As an introduction to formal analysis, Williamson takes the example of how advertisements link the product with other objects or with the potential consumer in such a way that the links appear entirely natural. There is nothing natural, however, about the ways in which this sense of the natural is constructed. If the links between things are made to appear natural, then it becomes very hard to see matters in any other way: so if advertisers can construct an apparently natural relation between their commodities and people, then the commodities can be seen as unquestionable parts of life, as the way things quite simply are. The fact that such connections are entirely manufactured becomes invisible.

Let us take the examples of the advertisements for Continental Soup reproduced as Figures 5.1 and 5.2. In each of these cases, the product is linked with the meanings of some other object and prepares a place within the ad for the reading subject. These ads are particularly good examples of myth in the sense understood by the French writer Roland Barthes (1989 [1957]), who was one of the first to take a semiotic approach to analysing the world of popular culture and thus one of Williamson's more important predecessors. 'Semiotics' comes from the Greek word for sign, and is a discipline that looks at how the world of signs works. A sign can be pretty much anything that carries a meaning – words, sounds, pictures, traffic lights, clothing. But what is the nature of a sign? The Swiss linguist Ferdinand de Saussure (1974 [1916]), who is generally credited with first putting the notion of a science of signs on the disciplinary map, saw it as follows. A sign is composed of a signifier and a signified, and is to be distinguished from a referent. For example, the written letters H-O-R-S-E or the sound stream [horse] are signifiers, the idea 'horse' that comes to us when someone utters the sounds or writes the letters is the signified, and the combination of the two is the sign. So a sign is composed of the unity of a signifier and a signified. The referent is the horse in its concrete existence. Note that there is no intrinsic link between a signifier and a signified – the relationship

Figure 5.1

between them is quite arbitrary. The signified 'horse' has no special connection with the sound stream [horse]: a French person would say *cheval*, a German *Pferd*, and a Swede *häst*. This means that signifiers are quite detachable from signifieds, and can circulate freely among other signifiers, thereby creating meanings that have nothing to do with their signifieds. This, for Barthes, is how myth works, and the same process lies at the base of many of Williamson's analyses. Barthes takes the example of a photograph of a bunch of roses: this is a sign that signifies, well, roses. But the roses can then be seen as themselves signifying 'passion' or 'love'. So the photograph of a bunch of roses has 'roses' as its signified, but this rose-sign then becomes the signifier of another signified, namely love or passion, and the unity of these two becomes a new sign. This phenomenon, when the sign of the first becomes the signifier of the second, is, according to Barthes, how myth works: it 'steals' something (the roses) and uses it to mean something else.

Figure 5.1 creates a place for the subject by inviting the reader to lift up the mug of soup lying in the bottom right-hand corner: there is only one mug, and nobody else portrayed in the ad. It's yours, take it! Left-handers, of course, might have problems with the way the mug is turned. The myth would seem to be that of the experienced international traveller, as we can see from the old and peeling labels from exotic places placed strategically over the suitcase. So to consume Continental Cup-a-Soup is to become this experienced traveller in exotic places. The placing of the soup packets on the case gives them similar status to the old labels – they borrow, or steal,

This soup is cracked up to be something special.

For a vegetable dish they'll be scrambling for, this soup is
eggsactly what your dish needs.

Fluffy Vegetable Bake

2 cups diced, grated vegetables: Zucchini, capsicum, corn kernels etc.
1 packet Continental Indian Mild Korma Curry Soup
4 eggs ~ 1 1/2 cups milk ~ 3 slices white bread buttered and diced

Place vegetables into a greased ovenproof dish. Whisk together the soup mix,
eggs and milk, pour over the vegetables. Sprinkle with diced bread and
bake at 180°C for 40-45 minutes, until set and golden. Serves 4.

Continental Soup. The start of a great meal.

Continental
INDIAN MILD
KORMA CURRY

Figure 5.2

perhaps, all that those peeling labels stand for. This process is quite common
in advertising: put two objects together, and the lesser one, in terms of prestige and value, will take from the greater one. So put your product next to
a famous person or thing and it will steal value from them. Put the cheap
eau de toilette you are trying to sell against the Eiffel Tower and you have
stolen chic Parisianness and given it to your product (see the discussion in
Williamson, 1978: 20–39).

The subject in Figure 5.2, also featuring Continental soup, is about to serve
him/herself with a nice helping of Fluffy Vegetable Bake. The myth here
would seem to refer to homeness and awayness in the one place: the exotic
soup seems to borrow homeness from the obviously home-embroidered

cloth while the homely cloth and dish borrow exotic awayness from the soup – there is a sort of continual exchange between homeness and awayness here, and you of course can have both at the same time by consuming that tempting portion of food that is about to be served.

Once the product has managed to obtain meaning from outside itself, it is a short step to taking over that meaning. As Williamson puts it, 'the product itself comes to *mean*. It may start off as a reflection of something exterior, but will soon come to represent it' (1978: 35). She gives a good example of this in the advertising slogan 'Beanz meanz Heinz' (Williamson, 1978: 36). 'Beanz' are here a subset of 'Heinz', and their existence is contained within the brand name. There are no beans outside Heinz, although this does not, of course, preclude Heinz from containing 56 things other than beans. This is clearly a very powerful technique: the product has captured reality, the real world emanates from the product. The product means reality, and if you want a real existence you need to buy the product.

Because it is possible to invest brand names with much more specific meanings and values than unbranded goods, the brand, such as Heinz, can impose itself over the actual good (beans) as principal carrier of meaning. The process has become quite familiar in English: instead of thinking about, say, chocolate, we might think about Cadbury's chocolate, or instead of thinking about a vacuum cleaner we might think about a Hoover vacuum cleaner. After a while, we might begin to think not of Cadbury's chocolate or a Hoover vacuum cleaner but of say, a bar of Cadbury's or buying a Hoover – indeed, in Britain and Ireland 'to hoover' is often synonymous with 'to vacuum clean'. The actual items themselves disappear behind the brand names, and the company names replace the 'real thing'. Once we start thinking like this, it becomes less likely that a glut of goods on the market will lead to the ruin of the manufacturer – after all, we are no longer interested just in buying chocolates or vacuum cleaners produced by anybody but in buying Cadbury's or Hoovers. The brand name gains a certain relative independence from the ups and downs of the market which makes it more difficult for rival manufacturers to capture territory (Windschuttle, 1988: 12). One cannot just market chocolates and vacuum cleaners any more; one has to market something that is also not Cadbury's or a Hoover and something that has better or different meanings and values than Cadbury's or a Hoover.

One of the best examples I know of the power of a brand name to eclipse the actual good it was branding was the marketing of a cider called Stag, which is sold in Ireland. Now cider does not have a particularly good name there, as it is associated with 12–15-year-olds sitting around waste ground getting very drunk very quickly. The advertising for Stag in the late 1980s never mentioned that it was a cider – all the marketing gave the impression that it was a lager, although it never explicitly claimed to be one. A number of my research methods students interviewed people about Stag, and found that most did indeed think it was a lager. Then, pursuing the research project, one of the group went up to a bar and asked for a cider – she was told no, and was asked to leave as the publican did not want that sort of person in the pub. Another of the group then went and asked for a Stag, which she had no problem in obtaining, and was no doubt exactly the sort of person that the publican wanted in the establishment. So a cider has managed to position itself as a sophisticated and desirable drink by being known only as its brand name and by marketing itself like a lager rather than a cider. Ask for a cider and you risk being thrown out of the pub, ask for a Stag and you are a valued customer. The good itself – cider – has completely disappeared behind the brand name. At the high consumer stage of capitalism in which we are now living, this may become the norm rather than the exception.

Advertising language and the protected consumer

We have just seen how advertisements rather cleverly manipulate various sorts of signs in order to project meanings that may bear no obvious relation to the goods being sold. But surely the law protects us from misleading advertising? Let us now consider if this is indeed the case.

According to the Federal Bureau of Consumer Affairs (1993: 3), Australian consumers have the right to be informed: 'To be given facts needed to make an informed choice, and to be protected against dishonest or misleading advertising and labelling'. The Trade Practices Act 1974 'provides power for public enforcement of the provisions prohibiting unfair, unconscionable, misleading and deceptive conduct' (1993: 5). But Richard Parmentier (1994: 142ff.), commenting on US consumer law, suggests that this type of legislation may well have the opposite effect to that intended. Instead of protecting consumers, it may leave them open to even more manipulation and deception. How can this be? Let us consider a few examples drawn from the 32-page *Innovations '96* New Year catalogue distributed with the *Australian* newspaper in January 1996:

amazing wonder mop
beautiful mahogany filing cabinet
brilliant sunshade pavilion
clever telescopic hose brush
delightful and versatile throws
elegant button-through dress
essential garden unbrella
eye-catching new Jersey Suit
fabulous gold-edged cutlery
fine Italian leather sandals
great space saver
high quality diver's watch
lovely sun and moon throw
neatest TV antenna
perfect choice for summer
remarkable breadmaker
remarkable reversible raincoat
revolutionary new sweeper

stylish storage tower
superb barrister bookcase

It is probably clear to most readers that terms such as 'amazing', 'beautiful', 'brilliant', 'clever', 'delightful', 'elegant' and so on are to be read as entirely matters of opinion rather than as factual descriptions. They are typical examples of what Parmentier (1994: 143) calls 'puffery'. He argues that in the *caveat emptor* era consumers were supposed to be able to distinguish 'puffery' for what it was, but new regulations on commercial language suggest that it is truthful and subject to verification:

> while the tradition of *caveat emptor* constitutes a general background warning that commercial speech is basically persuasive, the modern regulatory environment assumes, falsely, that commercial speech is primarily referential, contributing valuable information essential to rational markets . . . The regulated referentiality assigned to a portion of the ad is, then, transferred to expressions of puffery, attributing to them analogically the factuality previously dismissed by all reasonable people. (Parmentier, 1994: 145–6)

The regulations protecting consumers, then, play directly into the hands of advertisers by making it more likely that puffery will no longer be recognized for what it is. In other words, the 'amazing', 'beautiful', 'brilliant', 'clever', 'delightful', 'elegant' and other terms noted above will come to be interpreted as factual descriptions of the qualities of the items advertised rather than mere puffs to be taken with several grains of salt: it is no longer the seller's inherently contestable opinion that is being proposed, but a legally approved statement of fact. The elegant button-through dress is elegant because the law guarantees that it is, consumer opinion notwithstanding. Parmentier's reasoning may assume a rather naïve reader, but the legal structures that would allow such a reader to exist are now in place. Let the 'advertisee' beware.

6
Women's Magazines

Readership figures for mainstream women's magazines are impressively large: *Women's Day* reached 14,827,000 US female readers in 1982 (McCracken, E., 1993: 93), *Libelle* was read by 43.8 per cent of all Dutch women in 1988 (Hermes, 1995: 166), and some estimates place the readership of the *Australian Women's Weekly* at more than 20 per cent of the entire population (see p. 87 below). These figures suggest that women's magazines may take up an important place in consumer culture, and so this chapter considers a number of ways in which women's magazines prepare subject positions for their readers. We pay particular attention to the analyses of magazine titles and feature articles. Space considerations preclude a study of the ways in which such magazines are actually read in practice, and interested readers are referred to Ballaster et al. (1991: chapter 5), Frazer (1987) and Hermes (1995). Examination of the titles shows a historical drift from women as members of a class to members of a relatively undifferentiated mass, and then to a more complex collection of status categories. The family is seen as a major concept underlying titles and feature article content, but it is suggested that an even more fundamental concept governs all aspects of these magazines, namely the notion of transformation.

Class, mass, status and consumption

What sort of woman is the woman of women's magazines? Let us begin by treating this question at a level that is both broad in historical overview and quite narrow in focus: magazine titles. Can a simple examination of titles be informative about the ways in which 'woman' has been constituted as a social category? Ballaster et al. (1991) examine British women's magazines from the late seventeenth century through to 1988. If we extract the titles from this text and organize them according to the themes implicit in their names (Table 6.1), we find the following broad themes: General (17 titles), Class community (21 titles), Mass community (17 titles), Family and domesticity (14 titles), Status category (16 titles), and Lifestyle (21 titles). These classifications are approximate: some are hard to classify unambiguously, some fit into more than one, and I have not taken magazine mergers into account. But the broad tendencies are clear.

The category 'General' refers to titles that do not indicate specific categories of women, or even women at all, and so we will not discuss this. Now if we exclude titles that derive directly from parent magazines and invoke a

Table 6.1 UK women's magazines from the late seventeenth century

General	Class community	Mass community	Family/domesticity	Status category	Lifestyle
The Athenian Mercury 1691–97	Ladies' Mercury 1693	The Female Tatler 1709–11	The Family Magazine . . . 1789–?	The Mother's Magazine 1834–49	Court and City Magazine 1770–71
The Tatler 1709–11	Ladie's Diary 1704–?	The Female Spectator 1744–46	The Mother's Magazine 1834–49	The Mother's Friend 19th century	Bon Ton Magazine 1790–96
Records of Love* 1710	Ladies Magazine 1749–53	Englishwoman's Domestic Magazine 1852–79	The Mother's Friend 19th century	The Christian Lady's Friend 19th century	Town and Country 1769–96
The Spectator 1711–14	Lady's Magazine 1759–63	English Woman's Journal 1858–64	The Family Economist 1850s	The Young English Woman 1860s–?	Court's Magazine and Belle Assemblée 1832–48
The Nonsense of Common-Sense 1737–38	Lady's Museum 1760–61	English Woman's Review . . . 1866–1910	Englishwoman's Domestic Magazine 1852–79	My Weekly 1910–	The Leisure Hour 19th century
The Parrot 1746	Lady's Magazine 1770–1830	Woman's World 1887–1920s	The Illustrated Household Journal 1880–81	Peg's Paper 1919–?	The Saturday Magazine 19th century
Westminster 1772–85	New Lady's Magazine 1786–95	Woman: for all Sorts and Conditions of Women 1890–1912	Milliner, Dress-maker and Draper 1881–?	Bunty*	Paris Mode 19th century
Sentimental and Masonic Magazine 1792–5	Ladies Monthly Museum 1798–1806	Woman at Home 1893–1920	Woman at Home 1893–1920	Jackie	Vogue 1916–
Eliza Cook's Journal 1850s	La Belle Assemblée . . . Ladies 1806–32	Woman's Weekly 1911–	Home Notes 1894–1957	Honey 20th century	Harper's Bazaar 20th century
The People's Friend 1869–?	The Lady 19th century–	Women's Filmfare 1935–	Home Chat 1894–1957	Ms 20th century	Living 1960s
The Argosy 19th century	My Lady's Novelette 19th century	Women's Illustrated 1936–?	Home Sweet Home 1890s	Spare Rib 1972–early 1990s	Nova mid-1960s–1975
Belgravia 19th century	Lady's Magazine 1832–37	Woman 1937–	Good Housekeeping 1922–	Shocking Pink late 20th century	Slimming 1969–?
Time and Tide 20th century	Court Magazine . . . and Lady's Magazine 1833–47	Woman's Own 1957–	Homes and Gardens 20th century	Black Hair and Beauty 1980s	Patches 1970–
True Monthly 20th century	La Belle Assemblée, or Ladies' . . . 1848–59	Woman's Mirror 20th century	Family Circle 1960s	Just Seventeen 1983–	Cosmopolitan 1972–
True Story 20th century	The Queen 1861–63	She 1950s		New Woman 1988–	Company late 20th century
Loving* 20th century	The Ladies' Newspaper 1863–?	Elle 1980s		Working Woman 20th century?	Essentials 1980s
True Romance* 20th century	Lady's World pre-1887	Woman's Review 1985–87			Options 1980s
	Lady's Pictorial 1881–1921				Prima 1980s
	The Gentlewoman 1890–1926				Chic 1984–
	The Christian Lady's Friend 19th century				Bella 1987–
	The Servant's Magazine 19th century				Best 1987–

* Uncertain classification.
Source: after Ballaster et al., 1991

non-class male/female difference (*The Female Tatler, The Female Spectator*), it is clear that the earlier magazines addressed women as the *class* audience of aristocratic ladies (for example: *Ladies' Mercury, Ladies' Diary, Ladies Magazine, Lady's Museum, New Lady's Magazine, Lady's Monthly Museum, The Lady, My Lady's Novelette*, and so on), while the non-lady female – the woman – only appears in 1852 with the *Englishwoman's Domestic Magazine*, when industrialization was raising the status of the (non-aristocratic) middle class to formidable levels. It is only from that moment that we find titles like *English Woman's Journal, English Woman's Review, Woman's World, Woman: for all Sorts and Conditions of Women, Woman at Home, Woman's Weekly, Women's Filmfare, Woman's Illustrated, Woman, Woman's Own, Woman's Mirror*, and so on. Viewed through the lens of class, 'lady' and 'woman' were *not* interchangeable terms in the Britain of the nineteenth century but were related as binary oppositions (see discussion in Ballaster et al., 1991: 93–4). In this sense, magazine titles created two separately classed communities of female persons, 'ladies' and 'women', the latter eventually replacing the former as dominant term in this century. The transition from 'lady' to 'woman' may be located in the late nineteenth century. Ballaster et al. (1991: 93) note that *Lady's World* became *Woman's World* in 1887 at the insistence of the new editor, Oscar Wilde, while the claim made by 'woman' to include all categories of female persons seems quite explicit in the 1890 title *Woman: for all Sorts and Conditions of Women*. The fact that it *is* so explicit indicates that the claim is new and uncertainly grounded, but its eventual success can be appreciated by noting that the term 'lady' has almost disappeared from the twentieth-century British scene. Instead of two separate *class* communities of female persons, namely ladies and women, there now appears to be a generalized *mass* of women, the stability of this mass guaranteed by its opposition to a term not directly visible from our classifications, but implicit in every post-lady use of the term 'woman': 'The construction of women as a homogeneous group, or even a group at all, is primarily achieved by the invocation of its supposedly "natural" opposite – men' (Ballaster et al., 1991: 9). The woman/lady opposition has been replaced by the woman/man opposition, thus shifting differentiation from different classes of female persons to different classes of gendered persons. Now it begins to look as if all women are essentially the 'same', simply because they are not men.

Magazine titles, especially in the nineteenth century, located this mass of women in the domestic sphere. This mass, however, was eventually to become internally differentiated into a number of status categories, a process that seems to be accelerating in the present century. Nineteenth-century status categories such as 'mother' or 'Christian' (as in *The Christian Lady's Friend*) refer to the larger transcendent categories of family structure and religion, while 'young' (as in *The Young English Woman*) may be subsumed under the rubric of age categories. Although the latter persists in this century (*Just Seventeen*), family and religion disappear to be replaced by two different sets of status categories.

The first set, like the earlier ones, refers to larger transcendent categories: here, race (*Black Hair and Beauty*), feminism (the ironically titled *Spare Rib, Shocking Pink, Ms.*), and activity outside the domestic sphere (*Working Woman*). The second set, however, stresses personal positions rather than belonging to larger categories. For example, *My Weekly* is as immanent a title as one could imagine, while *Jackie* and *Peg's Paper* imprison the subject within a proper name that hails her (Althusser, 1971 [1970]) as, paradoxically, the essentially personal incarnation of the broader category 'woman'. Such first names, indeed, allow their holder to escape the broader category that provided them with gendered names in the first place: a woman named, say, Mary, can claim that she is the site of her own very individual bunch of experiences that do not quite match anybody else's – 'Mary' may refer to a unique person when considered in this light. So, gendered first names provide one with both a very general belonging to the broad category of, in this case, 'woman', and with a very specific personal status (*this* Mary or Jackie, not any other Mary or Jackie). Contemporary magazine titles, then, appear to indicate a possibly unresolved and unresolvable tension in women's lives between larger categories such as race, feminism and occupational status, and the more personal categories of private life. In general, terms of address such as proper names and titles (*Ms* again, possibly *Honey*) are among the most powerful means available for locating persons as subjects in particular social positions (see Braun, 1988; Brown and Gilman, 1960; Ervin-Tripp, 1986 [1972]). *Ms* is a good example of how a term from the larger discourse of feminism constructs an addressed subject in a particular way. *Honey*, if interpreted as a term of address, accomplishes the same thing but from a different, and possibly opposing, larger discourse.

Other magazines may be gathered under the loose term 'lifestyle'. Earlier titles tend to locate lifestyle in particular spaces (*Court and City Magazine, Town and Country, Court's Magazine and Belle Assemblée, Paris Mode*), or specific times (*The Leisure Hour, The Saturday Magazine*), excluding other spaces and other times. Later titles dissolve this compartmentalization, and life in general becomes open to lifestyling: the title *Living* could hardly be more general and all-encompassing, while the most recent titles place the accent on living in general (*Cosmopolitan, Essentials, Options, Best*). It is not clear why this shift has taken place, but it would appear to be in line with the civilizing process as theorized by Elias (1994 [1939]), where the domain of 'proper' ways of doing things extends over ever more aspects of human existence. *Bon Ton Magazine* may be an early attempt to lay down explicitly what these 'proper' ways are for rising social classes with an uncertain grip on cultural capital (Bourdieu, 1984 [1979]). The growth of consumption as a mode of claiming status (Veblen, 1975 [1899]) has placed the mass of people in a position of having more choices than ever over their objects and ways of doing things and spending time, so it may be rather useful for the reader to be informed of the *Best Options* and *Prima Essentials* that will allow her to pass as *Chic* in the most *Bella* and *Cosmopolitan*

Company. 'Etiquette may be defined as the technique of the art of social life,' writes Troubridge (1931 [1926]: v). Her *Book of Etiquette*, 'written for those whose "gentle" minds lead them to wish to do what is expected of them, and that which may be considered the right thing' (Troubridge, 1931 [1926]: vi–vii), has been replaced by the lifestyle magazine, which provides details on the technique of the art of social life in consumer societies. To be 'civilized' is to know how to consume appropriately. The recently noted importance of the body as consumer object (see Chapter 10) is explicitly present here only in the title *Slimming*, but becomes more prominent in US magazines, as we shall see below.

The tendencies emerging from the examination of British magazine titles become even more pronounced when US titles are considered. Table 6.2 reorganizes according to theme the list of US magazines that features on page 303 of Ellen McCracken's book *Decoding Women's Magazines*.

There is no class/mass distinction evident from the titles alone and the information provided precludes historical analysis, so it is not possible to claim that 'woman' has replaced 'lady'. Indeed, such an opposition may make little sense in the US, as it is a society founded on bourgeois notions of the equality of subjects (even if not all categories of person acceded to subjecthood at the same time) rather than feudal distinctions with their irreducible inequalities. Women are still located in the familial-domestic sphere, but there is an increased fracturing of 'woman' into more status categories than the UK sample. That is, more individual types of women are constructed by these magazine titles. Four create women as entirely contained either within the person (*It's Me, Self*), body (*Slimmer*), or body in assembly with other bodies (*Weight Watchers*), but the majority relate to broader categories. Several titles see the female subject caught up in traditional areas such as marriage and the family (*Brides, Modern Bride, Parents, Working Mother*) or age groups (*Seventeen, 'Teen, Young Miss*). Terms of address include *Mademoiselle, Ms* and *Young Miss*, and seem to indicate a tension between feminist and traditional approaches to locating women in titled social space. Of course, these terms of address may also be assimilated to the discursive field of marriage and the family, where the marital status of women may (or deliberately may not, in the case of *Ms*) be (pro)claimed publicly through naming practices. The woman as worker appears twice (*Working Mother, Working Woman*), and twice again as player (*Playgirl, Women's Sports*). *New Woman* hints at a break from past versions, while *Newsweek Woman* creates a woman informed about world events. As in the British sample, we find lifestyle titles, but here there are almost as many devoted to specific aspects of lifestyle, such as food, clothing and the body, as to general living.

So what sort of woman emerges from an examination of magazine titles? There has been a clear shift in the UK sample from women as members of a social class to women as members of a mass, this mass being then further divided into a number of status categories, the latter then shifting slightly from broad categories to more personal ones. Lifestyle concerns are present

Table 6.2   *US Women's Magazines in 1983*

Family/domesticity	Status category	Lifestyle–general	Lifestyle–specific
Better Homes and Gardens	*Brides*	*Bazaar*	*Bon Appetit*
Family Circle	*It's Me*	*Cosmopolitan*	*Cuisine*
Good Housekeeping	*Mademoiselle*	*Essence*	*Gourmet*
House Beautiful	*Modern Bride*	*Glamour*	*Shape*
House and Garden	*Ms*	*McCall's*	*Slimmer*
Ladies' Home Journal	*New Woman*	*Redbook*	*Vogue*
Parents	*Newsweek Woman*	*Savvy*	*Weight Watchers*
Working Mother	*Parents*	*Spring*	*Women's Sports*
	Playgirl	*Town & Country*	
	Self	*Woman's Day*	
	Seventeen		
	Slimmer		
	'Teen		
	Weight Watchers		
	Women's Sports		
	Working Mother		
	Working Woman		
	Young Miss		

Source: after McCracken, E., 1993: 303

throughout the historical period covered in the sample (from the late seventeenth century to the present day), but tend to become more diffuse and general as more and more aspects of life demand 'proper' forms. The US sample, although lacking the diachronic structure of the British, again indicates a large number of status categories ranging from those that link people as members of this category (*Weight Watchers*) to those that are immanent within the individual (*It's Me, Self*), and both general and specialized lifestyle titles. Specialization would appear to indicate the growing importance of the lifestyled woman (the woman as informed consumer and practitioner of life arts), as it implies that areas of consumption such as food now require more details on the niceties of proper usage than could be provided in a general magazine.

But it would be wrong to assume that the class-subject and the mass-subject have disappeared completely into the personal/status category-subject, even if the subject as consumer is, indeed, the individuated target of ever more messages. An examination of the content of magazines, rather than titles alone, shows that these subject statuses in fact co-exist: although we may be addressed as specialized sorts of subjects, we are also addressed as classed and massed subjects. Indeed, according to Ellen McCracken (1993: 84, 196–8), there has been a drift back to class coinciding with the emergence of groups of women who earn high salaries. This new class belonging is not constructed through titles, but by such techniques as targeting only women who live in upscale postal codes with certain magazines (*Newsweek Woman*), or advertisements that appear only in issues sold in those areas, or restricting circulation to the well-off by raising cover prices.

Actual items advertised also create a class/mass distinction within the general category of consumer: 'Lower-priced cosmetics ... are usually advertised in magazines that reach women with moderate spending power ... while ads for more expensive make-up lines appear on the pages of *Vogue* or *Town & Country* – magazines with upscale readers' (McCracken, E., 1993: 92).

A similar pattern emerges in Australian magazines. The Australian version of *Vogue*, for example, has far more upmarket advertisers than the mass-oriented magazine the *Australian Women's Weekly* (which is not a weekly at all, but a monthly): according to the 1993 figures (*Sydney Morning Herald*, 28 May 1993), the exclusive class of *Vogue Australia* purchasers numbered 76,420, a figure dwarfed by the 1,172,332 members of the masses who spent their dollars on the *Weekly* – over 15 times greater. These circulation figures would, of course, be exceeded by actual readership. According to Windschuttle (1988: 247), Australian publishers claim that each copy is read by three people. If this is so, then the *Weekly* would reach over 3.5 million readers. As the total Australian population in 1990 was only 17.169 million (Castles, 1992: 5), this seems to represent a truly mass audience.

Goldman (1992: 151) remarks that advertisements almost never self-consciously raise the question of class. This may well be so, but this does not mean that they do not construct class in more subtle ways. The items advertised usually connote 'mass' or 'class' (for example, cosmetics one can buy in a local supermarket as opposed to those available only in specialized outlets), or the characters are of a certain social type: 'The signs are subtle: French roast coffee and croissant, she's an editorial assistant, he an engineer. "Heroines" and "heroes" never work on the factory floor or live in council houses' (Winship, 1987: 75). This appears to change only in the exceptional circumstances of the 'war worker' doing the 'Victory job' during the Second World War, where notions of patriotism could be seen to override class concerns (see Bonney and Wilson, 1983: 259–61).

But this does not take aspirational reading into account for those magazines not targeted at the postal codes of well-heeled areas. The majority of readers of upscale magazines such as *Vogue* in the US have actually quite modest household incomes (McCracken, E., 1993: 169), and a similar pattern emerges in Britain:

> Magazine editors know their audiences to be largely from the C1–C2 British occupational groups (women with white-collar working husbands or fathers) ... magazines hold out to these women the 'opportunity' to spend at A and B levels ... a gap emerges between the reader's social and economic reality and that projected by the text she consumes. (Ballaster et al., 1991: 11–12)

This is not really surprising, and can easily be understood through theories such as those we met in the opening chapters of this book: lower classes are continually trying to pass as one class higher than the one they occupy, while the latter try to maintain their distance by changing their modes of consumption. In other words, only those who do not know how to consume in a manner appropriate to a particular class will need the help of a guide-book.

Editorial and feature articles

Although it has been argued that there is a great deal of overlap and some rather blurred boundaries between advertisements and editorial in women's magazines (Ballaster et al., 1991: 116; McCracken, E., 1993: 3–4, 38ff., 135), feature articles nevertheless appear worthy of examination. An early and crucial accomplishment of these publications was the creation from the mid-eighteenth century of 'an artificial imaginary community in which the readers could participate from the isolation of their homes' (Ballaster et al., 1991: 60). This artificial community was very much a 'woman's place', and in this section two principal questions will be posed: how is this artificial community constructed, and how, if at all, is it related to the wider world?

Ballaster et al. (1991) identified a number of themes that recurred across their 1988 sample, only some of which will retain our extended attention: femininity and masculinity; sexuality; home and family; leisure, lifestyle and consumption; employment; feminism and politics. Femininity and mascu-linity, as well as sexuality, refer to the ways in which these magazines tended to position women with respect to men, constructing the reader as a hetero-sexual woman. Furthermore, the magazines map the emotional work involved in relationships onto women. Women are made out to be the emotional workers in the realm of relationships with men, children, and the family generally. This brings us to a central theme of women's magazines: the family.

The importance of the family lies in its capacity to create an imaginary community of women transcending social divisions such as class that, in extra-magazinish life, present obstacles to the existence of any such com-munity (Ballaster et al., 1991: 9). Not only does this mean that women relate as mothers, wives, daughters or sisters (Winship, 1987: 75), but it also means that men, no matter what their social status may be, appear here wrapped up in the kinship terms of fathers, husbands, sons or brothers. It is almost as if the entire social world consisted of a single social institution. The family unites all sorts of women: rich and poor, readers and royalty, readers and editors, readers and readers – the family is the concept that unites all these categories of person who would otherwise be kept apart (Ballaster et al., 1991: 146). Almost everybody seems to be related to in terms of the family: Prince Charles may be a remote prince, but he is also a son, a father and a more or less ex-husband, categories that will be very familiar to the readers of these magazines. Similarly with politicians and celebrities of all types: their family side is emphasized, and they are made more real and more accessible to ordinary readers. If practically everybody is involved in family relationships, then they are no different to you and me really, are they? The family is a sort of common currency that makes exchange of incompatibles possible. Marx (1974 [1867]: 44ff.) argued that the only reason a quarter of wheat could be exchanged for x blacking, y silk or z gold was because all of these quite different objects had one thing in common, namely labour power. Similarly, the only reason readers can be exchanged in equivalence with the normally incompatible royals, politicians and celebrities of the magazines is because they have one thing in common – the family.

Magazines cover the next central theme, consumption, in a number of different places: fashion features, advice on new products, make-up and beauty tips. The 'what's in' and 'what's out' types of column often found in these magazines, as well as advice on what to wear with what to which occasion and what to serve and how to serve it, are clearly part of the tendency to establish particular lifestyles through particular modes of consumption.

Although the community of women constructed by these magazines may be an imaginary or utopian one, this does not mean that it exists in isolation from developments in politics and the economy. Indeed, Australian, British and US magazines have demonstrated strikingly similar trajectories since 1939. In all three countries during the war years women's magazines put a major effort into mobilizing their readers for the war effort by encouraging them to break out of the domestic sphere and enter the workforce. In the 1950s the reverse occurred, and domestic consumption as a mode of life became the supposed occupation of the magazine-reading women, a situation that has been modified only recently with the re-entry of more women into the workforce (Ballaster et al., 1991: 110, 121–2; Bonney and Wilson, 1983: chapter 7; McCracken, E., 1993: 178; Winship, 1987: 30–6). So if the war years saw women mapped onto production outside the family, the following decade saw the magazines mapping women onto consumption inside the family. For both Australian and British readers, the accession of Elizabeth II to the throne in 1953 cemented the new consumerist classlessness to the importance of the family as the proper site for women. The image of the queen as mother of a young family showed that she was just like anyone else, and advertisements showed that any young family could be like the queen's if they used the right goods (see the illustrations in Bonney and Wilson, 1983: 284–5; Winship, 1987: 36). In Australia, it could be argued that the notion of the royal family was the British cultural contribution to the increasing importance of American economic and political power in the region: your family can model itself on the royals, thanks to the availability of republican American commodities that were frequently and persistently advertised *as* American (see the examples in Bonney and Wilson, 1983: 241, 282).

The *Australian Women's Weekly* did not address the problems of the transition from production outside the home to consumption within it (Bonney and Wilson, 1983: 234). Had it done so, it might have been possible to see the political, economic and cultural processes involved in shifting from one to the other, and therefore to argue about the pros and cons of what was happening. Instead, both are made to appear as natural states of femininity, despite the glaring contradictions between them. That is one purpose of myth in the sense that Barthes (1989 [1957]) understood it: it turns the historically contingent into a state of nature that cannot be questioned. We have already seen that the notion of femininity as a natural state shared by all women is common to these magazines, but this seems to be accomplished differently in different contexts. It was argued above that the family is one way in which differences among women are obliterated and a shared sameness constructed. During the war, notions of patriotism and love of country served to link women together. In the 1950s, new access to consumer goods that previously only the rich could afford made it possible to think of women as no longer divided along class lines: after all, if everyone now has access to consumer items then this means that we are close to a classless society. If all women are consumers, then all are equal. This, of course, ignores the fact that the practices of consumption offer a vast number of ways, from the most subtle to the most crass, of demonstrating what Veblen (1975 [1899]) called 'invidious distinction'.

But what of the *Australian Women's Weekly* today? Let us consider the May 1993 issue and in particular the role of the family. It was argued above that the family allowed readers to relate to otherwise inaccessible persons like royalty or celebrities, and indeed notions of the family are quite prominent in this issue. The article on the singer Anthony Warlow's victory over cancer contains three photographs of Warlow and his wife; the model Rachel Hunter is in three photos with her baby, one with her husband Rod Stewart, and one with both baby and husband; there is a piece on Prince Charles with a photo taken when the family was together, which is contrasted with the present-day 'lonely prince'. We are invited to meet the husband of television personality Lisa Patrick (four photos of the two of them together); then we find two photos of the swimmer Duncan Armstrong and family under the title 'My Son's Disabled'. Next there is a feature on famous mothers and daughters (four pairs of photos); then something on Viscount Linley and current girlfriend, which could be called candidate-family: 'the match ambitious mothers' dreams are made of' (photos included). The possible Aboriginal ancestry of the television presenter Ray Martin is featured, and we discover an article on the Gorbachevs. There are three pages where mothers write about the experiences their children had in other lives, and then a 'Desperate Plea of Jack Nicholson's Dad: "I want to meet my son before I die"'. There is a quiz entitled 'How smart is your cat?', which I propose to treat as an instance of family because cats are, precisely, *domestic* pets: readers here relate to each other as owners of cats. The cat constructs readerly togetherness, which is perhaps a step up from sitting on the mat. Twenty-three of the 29 letters from readers to the 'That's Life' pages concerned incidents with family members, so here is another instance of readers relating to each other through that which they have in common, namely the family. There are still more examples in this issue, but perhaps the point has been made by now.

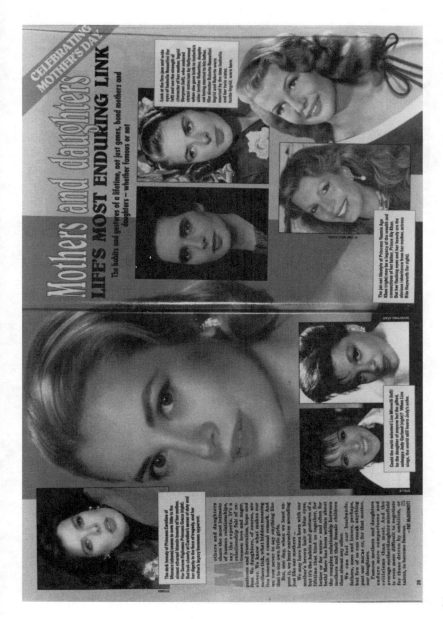

Figure 6.1

It might appear reasonable at this stage to argue that the family was the central concept underlying this issue of the *Australian Women's Weekly*. But there is something even more fundamental at work across the magazine, something that may not be evident at first glance. I refer to the notion of *transformation*, often presented as a magical transformation. Where do we find this at work? Let us look at some of the content again: Anthony Warlow

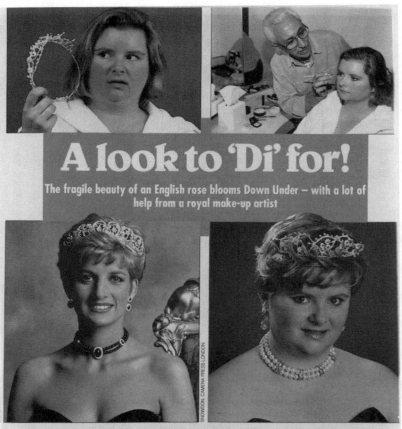

A look to 'Di' for!

The fragile beauty of an English rose blooms Down Under – with a lot of help from a royal make-up artist

A t a quick glance, it looked as if the Princess of Wales had an Aussie twin! The "twin" even captured the characteristic "shy Di" expression ... before she doubled up with laughter.

The "twin" was "Fast Forward's" Magda Szubanski who was, at first, nearly speechless when asked by The Weekly to test the skills of international make-up artist Clayton Howard. "Me? Be made-up to look like Princess Di? Are you serious?" she asked.

Clayton assured Magda – who will be seen on the Seven Network in "Full Frontal", a new sketch comedy series following the successful "Fast Forward" –

The real Diana (above left); Magda Szubanski as a Di look-alike (above right) after being transformed by royal make-up artist Clayton Howard (top).

that she looked like the Princess. "You both have two eyes and a nose in the same place, and a mouth. That's a good starting point," he said.

Clayton is in Australia to promote his book, "Look Like a Princess", which has been on the best-seller list in the UK for almost six months. The book takes readers discreetly into stately homes where Clayton has been make-up artist to members of the royal family for more than a decade. It also shows readers how

to apply cosmetics so that a mere commoner can look like a princess. Clayton first met the Princess of Wales when she was Lady Diana Spencer. He made her up for her first official photographs as the future royal bride, creating the now famous Di look.

Clayton completed Magda's transformation in a suite in Melbourne's Regent Hotel. Magda looked so "Di-like" that she offered to stand in for the Princess on Wales on her next royal visit.

– **VERONICA MATHESON**

Magda's wig by The Individual Wig, Chapel St, South Yarra, Vic 3141. Jewellery from Myer, Melbourne. "Look Like a Princess", by Clayton Howard, is distributed by National Book Distributors, rrp $24.95.

Figure 6.2

is a different person after surviving cancer – he is also an actor, which means that transformation of personality is his business. The latter point, of course, also applies to other actors who may populate the magazine. Rachel Hunter as mother is not the same person she was before being transformed by Rod Stewart's magic wand: 'I'm not as aggressive as I used to be. Having a baby puts life into perspective.' Prince Charles has been transformed from family man to 'lonely prince' and has himself 'transformed the once-derelict grounds of Highgrove into an experimental organic farm'. Lisa Patrick

Raisa Gorbachev's private HELL

Fragile and frightened, Raisa Gorbachev is the real casualty of the Russian coup. Moscow's one-time first lady is now a sad, drawn shadow of her former self

She was once the glamorous face of the new Russia. Confident and proud, Raisa Gorbachev, resplendent in her sables and silver fox, once jetted happily from the White House to the Elysee Palace to Downing Street.

Shopping in London or Paris was her idea of heaven. The scent of Estee Lauder would linger in the boutiques of Chanel, Yves Saint Laurent and Cartier long after the first lady of the former communist world left.

But today, the auburn hair, once coiffed and curled, is flat and unkempt.

The eyes no longer shine, the face is drawn. The "Tsarina's" distress echos the agony that has overtaken her country.

Raisa, 61, recently left a Moscow clinic after weeks of specialist treatment. It was her second stay in hospital since the 1991 coup which toppled her husband from power. Today, she is "virtually unrecognisable" as the once formidable wife of a charismatic Soviet president who created a crusade which changed the world.

Officials close to the Gorbachevs revealed that Raisa is probably suffering from atherosclerosis – furred arteries –

ABOVE LEFT: Raisa and Mikhail Gorbachev in happier days. ABOVE: Raisa as she is now.

of the brain which, coupled with her high blood pressure, could bring on a fatal stroke. Mikhail admits that his wife is very ill. "At times, she can't speak properly or control her movements," he commented sadly.

Those who saw Raisa smuggled out of hospital in a grey tracksuit were shocked at her appearance. One nursing orderly said: "She had become just another little old woman. Nobody took any notice. The Gorbachevs are history. So ▶

Figure 6.3

disappears from Australia's television screens but pops up here transformed from 'TV star' into 'newlywed'. Duncan Armstrong is changed from 'dedicated sportsman' to father of disabled child, while the article on famous mothers and daughters deliberately looks for resemblances (Figure 6.1). Indeed, the mother is transformed into the daughter: the strength of Ingrid Bergman is changed into the 'firm jaw and wide eyes' of her daughter Isabella Rossellini, while the 'flashing eyes and ... beauty' of Rita Hayworth are transformed into the shape of her daughter, Princess Yasmin Aga Khan. Then the well-known Australian comedian Magda Szubanski is transformed into the Princess of Wales by a 'royal make-up artist' (Figure 6.2). Ray Martin is a new person now that he has discovered his 'amazing past', while an article on a new TV series features people playing people who are not themselves. Raisa Gorbachev's transformation from the happy and confident woman who existed before the August 1991 Moscow coup attempt to the 'sad, drawn shadow of her former self' is dramatized through before-and-after photographs (Figure 6.3). The article on children who say they have lived previous lives can clearly be interpreted in terms of the notion of transformation. Of course we could also mention the transformations available through new clothes, fashions, lipsticks, hairdyes, and the 'magic make-over' mentioned in features and advertisements.

But why all this fascination with transformation? It is not an absolutely new idea – transformations are quite common in fairytales, where a frog becomes a prince, a wolf becomes a grandmother, a new status is created through new clothes (Propp, 1973 [1928]: 77–8, sees this as a standard function of fairytales). Indeed, Ovid's *Metamorphoses* (1955 [8 AD]) is about little else, and that has been part of our literature for 2,000 years. It is possible that there is a link to the conditions of life we lead under late capitalism. Identities are less stable than they used to be, although this is probably true of all historical transition periods: we are no longer guaranteed jobs for life in the same place, or even jobs at all, so we may have to change job identities quite a bit; feminism has made gender role identities less rigid and more fluid, so gender roles and, indeed, sexual identities, are not fixed in stone any more; the ever-increasing use of consumer objects to indicate identity means that we can keep changing the person we appear to be; mobility through social class may also mean that we have to learn to be different people. Transformation, which used to be restricted to such changes as, for example, child to adult, daughter to mother, has become a more everyday experience in a much wider range of contexts – indeed, it may be one of the central problems of everyday life in the late twentieth century. Not only were earlier transformations relatively infrequent, their special quality was often recognized by explicit ceremonies of the *rites de passage* type. The majority of the current proliferation of transformations, however, lack the earlier explicit recognition of changes of state, and so we miss the ritual forms that enabled earlier generations to handle such transitions. Uncertain, shifting identities seem part and parcel of the postmodern experience. In that sense, women's magazines may have their finger on the pulse of one of society's most pervasive problems.

Conclusion

This chapter began by posing the question, 'What sort of woman is the woman of women's magazines?' Perhaps the answer is rather paradoxical: she is a continually transforming, constant woman. Transformations occur at both broad social levels (the shift from class, to mass, to social status categories), and on much more personal planes (new food, clothing, the 'new you', and the like). The constancy seems to reside in two main areas: the woman as consumer and the woman as member of a family. The diachronic dimension of change seems to co-exist with the synchronic tendency to present the world as eternally the same. That seems to be as accurate a reflection of the contradictions of contemporary life as any.

7
The Home

Our contemporary notions of the home are creations of quite fresh date. In earlier societies, and indeed in early capitalism itself, much production took place at home and there was therefore no real distinction between place of work and domestic sphere. Industrialization, however, constructed them as spatially separate entities and as culturally polar opposites, at least for men. The workplace was the site of public productive life, and the home became the place of private consumption: a 'haven in a heartless world', where gentle loving domesticity supposedly reigned.

The objects populating the home world were caught up in the task of maintaining this new home/work distinction – domesticity was *designed*, and was to nullify all associations with work. Forty (1986) maintains that, over the last hundred years, domestic goods have also played a central role in transforming the home itself from a source of moral welfare and place of beauty to a source of physical welfare and place of efficiency. My own investigation shows that the home in the 1990s is portrayed as a place of communication and sociability.

If your home was about to be engulfed by a fire, what would you save from it? The large wad of cash hidden away in the drawer? Or would you prefer to take your photo album first, and risk letting the banknotes burn? A painting by a child, a birthday card from a distant friend, or your video recorder? What reasons could you give for your choices? In other words, what things in your home matter most to you, and why? This is the question posed by Csikszentmihalyi and Rochberg-Halton (1981), and we consider their answers with respect to the meanings of furniture, visual art and photographs. The question of why one would want to own a home in the first place is considered by Richards (1990) in her study of a new Melbourne suburb.

Where the home is, work is not: domesticity designed

It will be recalled from Chapter 1 that Colin Campbell argued that capitalist industrialization simultaneously created revolutions in both production and consumption, even if more sociological attention has been paid to the former than the latter. Similarly, we could argue that capitalist industrialization simultaneously created both the factory and the home as we have understood it for most of this century, even if, again, more sociological attention has been paid to the former than the latter.

Before the Great Transformation, many productive activities took place at home: people engaged in their crafts or trades there, and merchants did their buying and selling. What capitalist industrialization brought about was a concentration of paid labour in the factory, and a draining of recognized labour from the home. In other words, where once the home was also the site of productive activities, now such activities were taken out of the home and placed in the factory. The home became the site of something else: non-work, domesticity. This is not to say that there is no work involved for those at home, merely that the shift to the factory or the office makes it appear as if the home should be for something else. As we shall see, the home does not mean exactly the same thing for men who work outside domestic space and for the women who remain within it. For Victorian men, though, the home was a welcome haven from the pressures of outside work; it was a place where one could become truly oneself. This was particularly true for those who had jobs that allowed little space for self-expression and autonomy. One was oneself only outside work, and the home became a central component in the creation and upholding of one's 'real' self. The true job of the home under these conditions, then, was to be an area of non-work. No hint of the outside world of industry was to find any place, because we were now faced with a binary opposition. Binary oppositions insist on the purity of the opposing terms: work or non-work, not a bit of this and a bit of that. Any mixing produces confusion, fear and disorder. Given the above, what were homes supposed to look like? Forty (1986) suggests that the home was transformed into the site of non-work through the ways in which its contents were designed, and the most important principle of domestic design was that all associations with work should be removed.

A good example of the necessity for separating work and domesticity can be found in Forty's (1986: 94–9) account of the sewing machine and the difficulties manufacturers had in selling it. At first such machines were bought only by industrial users, but manufacturers found that this could be a limited market and they risked going out of business. So why not sell to homes? It became necessary to turn the sewing machine into a domestic appliance, but this was easier said than done. Initial attempts were not too successful, partly because they were expensive. But cost was not the only factor, for the industrial connotations had not been quite removed. As Forty (1986: 96) puts it, 'it was like having a machine tool in the living room'. The drop in prices and the advent of hire purchase made it easier for people to pay for a machine, but this was not enough to create the impression that a sewing machine's place is in the home. Unless this impression was created, the domestic market was never going to take on such a machine. This was partly done through advertising, and Forty (1986: 97) reproduces a fashion plate from 1867 showing a sewing machine in a prominent position in a domestic interior. The point of this advertisement is to show that the home is indeed an appropriate place for such a machine – it will fit in perfectly with general domestic doings.

But this classical advertising trick of placing things together in a context so as almost magically to produce an unquestionable link between them was perhaps not quite enough. Manufacturers went a step further and designed domesticity into their machines. How did they do this? The brochure for a Singer machine of 1858 writes of 'a machine of smaller size, and of a lighter and more elegant form; a machine decorated in the best style of art, so as to make a beautiful ornament in the parlor or boudoir' (quoted by Forty, 1986: 98–9). So: small, light, elegant, artistic and beautiful: not a machine, but an ornament. The machine must not look as if it actually does any work; instead it is to be of the same order as a painting or a piece of sculpture – the aesthetic dimension nullifies the industrial dimension. Further examples of some of the ways in which ornamentation becomes an integral part of the machine can be found in Forty (1986: 98). The very success of the sewing machine in the domestic arena made it less necessary to make it appear so totally different to its industrial counterparts, and after a while the differences lessened. There still remained, however, a higher degree of ornamentation in the domestic models.

Forty maintains that the home in the nineteenth century and the home in the twentieth century do not have the same role. Of course it is true that a house may still be for shelter, but we are not talking about houses here but about homes. Perhaps this is similar to the difference between sex and gender. 'Sex' and 'house' refer more to the physical characteristics of people and things, while 'gender' and 'home' refer to the ways in which sex and the house are transformed into meaningful cultural entities. The great shift, according to Forty (1986) was from the role of the house as a source of moral welfare to the role of the house as a source of physical welfare. This corresponded to a change from the home as a place of beauty to the home as a place of efficiency. Let us first consider the place of beauty in the home. Obviously, we are not tackling this question from the point of view of the philosopher of aesthetics, who is interested in topics such as 'What is beauty?' Rather, we are more interested in answers to the question: 'What are the social functions of beauty?' Perhaps the lowest form of beauty is good order. What is the purpose of this? Forty quotes the sanitary reformer Southwood Smith from the 1861 book *Recreations of a Country Parson*:

> A clean, fresh, and well-ordered house exercises over its inmates a moral, no less than a physical influence, and has a direct tendency to make the members of the family sober, peaceable, and considerate of the feelings and happiness of each other; nor is it difficult to trace a connexion between habitual feelings of this sort and the formation of habits of respect for property, for the laws in general, and even for those higher duties and obligations the observance of which no laws can enforce. (quoted in Forty, 1986: 108)

The point is not to agree or disagree with this passage, but to see the sorts of claims it is making. The most striking thing is the fact that order and cleanliness are presented as having a moral purpose: they make you sober, peaceable and considerate, and even respectful of property and the law in general. They make you a good family member and a good citizen at the same time. Who needs a police force when you can have a clean house?

But it was considered that mere good order was not enough, and beautification in the sense more familiar to us had its role. Forty (1986: 109) quotes from the journalist Loftie (1879): 'A few bare walls hung with pictures, a few flowers in the window, a pretty tile on the hob, would, in my opinion, do more to keep men and women at home, and to promote family love, than libraries of tracts and platforms full of temperance lecturers.' The pictures on the wall are not there just to give idle pleasure, they fulfil the greater purpose of family solidarity and a life led in the private sphere rather than on the public streets. Almost 80 years later, in the Sweden of the 1940s and 1950s, home aesthetics still had a moral purpose: 'The focus on the aesthetics of everyday life was strongly linked to ideas about mentality and morality. The peaceful and light, the restrained and low-key, the orderly and practical home should create a setting for light-hearted, open-minded, harmonious and rational minds' (Löfgren, 1994: 58).

If the nineteenth century was the century of the drawing room, the twentieth century was the century of the kitchen. Why did the kitchen become more important and the drawing room less? This shift reflects a change of emphasis: since the nineteenth century was quite caught up in ideas about the moral, civilizing virtues of beauty, the drawing room, built for display as much as anything else, was the key room in the house. But the twentieth century has been more interested in physical welfare and health, and so it is hardly surprising that the kitchen overtook the drawing room as the most important room in the house. We can also see a shift from the inculcation of collective sentiments of good behaviour, honesty and respect for property through drawing room beauty to the efficient production of individual human bodies. This originally had nothing much to do with the welfare of individuals' own health, although that is generally how we spontaneously think of it now (I modify this point below). Rather, the health of individuals became a matter of national importance. This is particularly clear in the British case, where a quarter of Boer War recruits were discovered to be unfit and the ability of the population to defend the Empire began to look doubtful (Forty, 1986: 115).

The secret to the importance of the kitchen, then, lies in questions of race and empire. Here the individual body belongs not so much to the individual as such as to the state, and it is the role of the home to produce proper bodies to state specifications. Fighting machines as much as moral machines were required for the Boer War. From this time on, when the demands of the state for healthy bodies have grown less in the military sense, it has been possible for this initial state interest in individual health to slip into the background and the idea take hold that the body is indeed the individual's. The health aspect remains, but it is health for the individual rather than health for the state. This is not to say that the state has no interest in the health of the individual any more. Far from it, indeed. Otherwise, there would be no campaigns against smoking or drink-driving, and presumably no Medicare or National Health Service. But individuals now see the health of their bodies as their own business, and the notion of healthy eating has of course expanded greatly over the last couple of decades in all Western countries. It seems, though, to be still entirely in the interests of the state to foster this ideology, if only to save on medical bills. There may well be a semi-permanent tension in the answer to the question: to whom does the individual body belong – the individual or the state? In earlier historical periods, the tension might have been between the individual, the state and God. The answer is not either/or, but shifts in one or the other direction according to various factors we cannot explore here. But in either case, the kitchen still remains the central room for the production of the healthy individual body.

We have just seen that there is a tension or a contradiction between the individual and the state. The home in general may also be understood in terms of a tension between individual expression and ideas that come in from the outside. It seems as if we are always going to be stuck with a tension between the inside and the outside when we furnish our homes, between individual taste and expression and the political values built into the furniture we purchase. After all, those of us without advanced craft skills are going to get most of our furniture on the market, so the choice will be limited anyway.

Perhaps I should give you an example of a dilemma I faced recently. I needed to purchase a desk for the computer I work with at home. What were the choices on the market? On the one hand, there were desks made of metal and plastic in black and grey colours, and on the other there were solid timber desks with soft rounded corners. What sorts of things are built into these designs? The metal and plastic desks were well adapted to the purpose: rational, efficient and cheap. They connoted industrial, rational work, and their design responded well to the high tech image we associate with computers. They appeared made for each other – I knew it made sense. These are clearly the values of capitalist work and the office, so such a desk would import these values into my own home, turning it into a place of rationally organized work. It would admit that these were the values that guided my work, and that the production of lectures, books and academic papers was a rational, bureaucratized task. The high tech aspect would claim that my work was the product of machines. The characteristics of my work should reflect this: it too should be rational, efficient, and conform to the demands of technological work.

What about the solid timber desk? This was functional in the sense of well designed to hold a computer, but expensive. It did not connote industrial work at all but craft work, as it was made by hand. There was nothing high tech about it, and so it did not respond harmoniously to the computer – if anything, it was low tech and traditional. The soft rounded corners required expensive labour and so were not rational from a cost point of view, but they were nice to look at and to touch. It did not have the values of an industrialized workplace, but more those of a novelist or a poet. It said that my work would not be of the rational-efficient variety, but of the creative-unquantifiable and not necessarily efficient sort: craft rather than industrial – I knew it made sense. Where the metal and plastic desk shared the aesthetic of the computer and imposed the notion that the machinery governed the writer, the solid timber desk neutralized the high tech image of the computer and seemed to allow the writer the possibility of dominating the machine. The two types of desk, then, created quite different notions of work in general, quite different versions of the sorts of work that academics are supposed to do, and different relations to the machine. I knew what made sense. So next time you buy a piece of furniture, consider what sorts of values and ideologies are built into the designs from which you can choose. It appears that there is more to this than individual taste.

But it is now time to consider questions of hygiene and cleanliness in the home.

The clean and the dirty: homes and hygiene

Have you ever asked yourself why your fridge is white? So accustomed are we to this that the whiteness of fridges seems to have the status of a fact of nature. But fridges were not always this colour. There is an instructive contrast to be found on page 156 of the Forty book. The Leonard refrigerator of 1929 came in the form of a varnished wooden cabinet. How would you react to the appearance of such a fridge in your kitchen? The Leonard may have been perfectly efficient at its job of keeping food at a particular temperature, but it was perfectly inefficient at giving the impression that it was hygienic. That is not to say that it was not hygienic – merely that it did not have the look to convince people of its cleanliness. Contrast the Sears Roebuck Coldspot refrigerator of 1935: it was made from steel, had smooth corners rather than angles and was, of course, brilliant white. In Forty's words, 'it looked the physical embodiment of health and purity' (1986: 156), and we can easily see in the design of this fridge the precursor to those we have in our kitchens today. Indeed, fridges are not the only household good to be designed in this way, as a glance around the modern home will show. So the ideas of health and purity take concrete form in the design of this particular piece of domestic apparatus. But why did questions of hygiene and cleanliness become so important and influential, so that the beauty of many kitchen appliances for us lies in the ways in which they embody such ideas?

The change to ideas of cleanliness is located by Forty at the end of the nineteenth century, when baths and bathrooms began to appear in houses and interior colours changed from browns and reds to white. As he points out, this did not mean that people were necessarily cleaner in practice, but the idea that cleanliness was a good thing certainly took hold. We know that there is nothing natural about cleanliness in humans: generations and generations would have been horrified at the thought of bathing themselves (see Vigarello, 1987 [1985]). So a reasonable question to pose is: under what circumstances do we become interested in cleanliness? Why does it become so important? The anthropologist Mary Douglas 'expresses the idea that anxieties about pollution arise when the external boundaries of a society are threatened, or when the lines defining the internal relationships in a culture are threatened, or when dangers arise from internal contradictions within the morality of the culture' (Forty, 1986: 159). Forty suggests that we can use this approach in the case of the late nineteenth century: there was rapid social change and boundaries became uncertain as the working-class movement increased in power, and in this perspective it was not unexpected that the bourgeois classes felt under threat and became preoccupied with cleanliness. It was a way for them to re-order life and defend their borders against the dangers they saw threatening them. In the face of revolution, install a bathroom. Put so bluntly, this may seem crazy – but it is not as crazy as it appears, provided the revolutionary class can be persuaded to install bathrooms as well. It is through the ways in which the revolutionary class can be so persuaded that the water of cleanliness can douse the flame of revolution.

A second element that went towards establishing the hegemony of hygiene was a change in the theory of disease. Disease was once thought of as the result of 'spontaneous combustion that was supposed to occur in foul, stagnant air' (Forty, 1986: 160), and so the best way to prevent disease was to make sure there was ventilation everywhere. This theory had a direct impact on the architecture and design of houses, as Corbin makes plain:

> The influence of aerist theories on Enlightenment architecture is well known . . . The building must be designed so as to separate putrid exhalations from currents of fresh air, in the same way that fresh water had to be divided from used water. The idea was that the shape of the building itself would ensure satisfactory ventilation, thus rendering traditional methods redundant . . . This obsession caused cellars, vaults, and secret rooms to be denounced on two fronts: they were subject to emanations from the earth, and they lacked the requisite circulation of air. Caverns inspired terror. Abandonment of the ground floor in favor of the first story began to be advocated . . . Such beliefs provoked new criticism of the rural norms of habitation. The sanitary reformers' advice was heeded, as changes in both living patterns and architecture attest. Jean-Claude Perrot has noted the beginnings of migration to the upper stories in the city of Caen. Newly built apartments were ventilated better than old dwellings. Claude-Nicolas Ledoux praised the steps that gave access to raised buildings; they not only symbolized the grandeur of the construction but also attested to the belief in the purifying quality of air. (Corbin, 1994 [1982]: 98–9)

Note that cleanliness of persons or surfaces is of no importance in this view. But then, following the work of Pasteur and Lister, disease was understood as coming from germs – mere ventilation was not going to help. The result of this was a shift towards the removal of dirt and germs from both the house and the person. This opened up spaces both for the increased importance of the bathroom and for the selling of household appliances that would clearly show up dirt, and other household machines that would remove it: vacuum cleaners, soap powder, washing machines, and so on. This gives marketers a powerful weapon because practically everyone now accepts that cleanliness is an important objective. If it seems eminently reasonable to be clean, then it seems eminently reasonable to purchase that which will make the attaining of cleanliness possible. And if all your main household kitchen and bathroom items are designed in white, then any dirt is going to be very obvious indeed.

The home of the late 1990s: beauty, efficiency, sociability and communication

So much for Forty's account. But what beliefs and ideologies are attached to the home in the late 1990s? Considering a sample of houseware magazines available on the market in January 1996, it was found that a limited number of themes recurred over and over again in both advertisements and feature articles: aesthetics, the notion of the ensemble, functionality, the importance of light, pleasure in the bathroom, the self, and sociability. Aesthetics and functionality were usually found together.

The following reference system has been adopted for this section only:

AHB = *Australian Home Beautiful/Your Garden* 1996 Annual
HD = *Home Decorator* 4, Summer 1996
HLR = *Homes and Living Renovations* 1996
KBQ = *Kitchens and Bathrooms Quarterly* 2(3)
LY = *Lifestyle Yearbook* 1996

Aesthetics and functionality

How do these apparently unconnected qualities come together? Advertisements make statements such as the following:

Introducing the perfect blend of style & function (Finesse, *HD*: 87);
Style, design, tradition, features and functions all combine to make a Russell Hobbs Classic kettle one of the world's favourites (*HD*: 99);
Besides all these functional advantages we've also paid special attention to the beauty of appearance . . . Engineered for Fine Furniture (Metabox, *KBQ*: 4);
The Ceran cooktop, which is easy to clean, quick to heat, and combines toughness and elegance (Chef, *KBQ*: 14)
For style, elegance and practicality that will add thousands to the value of your home, insist on a Dana Design Kitchen (*KBQ*: 80);
Kitchens with style, distinction and practicality (The Kitchen Place, *KBQ*: 93);
These superbly crafted shower cubicles have been designed to be both functional and beautiful (Showerline, *KBQ*: 115).

Feature articles are very similar:

Classic desk accessories combine beauty, function and efficiency (*HD*: 84);
a new product that combines design flexibility with durability and practicality . . . with gorgeous results (*KBQ*: 12);
long life and easy cleaning . . . looks simply wonderful (*KBQ*: 16);

> The resulting kitchen is one with the efficiency and elegant styling of a contemporary kitchen, and the perennial beauty of good design and quality materials (*KBQ*: 54);
> The kitchen is a spacious and modern, not just a pretty place – it actually works well for these busy parents of twins (*HLR*: 54–5).

Only the last citation even hints that there might be a contradiction between the aesthetic and the functional, but this contradiction is clearly not present in the kitchen under discussion. The contemporary consumer does not have to choose either one or the other, but can have both. Those who tend to aesthetically based decisions are rewarded with the bonus of perfect functionality, while those who prize functionality above all are rewarded with the bonus of beauty. Aesthetes and functionalists may be imagined as opposing types of person, but today's housewares transcend this opposition. Thus Veblen's (1975 [1899]) account of the inverse relationship between the useful and the beautiful no longer holds, for we no longer find something beautiful to the extent that it is useless. For the consumer, the ethics deriving from work and aesthetics merge into one. Nobody has an excuse for despising modern commodities, for they answer objections from both sides of the aesthetics/functionality divide by removing the grounds for division.

Where aesthetic considerations are found without relation to functionality in any direct way, they are nevertheless resolutely 'unarty' in the sense that there is no hint of an 'art for art's sake' approach that would be independent of other considerations. For example,

> The courtyard with its gravel covering brings to mind a Japanese Zen garden. There is no artifice; the gravel is what it is . . . But [the home's] most memorable aspect is the honest way in which materials have been used. It is a fine example of the dimensions and possibilities of concrete, provided that it is not painted or transformed into something it is not. This is art without artifice . . . honest architecture. (*HD*: 38, 42)

Rather like the nineteenth-century furniture mentioned above, the role of art here is to transmit the moral virtue of honesty. Elsewhere, beauty serves to display one's (Kantian?) taste ('a choice of finishes designed to reflect your impeccable taste in the kitchen': Miele advertisement, *KBQ*: back cover) and the values of casualness ('make this kitchen casual, while not compromising its obvious elegance': *KBQ*: 83) and comfort ('The result is elegant and disciplined but at the same time gloriously comfortable': *AHB*: 8).

Even when we find something very close to a pure interest in art, it is by no means portrayed as an essentially elite interest:

> 'I'm interested in excellent design from all periods', explains one of the new owners, 'but especially enjoy the fifties for the lightness of design and sparseness of form. I love what was then avant-garde – clean modernist lines'; 'Most people don't have enough training in aesthetics – the last art they did was probably lower high school. It's an illiteracy – people don't know enough about colour, form and style because our society doesn't think it's worth teaching.' (*HLR*: 97, 103)

Here we have a cry that is much closer to 'art for all' than 'art for art' or for an elite. 'Society' is criticized for failing the people's aesthetic education.

Beauty is honest, tasteful, casual, comfortable and striving to be democratic – no fraud, vulgarity, formality, lack of appreciation of bodily needs, or elitism. Home aesthetics, then, seems to exist to display certain core values of the Australian middle class. It may display rather different values in the somewhat less casual societies of Europe, but that is for the European reader to determine. North American home aesthetics may be different again.

The ensemble

Consider the individual pieces of crockery, particularly drinking vessels, in your home. I suspect that there is a very high probability that these are of two fundamentally different types: cups that form part of a larger overall set of matched pieces, and mugs that form no part of any larger system of co-ordinated items. What principle of unity is at work here? In the case of the matching cups, the unity derives from the aesthetic characteristics of the set itself – from the sharing of colour, form and design. The mugs, by contrast, were probably picked up here and there and represent such things as visits to various locations, particular social occasions, or membership of organizations. The principle of unity of the mug collection derives from the peculiar biography and experiences of the owner. On the one hand, then, we have unity based on the objects; on the other, we have unity springing from the subject. Consumers who choose the latter path as a general principle for all purchases clearly impose their own principle of unity and make it more difficult for manufacturers to sell more than one item from a range. But if we are persuaded that everything should match, then entire ranges can be sold much more successfully. Six different chairs from totally different places arranged around the same dining table may tell a fascinating story about the owner's varied life and times; six similar chairs forming an aesthetically based set tell us more about the manufacturer's story. Here, aesthetic considerations serve an entirely commercial purpose. Marchand (1985: 132), indeed, remarks that 'More than any other phenomenon of the era [1920s], the success of advertisers in selling the esthetic of the ensemble to consumers epitomized the contributions of color and style advertising to the ascendance of a mature consumption ethic.'

The ensemble is alive and well in contemporary houseware magazines:

Kleenmaid Fridges and Dishwashers Offer the Art of Perfect Integration (*HD*: 7);

This sleek, European-style kitchen with matching appliances, in stunning stainless steel, glamorous black or perfect white is just one of the looks from Chef (*KBQ*: 14);

If the appearance of white refrigerators leaves you cold, you're sure to like the look of a General Electric. With our unique Decorator Kit you can now have a beautifully co-ordinated kitchen. All you have to do is give us details of your preferred style and we'll take care of the rest (*LY*: 59).

The first two seem to impose the idea of the ensemble in the classical manner, but General Electric are more subtle in showing how they can co-ordinate their appearance to suit one you have already chosen. This returns discretionary power to the consumer, but at the same time suggests that only General Electric has sufficient chameleon quality to do the job.

An anti-ensemble view is articulated in a feature article:

> 'There's a basic theme at Corso', says Paul, 'to be adventurous, to put things you don't imagine together, together ... Australians have really moved on in that sense. They no longer have to have this sofa that goes with that side table that goes with that wall unit ... That's what the house is about. It's more than furniture and decoration. It's a projection of yourself and your character'. (*HD*: 65–6)

Dropping the ensemble mentality is seen as a progression that allows one to project a personal story through household items. Taken along with the General Electric advertisement, there is a suggestion that the principle of unity of a collection is swinging back towards the consumer. Such a development, if it continues and spreads, may replace the 'master narrative' of the ensemble with the personal epic of the subject as the general principle of consumer society.

Light

Two main themes are associated with light in our sample of magazines. Firstly, contrasts with past practices are drawn:

> A combination of natural and mirror lighting illuminates a room that was once dim and cramped. Rising Phoenix-like from a room that was dark and small, comes a bathroom that shows how efficient design and imagination can create light and space (*KBQ*: 103);

> Though rich in character, houses built in the 1920s and '30s have a tendency to be gloomy. In those days, it was the fashion to keep out the light and create cosy interiors. Since then, ideas have changed and today's renovators of old houses are usually keen to find ways of maximising the light while maintaining the charm. (*AHB*: 124)

Dim, dark, gloomy, and directed away from the outside: such are the home worlds of earlier generations seen from today's vantage point. This will not surprise after Forty's (1986) discussion of the nineteenth-century attempt to make as large a distinction as possible between the home on the one hand and work and the outside world on the other. The turn towards the light would seem to indicate that such distinctions have broken down, and that now there are no dangers to be feared from the outside – or at least the outside understood as nature. 'Natural light' in the home was mentioned six times in the sample, which would seem to strengthen the new link between the home and nature.

Secondly, light seems to be particularly associated with the kitchen, with seven instances linking the two. A Formica advertisement portrays light as the primary requirement in a kitchen:

'It's light that should be flooding your kitchen'. A thousand women can't be wrong. That's how many our research people talked to about what they wanted in a kitchen. And, to a woman they replied that their first priority in their new kitchen was a light, airy place to work in (*HLR*: 41).

The primacy of light is repeated in a feature article: 'One of the first questions your kitchen designer might ask is whether the kitchen can be relocated to maximise natural light' (*KBQ*: 32). The naturally lighted kitchen is taken to be such a 'natural' desire that it is not specifically accounted for. Light clearly makes it easier to see what one is doing, and can therefore be understood in functional terms. It also means that any dirt will be visible, and thus can be seen as an agent of hygiene. But the repetitions of 'natural light' suggest yet again that the kitchen partakes of a greater naturalness that lies beyond the cultural dimension of the home.

Pleasure in the bathroom

The act of washing oneself appears to be interpretable in two opposing ways. The nineteenth-century hygienists saw water as a way of ridding the body of the dirt that could cause disease by blocking the passages that allow transpiration, while the later disciples of Pasteur understood water as a means of ridding the body of the invisible 'dirt' of disease-causing microbes (Vigarello, 1987 [1985]: 154, 217). Here, washing can be understood as a purely hygienic, possibly even ascetic (especially if using cold showers), practice. One washes to maintain a healthy body. In fifteenth-century France, however, both public and private baths were seen as places of fun and sensual pleasure (Vigarello, 1987 [1985]: 45). On the one hand, hygiene; on the other hand, pleasure. What about the present-day bathroom as portrayed in houseware magazines? The following citations are from feature articles:

As one of the hardworking hubs of the home the bathroom provides deserved pleasure when it too is nourished (*HD*: 100);

A luxurious bathroom for a new house was created to give pleasure and refreshment at the end of a long day (*KBQ*: 98);

Bathing in a jet of bubbles or a scented, steaming bath is one of life's more exotic pleasures and a great way to relax and unwind. With the introduction of baths and spas made for two, you can now share the pleasure (*KBQ*: 109);

With new designs that banish the mean, grouted shower stalls of old in favour of spacious, steaming pleasure capsules, the shower is back, and a serious rival to the bath in the luxury stakes. (*KBQ*: 113)

Hygiene and cleanliness hardly have any place at all, except perhaps in the rather distorted form of 'refreshment'. 'Steaming pleasure capsules' would sound foreign indeed to those interested in bathing as a weapon against dirt and disease. It is perhaps because bodily cleanliness has become so taken for granted that the hygienic functions of bathing no longer need to be mentioned. After all, nobody is arguing that their shower cleans better than some other manufacturer's shower, for to do so would sound faintly absurd. Cleaning efficiency is not the point. The bathroom accomplishes its hygienic functions silently, speaking only of pleasure. And pleasure, as we saw in Chapter 1, is central to the dynamic of consumer societies.

The self

Forty (1986), as we have seen, shows how the home is a site where many external values may enter through, for example, the design of furniture. The home in this perspective expresses not an individual family but society more generally. Houseware magazines promote rather different views of the home. Here, the stress initially appears to be on how much a home is an expression of 'yourself and your character' (*HD*: 66). Manufacturers position themselves as partners who will help you attain your (not their) idea of how your home should be. De Gabriele kitchens 'will build on your ideas and develop them into the right design for you' (*HD*: 17), the Kitchen Place admits that 'You know what you want in your new kitchen. You've probably been thinking about it for months' (*KBQ*: 93), Miele designs 'reflect your impeccable taste in the kitchen' (*KBQ*: back cover), and Designing Women in the Kitchen cultivate a 'personal liaison with each client and [an] in-depth consideration of individual needs, taste, lifestyle and budget' (*KBQ*: 79).

With the exception of the Designing Women team, however, each of the manufacturers manages to remake your taste in their image. Your ideas will not overflow De Gabriele's 'largest possible range in styles and colours' (*HD*: 17), and it is the Miele Classic Collection that provides the mode of expression for 'your' taste (*KBQ*: back cover). The Kitchen Place is 'concerned about the small things that you may overlook – the way you work, your style of cooking, the decor of your home and so on' (*KBQ*: 93), suggesting that it can give a better account of your needs than you can. So even if the home is an expression of the self, it is a self that carries a manufacturer's signature.

Sociability

One might imagine that the social centre of a home was to be found in one of the spaces traditionally referred to as 'living room' or 'dining room'. Family or guests might be imagined to gather in the dining room to enjoy the food prepared in a separate space called 'kitchen'. On a Veblenian reading, the undignified work that went into preparing the meal was as well kept out of sight for no prestige would spring from it – especially if the food was prepared by servants. On a Goffmanesque reading (1972 [1959]: 109–40), front and back regions would be kept apart to the benefit of all sides: unsightly utensils streaked with unmistakable signs of use would be kept from the gaze of delicate sensibilities, kitchen mistakes could be covered up, and the general back region would be under the unquestioned control of the cook. Two things seem to have led to a change in middle-class houses. The advent of the servantless kitchen meant that family members, classically the wife/mother, needed to do their own cooking, and the idea of cooking as a creative middle-class pursuit, as opposed to a working-class chore, took hold. Instead of being hidden away as a task suited to lowly servants, cooking became a proudly visible activity of (usually) the mistress of the house herself.

Houseware magazines stress again and again that the kitchen is not somewhere obscured from view, but the most open and important room in the house. In particular, the cook is not isolated from social activity:

> The philosophy of the kitchen has moved on, too. It's what Vicki Poulter from Designing Women in the Kitchen calls the 'sociable kitchen'. It is often open to, or part of, a dining or family room area . . . 'Today's cooks don't want to be locked away', she said. 'They want to be able to have a chat with the family or sip a glass of wine with guests while they are cooking' (*KBQ*: 32–3);

> This clever, stylish kitchen simultaneously includes the cook in the activities of the dining room and, via the generous window over the sinks and preparation areas, the leafy garden outside (*KBQ*: 62);

> The owners realised all aspects of a social gathering should include the cook (*KBQ*: 71);

> lets the cook be involved with the rest of the family activities (*KBQ*: 77);

> The central island bench cleverly encourages others to converse with the cook (*KBQ*: 87);

> The kitchen is centrally located to the lounge, dining and informal living, allowing the hostess to always be part of the entertaining activities (*HLR*: 170).

The theme of openness, already present in some of the above citations, is also persistent:

> They [kitchen designers] will also want to know whether they can open the kitchen up to the rest of the house (*KBQ*: 32);

> [the kitchen] had to be spacious and open, an integral part of the living area and excellent for entertaining (*KBQ*: 70);

> The result is a much more open kitchen that connects to the rest of the house through doorways and arches, creating a flow rather than a dead end (*KBQ*: 77);

> An ideal kitchen for a large, open-plan home, and designed with family life in mind, it is equally the focal point for informal living and formal dining areas (*KBQ*: 83);

> 'Although the kitchen is open to the dining room, it's fine when we entertain because everyone ends up in the kitchen anyway' (*AHB*: 127).

There is clearly a collapse of boundaries between the kitchen and other areas. Instead of being a unit compartmentalized into sub-units each with a specific function, the contemporary home turns living, dining and cooking areas into a continuous semi-differentiated space. Furthermore, this new space is not so much a space for the accomplishing of discrete household tasks, as in the earlier compartmentalized model, but rather a space of

Table 7.1   *The changing functions of the home*

Historical period	Key function(s)	Key value(s)	Key room(s)
19th century	Moral welfare	Aesthetics	Drawing room
Most of 20th century	Physical welfare	Efficiency	Kitchen
1990s	Communication	Aesthetics	Kitchen, living and dining rooms collapse into semi-differentiated space under dominance of
	Sociability	Efficiency	kitchen
		Pleasure	Bathroom

general social communication for family and guests, with the most dense points of communication located in the kitchen area. A consequence is that this entire space is now on display, with no back region hidden from others. A much greater space now has a general communication function, and so more money, care and attention needs to be lavished on more parts of the home than before, which of course opens up more areas to be consumerized.

It will be recalled that Forty (1986) argued that there has been a transformation from the home as a place of beauty to the home as a place of efficiency. Our examination of contemporary houseware magazines shows, however, something slightly different. Now the home manages to be a place of *both* beauty and efficiency without contradiction or mutual exclusion, *and* has added a new dimension: the home as a place of sociability and communication. The changing functions of the home are summarized in Table 7.1.

The meanings of owning a home

What does owning a home actually mean to the people living in it as opposed to the accounts of houseware magazines? Lyn Richards (1990) asked this question in her interviews with the residents of the new Melbourne suburb of Green Views. As we shall see in a moment, the major meanings of home ownership can be understood in relation to just two main concepts: family life and security. Women and men, however, had different perspectives on what these concepts actually stood for. But perhaps we should first note the fact that almost everybody in the suburb thought that purchasing a house was a goal for everyone. This was so strongly felt that the 'purchase of the house was the overwhelming preoccupation and justification for decisions and the common link felt with other residents' (Richards, 1990: 115). So not only was the house central to the thinking and decision making of the owners, it was also what allowed people in this suburb to see links among themselves. To some degree at least, then, social solidarity in Green Views was dependent upon a shared identity as home owners. This seemed to make for an ambivalent attitude towards renters: people said ' "they don't worry" or "don't bother" us' (Richards, 1990: 116), or even 'some of our best friends' are renters – Richards suggests that these are all terms typically used for lower classes and migrants, while the 'some of our best friends' cliché is a traditional way of denying a prejudice that is probably actually held. Renting while saving for a deposit on a house was acceptable enough, but a negative view was taken of those who rented without home ownership in mind – a proper family, for these people, *means* owning a house. If this is not your aim, then your family is distinctly improper and is not likely to be included in the social life of Green Views.

The most common answer given to the question 'Why own your own home?' was security – indeed, sometimes the answer consisted of that single word alone. But what exactly did the residents of Green Views understand by the word 'security'? It seems to have been caught up with ideas of the family even when financial security was the topic. So there were replies such as 'It's something to own and can't be taken away from us. It's a home for the children and we don't have to move around any more'; or 'Security in the future – not only for us, but for the kids later on in life', or 'We want to be a family, and a good foundation is owning your own home' (Richards, 1990: 121). Ideally, you save, you buy your own home, and you then have children. So home ownership does not seem to be interpretable in terms of pure financial investment, but perhaps can be seen as a financial investment that is at the same time an emotional investment in the idea of the family. There seems to be nothing in Richards's sample about those who keep selling their houses in a succession of moves up market, so we have no information on the place of family, finance, and status among that particular group.

'Security' also meant control and independence. The negative version of control (lack of control) can be seen in repeated phrases like 'no one can put you out' – 'If you own, "You don't have to worry about the landlord throwing you out all the time"' (Richards, 1990: 124). But if you own a house you can do what you want with it – put a nail in the wall, have wild parties, or throw a brick through your own window: this is the positive side of control. There were gender differences, however, in the meanings of security – for men, it had a tendency to mean financial security and for women it tended to mean stability more than anything else. The stress here is on 'tendencies', as these differences were not absolute. Richards remarks that 'The security of not renting, for women, was about stability and space for bringing up children. No men say this' (1990: 131). So women tended to include children in their version of security, but men did not. She also maintains that 'It is hard to resist the summary that women see themselves as *living*, with families, in homes; men stress *leaving* the home to the children' (1990: 132). Family is important to both here, but one sees the family as something to live with and the other sees the family as something to leave the house to – rather different views of the family–house relation.

What does the phrase 'this house is mine' mean? It meant different things for the women and men in the sample. For men, the 'meanings of "mine" were those associated with security – my money, mine to remain in, mine to control' (Richards, 1990: 133). Men generally did not include others in the 'mine', but women tended to speak of 'we' and did include others in the meanings of ownership. Women also tended to mean 'mine' in the sense of the house as an expression of their own taste made manifest through doing it up in various ways – a number said they loved their house and it made them happy, but none of the men said this. The house was a symbol of success or ownership to the men, but for women it was the embodiment of the work they put into it through decoration and housework and the jobs they took on to pay the mortgage. It is not hard to see why men tended to see the home as a haven from work, while women saw it as a site of work.

Such, then, are the gendered meanings of home ownership as they arise from Richards's study. It is now time to consider the meanings of the actual objects to be found in people's homes, and so we turn to Csikszentmihalyi and Rochberg-Halton's (1981) account of the matter.

The meanings of domestic objects

The material in this study comes from a series of interviews held in 1977 with 82 families living in the Chicago metropolitan area, half being described by the researchers as upper middle-class and half lower middle-class. In particular, they were interested in answers to the question 'What are the things in your home which are special to you?' They came up with 1,694 things which they classified into a number of categories. The main ones were as follows, along with the percentage of the total sample mentioning at least one special object in each category: furniture (36 per cent), visual art (26 per cent), photographs (23 per cent), books (22 per cent), stereo (22 per cent), musical instruments (22 per cent), television (21 per cent), and sculpture (19 per cent). We consider only the top three.

Furniture

The meanings of furniture tended to depend on one's place in the life cycle. For children and teenagers, for example, furniture meant comfort and enjoyment and a stress upon the self. A kitchen table and chairs would be for the momentary comfort and enjoyment purposes of this class of person. Meanings are rather different for adult women, as can be seen from the comment of one: 'They are the first two chairs me and my husband ever bought, and we sit in them and I just associate them with my home and having babies and sitting in the chairs with babies' (Csikszentmihalyi and Rochberg-Halton, 1981: 60). Here, then, memories of times past and associations with babies are the primary meanings. The chairs are also part of family history, as they bring to mind both babies and husband; social ties, absent in teenage accounts of furniture, become quite important here. This was typical of the women in the sample, and their husbands also shared in this. The latter, however, also sometimes looked upon furniture as a personal accomplishment. The meanings of furniture, then, tended to see children associated with enjoyment and egocentricity, adult women with social networks, and men with accomplishment and abstract ideals.

Overall, the actual practical uses to which items of furniture might be put were less important than other considerations: of the '638 meanings given for why furniture was considered special' (Csikszentmihalyi and Rochberg-Halton, 1981: 62) only 5 per cent were utilitarian. Experiences counted for 11 per cent, stylistic reasons for 12 per cent, and memories made up 15 per cent of the reasons given. What is a chair for? If you ask the first person you meet on the street they will probably reply, 'For sitting in, of course!' As a sociologist, you will no doubt be pleased to inform them that they are greatly mistaken.

Visual art

Visual art in this research did not just mean original works of art but included 'Any two-dimensional representation other than a photograph . . . ranging from an original Picasso to the cheapest reproduction of the *Last Supper*' (Csikszentmihalyi and Rochberg-Halton, 1981: 63). There were class differences in the number and quality of pictures, with the upper classes having more pictures and more expensive ones, but the researchers suggest that this may have little to do with wealth differences because lower-class families often had expensive objects like cameras or stereo sets. Perhaps we can invoke Bourdieu's notion of cultural capital here to explain this: one needs higher cultural capital in order to feel comfortable with pictures in the house. Lower-class pictures tended to indicate social and religious values directly, such as pictures of 'Martin Luther King, John F. Kennedy, *The Last Supper*' (Csikszentmihalyi and Rochberg-Halton, 1981: 65), whereas higher social classes would have more abstract representations. This seems to fit low and high degrees of cultural capital quite well, and we will recognize the difference between an upper-class Kantian aesthetic and a lower-class anti-Kantian aesthetic in the sorts of pictures chosen.

One might expect aesthetic value to figure highly in the meanings of pictures, but again memories seemed highly important, at 16 per cent of responses, and the same percentage referred to immediate family. Twelve and a half per cent referred to non-kin relations so, as the researchers remark, pictures are a main symbol of friendship. They suggest that

> the bulk of significations carried by visual 'works of art' is not connected to aesthetic values and experiences but refers to the immediate life history of their owners: reminding them of relatives and friends or of past events. People pay particular attention to pictures in their home because in doing so they relive memorable occasions and pleasing relationships. (Csikszentmihalyi and Rochberg-Halton, 1981: 65)

We know of course that pictures are indeed bought for investment purposes, but there seems to be little, if any, of this here. It seems that people in the sample do not purchase pictures through the eyes of the art critic or valuer, and the philosophy of art for art's sake does not appear to have much of a place in this picture of the meanings of pictures.

Photographs

More than any other objects in the home, photographs referred to memories (27 per cent) and immediate family (26 per cent). The authors remark that 'photographs are the prime vehicle for preserving the memory of one's close relations . . . they are often described as being "irreplaceable" by older respondents. When the picture represents a deceased relative, it often bears a freight of vivid emotions for people in the middle generation as well' (Csikszentmihalyi and Rochberg-Halton, 1981: 67). It should be clear, then, that photos were less important to children than older people. Photographs allow the great majority of people in society the possibility of actually retaining an image of their dear departed ones, and so it is hardly surprising that they can take on an almost sacred status. In sum, the Chicago research seems to have found a strong relationship between precious objects and either the self or family relationships, rather than links to non-familial aspects such as aesthetic qualities.

We can see, then, that the meanings of the home and its objects can be approached from two quite different angles. The account by Forty shows how the interior of the home is moulded in all sorts of political and ideological ways by the design of home objects, but says nothing about the personal meanings of items to the people who live there. The Chicago study shows what objects mean to people, but cannot give us any way of grasping how the objects that are meaningful got to have that form in the first place, nor can it show the subtle links with the broader world that Forty can.

8
Food and Drink

Recent sociological accounts of food and drink have tended to be of two different sorts. Writers such as Stephen Mennell (1985, 1987) attempt to locate changes in eating and drinking practices within the overall changes in social structure that sprang from the transition from agricultural to industrial societies, a process that has by no means come to an end in our constantly transforming period of history. This socio-historical approach was inspired by the work of Norbert Elias (1994 [1939]) on the civilizing process, and traces the increasingly refined ways in which we accomplish our daily consuming activities. For example, there has been a tendency for meat to appear on our tables looking less and less like the animal that it was, and more and more as small inoffensive pieces that could have been processed anywhere from anything. The anonymous minced beef of the hamburger replaces the boiled calf's head resting proudly on the plate. Mennell tries to show why it would now be impossible for most of us to serve up the latter: revulsion is socially constructed, not naturally acquired.

The second main approach to food and drink is grounded in the structuralism of Claude Lévi-Strauss, and is here represented by Mary Anna Thornton's (1987) account of drinking practices in an Austrian village. Sekt and schnapps are the polar opposites structuring the drinking system, and may be mapped onto oppositions such as formal/informal, city/country, professional class/working class, special occasions/any time. Other drinks belong more or less to one of these two classes, with some overlap and ambiguity. Structuralism has been particularly popular among anthropologists, who are perhaps less handicapped than sociologists by the atemporality implicit in this way of thinking. Marshall Sahlins (1976) also takes a structuralist stance in his account of the US meat-eating system.

This chapter also considers Mennell's account of food dislikes, the refusal to consume food characteristic of anorexia nervosa, and the place of pets on the table.

On the civilizing of appetite: the work of Stephen Mennell

Stephen Mennell's approach to food grows out of Norbert Elias's (1994 [1939]) work on the civilizing process. Elias noted a tendency in society for more and more aspects of everyday behaviour to come under more and more control as society became increasingly rationalized. Some of these controls could be external, such as rules made by the state to regulate the sorts of clothes one might wear, but many of them came to be internalized and thus we finish by controlling ourselves rather than being controlled by outside bodies. We are much less likely than our ancestors to eat everything with our hands, blow our noses into the nearest curtain or receive guests while sitting on a chamber pot. We have become civilized in the sense of controlling those of our functions that we rather obviously share with other animals. We impose a distance between ourselves and our food by eating with knife and fork and we relegate defecation to a place hidden away behind closed doors. Being well brought up, we probably do not even think that we are exercising great control over ourselves here, but act as if these sorts of behaviour are in the very nature of things. Bringing up children might, however, remind us that there is little natural about our ways.

The rationalization process first noted by Weber appears to invade practically all aspects of social life. Trouble-making extremes are levelled out and the necessity for calculability tends to require reliably organized persons who appear not as the unruly products of nature but as the (ideally) self-ruled products of a *cultural* creation. The less purely natural and the more purely cultural we appear, the more we are suited to rationalized society. And the more areas of life that come under a cultural discipline, the less likely are we to have any aspects of our selves that may be unpredictable and hence potentially troublesome. Externally imposed rules are needed at first, but once the process is set in train self-regulation begins to take over – we behave as 'civilized' persons without having to be forced any more.

So in what ways has appetite become civilized? The aspect that retains Stephen Mennell's (1987) attention is the question of the quantitative regulation of appetite: why did we move from the gargantuan feasts of earlier Europeans to the relatively small amounts we eat today? One reason seems to lie in the shift from the feast–famine fluctuation in medieval Europe to the more even spread of food intake today. A stable quantity of food was not guaranteed all year round even for the upper classes, and the poor were of course even more at the mercy of variations in food availability. Allied to relatively poor transport and preserving facilities, these fluctuations made the 'feast while you can' philosophy quite suited to the social conditions of the time. Medieval life was insecure in all sorts of ways besides food availability, and indeed insecurity was probably an almost permanent state. It was hard to plan reliably and so one took what one could when the opportunity arose, for it might not be there tomorrow.

More trade and improved transport made general famines less likely, as food could be moved about more easily. This had some paradoxical effects:

> In the industrialized countries it was eventually to bring about increased diversity for available foods and improved diets for lower as well as upper social ranks; in the less industrialized world, in contrast, the same process has led through commercialization to concentration in many regions on only a few cash crops with a concomitant reduction in food diversity. In a shorter-term period of transition, the same sort of contrast could be seen *within* the countries of Europe. This conflict between national markets and local needs was one reason why food riots were still common in eighteenth-century England and France. (Mennell, 1987: 381)

So not everybody benefited from changes in trade and transport. At an earlier stage one gets inequalities at local levels within a given country; at a later stage the inequality appears to be between cash-crop economies and First World countries.

Even if famines appeared to become less likely, there was still the fear of going hungry which had been fed by the many centuries when supplies were not at all reliable. Such a fear was hardly likely to disappear instantly. Mennell (1987: 381) quotes the historian Mandrou (1961: 26–7) who observes that a central feature of the time was 'the obsession with starving to death, an obsession which varied in intensity according to locality and class, being stronger in the country than in the town, rare among the upper-classes and well-fed fighting men, and constant among the lower classes'. The same obsession was continued through folktales and stories about saints performing food miracles. It was clearly going to take some time for these fears to disappear, hence a continuation of the tendency to pounce on any food available and gorge oneself on it.

Given this insecurity, it might seem unlikely that medieval Europeans had much chance of controlling anything. But there were three agencies that had their own reasons for controlling food intake in certain directions: the Catholic Church, the state, and the medical profession. Mennell considers these briefly. The constraints on appetite brought about by the Church, such as fasting, appear in general not to have been internalized. Fasting, through its control of sensory urges, is presumably designed to submit mere humans to the spiritual designs of a god. As we shall see later, the notion of control through fasting may be turned to other uses in the case of anorexia nervosa. But Church rules had no effect on bingeing on days when people were not required to fast, and even when one did refrain from meat and eat fish instead it was perfectly possible to indulge in most copious fish dishes if one was a member of the better-off classes. Mennell sees this as evidence that these constraints had not been internalized, and were thus the sign of a low degree of civilization.

Although people later learned more self-control with respect to food, Mennell maintains that the teachings of the Church did not play a significant part. He sees the secular authorities as more important here – just as there were sumptuary laws regulating clothing, so there were sumptuary laws regulating food. These seemed to be directed more at social display through over-elaborate banqueting than at actual physical appetite. Earlier banquets could be excused as the excess went by custom to the poor for whom the upper classes had some sort of responsibility, but the rising social classes had no such clearly defined obligations towards others and so their banqueting seems to have been for display only. Such laws, of course, were almost impossible to enforce, but they appear to have established a political right to rule appetite.

This right seems more important today than ever, with various bits of state-related apparatuses seeing it as their right to control our food intake. I remember being quite taken aback when I first came to Australia to find that I could not obtain unpasteurized Camembert because it was illegal to sell it, despite the fact that the French have been eating it for over a century with few ill-effects. State subsidies and fines influence the consumption of certain types of food through regulating production. Wartime rationing is another more direct example. So although the state may have failed in its attempts to regulate food consumption through sumptuary laws, it appears to have established successfully its actual right to regulate food. A food policy becomes something legitimate for the state to have, and it can be propagated through agencies such as the school and the media.

Mennell's third institution after the Church and the state is medical opinion. He comments that 'Throughout the Middle Ages medical opinion . . . had favoured moderation in eating in the treatment of numerous illnesses' (Mennell, 1987: 385). However, this did not seem to have much effect on the majority of the population – medical power at this stage was effectively exercised only over those who were already ill, and so nobody else paid much attention to medical arguments about food. Even within the hospital there were contradictory approaches:

> nursing sisters had traditionally seen their role as a charitable one and, aware that many illnesses had resulted from repeated subsistence crises, saw it as their duty to feed up the poor and needy ill . . . [A doctor in Montpellier] in the 1760s documented how overfeeding by the sisters had led to patients' premature deaths, and 'gave the impression that over-eating was one of the major causes of hospital mortality!' (Mennell, 1987: 386)

Medical opinion only began to have any widespread influence once it had vanquished opposing locations of knowledge, skills and power as represented by, in this instance, the nursing sisters, and became a profession allied with the state, collaborating with it in spreading control over more and more areas of life. Many eventually accepted the medical model of health, and drew upon it when regulating their own consumption of food and drink. Here we see a shift again from external controls to internal controls as indicative of an increased degree of civilization.

An important change that contributed to the civilizing of appetite was the shift from stressing the sheer *quantity* of food consumed to the more delicate and complex question of the *quality* of the food. When supplies were insecure and irregular, quantity was a way of distinguishing the powerful from the others – there was no need of a refined taste to indicate social difference at this stage. By the mid-eighteenth century, however, mere quantitative excess was considered rather out of place. Why did this happen? The familiar argument about social distinction comes in here again: once food supplies become more regular and reliable and accessible to more and more elements of the population, the upper elements must act to distinguish themselves from the lower orders who have begun to copy their eating habits. Mennell (1987: 389) points out that 'By the sixteenth or seventeenth centuries, for the nobility to eat quantitatively more would have been physically impossible', so a limit appears to have been reached. How was this overcome? The emphasis came to be placed on the skill of cooks to produce 'an endless variety of ever more refined and delicate dishes; when the possibilities of quantitative consumption for the expression of social superiority had been exhausted, the qualitative possibilities were inexhaustible' (Mennell, 1987: 389).

To put this in the more philosophical terms used by Bourdieu in an earlier chapter, an anti-Kantian strategy is replaced by a Kantian one once the former can no longer successfully fulfil the function of invidious social distinction. Delicate, refined dishes replace the unrestrained blow-out. We find a battle of the ancients and the moderns in the mid-eighteenth century, 'in which defenders of old styles of cooking and eating railed against the preciousness, pretentiousness and overdeveloped sense of culinary propriety of the proponents of the *nouvelle cuisine*' (Mennell, 1987: 391). But as the latter spreads its influence and is copied by broader social classes, a reaction again sets in, and so it may well be possible to interpret the late twentieth-century form of *nouvelle cuisine*, with its reaction against heavy sauces and over-elaboration in presentation, in a similar light: for the chef Paul Bocuse, 'I find that meals are always too large. I think one should leave the table still feeling slightly hungry' (Bocuse, 1988 [1976]: xvi). This clearly claims that the point of food is not to feed the stomach and is, as we have seen from Bourdieu, typical upper-class Kantianism: refined and delicate stomachs should be permanently hungry, never stooping to the vulgarity of giving in totally to physical demands.

Knowing one's way around a selection of delicate dishes was a sign of higher social status, and entailed the practice of restraint. The French court of the mid-eighteenth century still retained to some degree the tradition of lavishness, and it was up to the bourgeois class to lay the stress on delicacy. Aristocrats had the capacity to indulge in both quantity and quality, but the bourgeoisie could afford only one or the other (Mennell, 1987: 391). The switch from quantity to quality also brought about a new kind of ideal body for the upper classes: a large body was a sign of a large food intake and would have been a very prestigious thing to possess in those periods when food supplies were unreliable and uneven. But the new regime demanded a body that provided evidence of delicacy, refinement and restraint – slimness was in. The slimmer body began among the upper classes, and indeed even today is more likely to be found among the better-off classes than among the poorer in the affluent societies of the West. The reverse may be the case in some Third World countries where food supplies are still uncertain (Mennell, 1987: 397).

Food avoidance and food dislikes

Almost everybody avoids and/or dislikes certain sorts of foods – but why is this? Many of us might maintain that it is merely a matter of personal taste for which, proverbially, there is no accounting: *à chacun son goût*. This is a historically recent stance, however. Pasi Falk argues that, we can give the well known slogan of the old scholastics – *de gustibus non dis-putandum* (one cannot dispute about taste) – two quite opposite meanings. In the (primitive) case of the strong alimentary code – to which it was never applied – it would refer to the fact that the judgement of what to eat and what not is made by the 'mouth' of the community according to the rules that are beyond doubt. In the modern case of individualized judgement the slogan may be conceived of in a way closer to the scholastic stance: taste cannot be disputed because it is based on the 'nature' of the individual being (body) and not in culture. (Falk, 1994: 13)

In earlier societies, then, the community decided what could be taken in and the idea of an individual taste would have made no sense for there were no strongly developed individuals as such. 'Individual' taste would have corre-sponded precisely to 'community' taste: differences between them would have been unthinkable. Translating Falk into Durkheim might make matters clearer. It will be recalled that Durkheim (1984 [1893]) drew a dis-tinction between mechanical and organic solidarity, the first characterized by sameness among the elements of a social system and the second by func-tional differentiation among the elements. It is only the latter that allows 'individuality' to flourish. Taste under conditions of mechanical solidarity would be the same for everyone, while taste under conditions of organic solidarity at least has the possibility of becoming differentiated in such a way that it can be mapped onto individual elements who thus appear each to have their 'own' taste. Whether this differentiation of taste is functional or not is another question, which cannot be pursued here. For the food industry, perhaps, it is.

But even the individuality of 'individual' taste may be an illusion in con-temporary society. As we may recall from Bourdieu, there is little that is personal about a taste caught up in struggles over class positioning. In the present context, perhaps we should say that there is little personal about *dis*taste. If we look at this in terms of the civilizing process, we can see that the more refined we become the more likely we are to find disgusting food that has, through this process of refinement on our part, become newly classified as 'unrefined' (unrefined in the social sense, not in the sense of, say, unrefined sugar). The distance we have travelled into 'refinement' can be seen in the remark of Elias that:

> From a standard of feeling by which the sight and carving of a dead animal on the table are actually pleasurable, or at least not at all unpleasant, the development leads to another standard by which reminders that the meat dish has something to do with the killing of an animal are avoided to the utmost. In many of our meat dishes the animal form is so concealed and changed by the art of its preparation and carving that while eating one is scarcely reminded of its origin . . . people, in the course of the civilizing process, seek to suppress in themselves every charac-teristic that they feel to be 'animal'. They likewise suppress such characteristics in their food. (Elias, 1994 [1939]: 98)

Following a similar logic, even the site/sight of slaughterhouses has shifted further and further away from the centres of towns, finally to reach a sort of invisibility: 'nowadays all you see is a high wall with a number of rooftops peeping over it; it is rare for the entrance to bear any kind of inscription, and even rarer for there to be signposts showing how to get there' (Vialles, 1994 [1987]: 22). Now we find it almost impossible to bear the sight of meat that pretty directly resembles the animal it originally came from. The head, of course, is probably one of the first things that falls to the civilizing process – the eyes, ears and mouth remind us like nothing else that this was once a living animal that, just like us, had eyes, ears and a mouth. Other cuts remind us rather less of this, although the testicles of cattle and sheep are also likely candidates for early victims of civilization. The general point here is that food that at an earlier stage appeared quite acceptable now becomes disgusting. This has little to do with personal taste as such, illustrating rather the point that taste and distaste are shaped by developments in the civilizing process.

Mennell proposes four main reasons for the avoidance of certain types of foods: 'the trained incapacity to enjoy food; fear of the after-effects of eating certain foods; fear of social derogation; and moral reasons for revulsion' (Mennell, 1985: 294). Several of these reasons might occur together. A number of Mennell's comments contrast specifically French and English ways of doing things with food, but it should still be possible for the reader to translate his observations into the context of their own culture.

What is meant by 'trained incapacity to enjoy food'? Clearly, the fact that people are brought up not to enjoy it. He sees this as an English phenomenon, for France appears very different. The English probably invented the notion of 'nursery food', and one certainly still finds children's menus in restaurants that are qualitatively different to adult menus, and items such as fish fingers are widely marketed as food especially destined for children. Children's food is constructed as different in kind to adult food, and is not merely the same food in smaller portions. Serving 'children's food' at an adult dinner party would be a serious insult in England, but the question would probably not even be posable in France. Mennell sees the origin of nursery food in Victorian ideas about the proper treatment of children and teenagers. He writes: 'A special kind of diet appears to have been considered appropriate for young people, not just literally in the nursery but at boarding schools and more widely, for the notion spread also to the less well-to-do homes where children were not segregated in an actual nursery' (Mennell, 1985: 295–6).

And what was the main characteristic of this food? It was plain, monotonous and dull – very unexciting. So food was something that was almost tasteless, and the concept of enjoying such body fuel was not likely to develop. It is possible, speculating a bit, that seriously unexciting and bland food might have been seen as a way of controlling children: developing one aspect of sensuality through developing the palate might have opened the door to the development of other aspects of sensuality, especially among teenagers. If the tongue can find excitement in food then maybe it can find excitement in other areas as well, but it may not be relevant to elaborate on that particular matter here. Children may well have disliked this sort of food, and Mennell suggests that this may have been a deliberate strategy to break a child's will through forcing them to eat what, according to adults, was 'good for them'.

Medical beliefs also propagated the notion that anything other than bland food was dangerous to children's health. This appears to have been peculiarly English; French children seem to be nowhere near as faddish or picky. Mennell's evidence for this is a bit impressionistic, although I have to say that it accords with my own perceptions of French and English food practices. He compares answers to questions on food in a survey of the mothers of 22 French children and 23 English children aged between 13 and 15 who were involved in exchange visits between schools in Exeter and Rennes in 1984:

> of the 22 French children, not one of the mothers had recorded any food aller-
> gies, nor mentioned any difficulties about food . . . In contrast, of the 23 English
> children, 14 mothers had mentioned foods their children could not eat. Most of
> them stated more than one food – the 14 produced a total of 27 mentions of non-
> acceptable foods. (Mennell, 1985: 300)

England 27, France 0. Perhaps surprisingly, these food dislikes did *not* refer to 'foreign food' but to everyday English things like tomatoes or carrots. English children are not trained to enjoy food; French children are. As a result, the French children treat eating as an occasion for enjoyment, and appreciate practically anything that is edible: everything gives its own special pleasures. The English children seemed to lack this positive attitude to food, and appear to see food not as a source of many pleasures but as divided into things they can cope with and things they cannot. Children are socialized through food practices in both cases, but the outcomes are quite different. Food dislikes here have little to do with personal (dis)taste and a lot to do with the ways particular societies treat food, using it to construct children and adults as being more or less similar to each other. The influence of Puritanism is, of course, stronger in England than in France, and this may be another factor at work. I will leave it to the reader to try and fit their country into this model.

The second reason proposed by Mennell for food dislikes is the fear of after-effects and the social embarrassment these may cause. Again this appears more an English fear and seems as if it may be a hangover from the stodgy food that characterized the English diet until relatively recently: there was a low intake of fruit and vegetables, and, as a consequence, the breath was likely to be bad. Leeks, onions and garlic would have made their presence very obvious to others, and so were either avoided or cooked almost out of existence. With a diet encouraging bad breath and bad digestion, there was a tendency to avoid any food that might speak loudly through one or several of the orifices that grace the human body. Mennell sees this as further evidence of the civilizing process, where people 'learned to anticipate [the] social embarrassment' (1985: 302) that certain foods may cause. Again, distaste is not so much a personal matter as a social one.

Mennell's third reason for food avoidance is fear of social derogation – the fear of appearing to be of a lower class than one actually is, or, more likely, aspires to be. Just as a particular choice of word, phrase, emphasis, grammatical form or accent can betray one's 'real' class (and this is especially important in class-sensitive societies such as England), so can a particular choice of food indicate one's social class. Mennell notes that 'There are countless cases of foods being dropped by higher social ranks when adopted by lower. One example is sago, in 1850 a rarity . . . later adopted by the poorer classes and dropped by the better-off as simply being dull' (1985: 303).

I would suggest that this principle holds not just for social classes but for age classes as well, particularly in those societies where, as in England, the notion of children's food exists. The older children get, the more likely are they to avoid certain foods because they are associated with the dietary practices of younger children. The same principle may be applied to gender. This can be seen in a fairly unserious way in the phrase 'real men don't each quiche' – to eat quiche would be to lose prestige by opting for a food for unreal men. Work on the gendered distribution of food within the family, as discussed by Nicola Charles and Marion Kerr (1987), shows definite male and female patterns of consumption where meat is a prime way of establishing superior and inferior relations. They studied the food distribution patterns of the families of a sample of 200 women who were bringing up young children. The women had the main responsibility for purchasing and preparing the food in these families. Now one might assume from this that they also controlled the choice of food purchased, but this was not the case – choice tended to be dictated primarily by the food preferences of the husband and secondarily by the food preferences of the children. When the father was absent the women tended to let the children decide the food. In fact, Charles and Kerr go so far as to say that many of the women often found it difficult to describe their own food preferences, and in some cases denied that they had any tastes at all. So despite doing the purchasing and the cooking, they had no real input of their own into the choice of foodstuffs. Even when they were alone, they often did not cook for themselves, considering it a waste of time and energy. Indeed, if everyday cooking consists of cooking for others and not for oneself, then perhaps this is not surprising: there is nobody left to cook for.

Charles and Kerr found a distinction between various status groups of meats: high status consisted of a joint, steaks and chops, medium status was made up of mince dishes, stews, casseroles, liver and bacon, while low-status meats, which were often associated with children, included sausages and burgers. There was a tendency for men to consume the high-status meats and women more to approach children's mode of consuming. The ways in which food is distributed tells us something about how people go about being mothers, fathers and children: being a 'proper man' involves the consumption of more high-status meat than women and children so men would tend to avoid eating medium- and low-status meat when they could. The social status of the food, here linked to gender, guides choice more than apparently personal preferences. Once more here we come across the notion of children's food as something distinct from adult food. So again, food dislikes and preferences do not appear particularly personal, but are more the result of the ways in which social distinction operates within class, age and gender.

There is no space here to discuss Mennell's account of the fourth reason he gives for food avoidance, namely moral issues. Now we turn to consider the related question of why most of us seem to have a tendency not to want to eat our pets, and why certain other animals are also unlikely to be on the menu.

Noëlie Vialles remarks that

> traditionally, animals raised for the family to eat are not individualised by giving them a name. A herd of cows may all have names, but they are not destined for the table. On the other hand, calves that are raised for sale as meat remain anonymous. Similarly, pigs, hens, and rabbits are never given names, and if they do happen to receive one it excludes them *ipso facto* from being eaten. (Vialles, 1994 [1987]: 115–16)

So long as something is unnamed it is at least potentially edible, but once an animal is named it becomes familiar to us, and such animals tend to be avoided for food. What animals familiar to urban dwellers are named? Primarily, pets. Pets appear to us as subjects with which we communicate, not objects destined for the slaughterhouse. As Nick Fiddes writes,

> By caring for pets, tending them, giving them proper names, we endow them with semi-human status. The foods we allot them are largely modelled on human tastes: no manufacturer markets the mouse or bluebottle flavour cat food for which, given free choice, eight out of ten cats might express a preference (nor cat-flavoured dog food!). We allow pets into our houses, and sometimes even into our beds; we talk to them; we give them special affection, special medical care, special exercise; we fret when they are unwell and weep when they die; we may even bury them alongside us. We treat pets more like individual subjects than the abstract objects as which we officially regard edible animals – although some species we treat more favourably than others, allotting them a closer relationship to ourselves. (Fiddes, 1991: 133)

Fiddes's comment on the marketing of pet food is perhaps the most revealing of all: it is usually sold as fish or chunks of meat, in other words the sort of food that we ourselves are likely to eat. In this way, pets are constructed as being part of the same class as ourselves through the exclusion of flavours that we might find disgusting but cats might find wildly attractive. We prevent cats from being just cats by replacing cat preferences in food with human preferences: not only do they have names and live with us, but they also eat like us. At this rate, to eat a cat (or a dog) would be like eating a member of the family.

Social proximity protects the cat. But there is another sort of proximity that makes it difficult for us to eat certain animals: our physiological proximity to primates such as monkeys and gorillas. It would be like eating a distant cousin. I suspect that this may be more the case in societies that have embraced Darwin's theory of evolution as the natural way the world is, for it was not until Darwin that anyone put forward the idea that humans and primates were very closely related. Christian writers had long argued that humans were naturally superior to animals, which had been put on earth for the benefit of humans. In this light, it would have been difficult for people to identify with primates. Darwin proposed a continuation rather than a rupture between humans and animals, and so they became more like us (and we like them) and as a consequence it began to become more difficult for us to eat them – slowly they began to take on the trappings of subjects with rights of their own. So whether we are talking about the social proximity of cats and dogs or the physiological proximity of primates, the idea of cannibalism seems to suit both. Of course some societies find the eating of monkeys or dogs acceptable, but they are likely to hold these animals at much greater social distance from humans than we do. Monkeys are eaten in parts of Africa and the Amazon, while dog is a delicacy in Korea: it is unlikely that such animals are 'humanized' as they would be in Western countries.

So to the next item on our menu of inedibles, after dog on toast and monkey pie: it appears that we do not normally eat carnivorous animals (Vialles, 1994 [1987]: 128). Fiddes (1991: 139) reports that the revulsion at this idea came to the surface in debates over two food scares in Britain in the late 1980s: the salmonella in eggs scandal of 1988 and the bovine spongiform encephalopathy (BSE) outbreak in cattle ('mad cow disease') the following year. In both cases, infection had been traced to the feeding of animal flesh to chickens and cattle, neither of which is a natural eater of meat – chickens were fed the carcasses of inadequately sterilized dead chickens as a protein supplement and cattle were fed the remains of sheep, some of which presumably suffered from scrapie, which is the ovine equivalent of mad cow disease. Fiddes (1991: 139) writes that 'Whilst scientific research focused upon the possibility of the agent transferring, in turn, to humans, an indignant public deplored the principle of feeding herbivores with animal remains at all.' Agribusiness practices had transformed both cattle and chickens into carnivores, and had even turned the latter into cannibals. This seemed to be what upset the public: cattle and chickens were now acting unnaturally, and if we continued to eat them we too would be acting unnaturally. By March 1996, the public had more than symbolic relations to worry about: the British government admitted that BSE could be transmitted to humans through the eating of beef (*Weekend Australian*, 23–24 March 1996).

But why do we not eat carnivores? Again the reason seems to have to do with their proximity to humans, this time in the sense that they appear to share our position with respect to other animals: many of us eat meat, and eating another carnivore would be like eating one of our own. Fiddes (1991: 141) remarks that 'We respect them since they do not fit neatly into the scheme of things whereby humankind is at the unchallenged apex of a pyramid of power.' We are alike in sharing the same position of power with respect to killing and eating animals. Fiddes points out that 'some animals fall into more than one category, such as the especially privileged cats and dogs who are close to us both socially and due to their carnivorous habits' (1991: 141), so here is yet another reason for not eating our favourite domestic animals. Similarly, Sahlins (1976: 175, fn. 7) refers to the case of dog-eating Hawaiians: dogs destined for eating are never allowed to touch meat. In this case, dogs are deliberately removed from the class of carnivore, and so become more easily edible. I do not know if this is the case in other dog-eating societies, but if so it would certainly seem to support the 'humans do not eat carnivores' rule in a striking way. Closeness to carnivores seems to break down a little when we speak of reptiles: it is less difficult to think of eating crocodile. This may be because we cannot identify with a cold-blooded creature, which is not 'one of us' in the sense that a warm-blooded animal is. Perhaps this cold-bloodedness is what also allows us to eat fish that feed on the flesh of other fish. So where warm-blooded carnivores never make it onto the menu, cold-blooded carnivores just might find themselves being served up to appreciative humans.

The reasons for avoiding certain foods are summarized in Table 8.1.

The food system in the US – a structuralist approach

The anthropologist Marshall Sahlins (1976) takes up some of the above themes about which animals we eat and which we do not in a systematic structuralist manner, and I have sketched his analysis in Figure 8.1. He proposes that a series of binary oppositions governs the way in which Americans decide what is edible and what is not, and it is quite likely that the model can be applied in other English-speaking countries with more than slight success. A key idea is the relation of a given species to human society, and he takes the example of the domesticated series cattle–pigs–horses–dogs. These are all close to humans, but in different ways, and these different ways correspond to different degrees of edibility.

Table 8.1 *Reasons for avoiding certain foods*

Trained incapacity to enjoy food
Fear of after-effects and consequent social embarrassment
Necessity of maintaining social status:
- age: adults will avoid eating 'children's' food
- class: higher classes drop foods adopted by lower classes
- gender: specific food practices prove that one is a 'proper' man or 'proper' woman
Social proximity of animals:
- impossibility of eating animals with given names
- cat food and dog food are made to resemble human food: thus such pets take on human qualities and are therefore inedible
Physiological proximity of animals:
- primates are perceived to bear a close resemblance to humans in Darwin-influenced societies, and to eat them would be a form of cannibalism
Formal proximity of animals:
- shared membership of class of (warm-blooded) carnivores

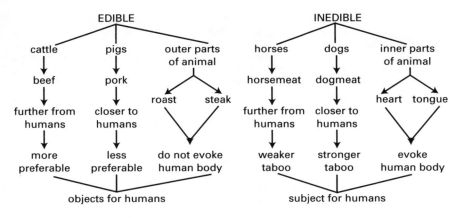

Figure 8.1   *Edible and inedible meats in the US (Sahlins, 1976)*

The first binary division is between the edible (cattle and pigs) and the inedible (horses and dogs). These classes are further divisible 'into higher and less preferable categories of food (beef vs. pork) and more and less rigorous categories of taboo (dogs vs. horses). The entire set appears to be differentiated by participation as subject or object in the company of men' (Sahlins, 1976: 174). The same logic of differentiation can be applied to the opposition of 'meat' and 'internal organs' in the case of the edible animal. I mentioned above how dogs are treated as part of the family, and Sahlins draws upon a similar notion to account for the differences between dogs and horses:

> Traditionally horses stand in a more menial, working relationship to people; if dogs are as kinsmen, horses are as servants and nonkin. Hence the consumption of horses is at least conceivable, if not general, whereas the notion of eating dogs understandably evokes some of the revulsion of the incest tabu. On the other hand, the edible animals such as pigs and cattle generally have the status of objects to human subjects . . . neither the direct complement nor the working instrument of human activities. (Sahlins, 1976: 174–5)

But pigs are closer to humans than cattle in the sense that they are scavengers of human food, and so are less prestigious to eat than cattle.

The division between the inner and outer parts of animals is mapped onto an assimilation to and distinction from parts of the human body. That is, speaking of roast, steak or chops – the outer parts – does not evoke notions of the human body, but heart, tongue, liver or kidney – the inner parts – does. It follows, then, that the innards of animals are symbolically closer to humans and therefore less edible – in the US, *considerably* less edible – than the outer parts. This explains an apparent paradox: why is steak in most countries considerably more expensive than the innards of animals, despite the fact that there is far more of it on an animal than there are various inner meats? Cattle have only one tongue, after all – should this not therefore be more expensive than steak? Sahlins writes that:

> It is . . . symbolic logic which organizes demand. The social value of steak or roast, as compared with tripe or tongue, is what underlies the difference in economic value . . . the symbolic scheme of edibility joins with that organizing the relations of production to precipitate, through income distribution and demand, an entire totemic order, uniting in a parallel series of differences the status of persons and what they eat. The poorer people buy the cheaper cuts, cheaper because they are socially inferior meats. (Sahlins, 1976: 176)

The symbolic logic of food, then, succeeds in standing apparent economic logic on its head.

The drink system in an Austrian village – a structuralist approach

Structuralist approaches tend to treat the social world as a world of signs and symbols, and Mary Anna Thornton (1987) applies structuralism to the analysis of the role of drinks in the marking of the social structure of an Austrian village. The polar opposites to be found in the region consisted of the class of subsistence farmers and the class of professionals, with an intermediary group of clerical and industrial workers. The farming group was characterized by the direct exchange of goods and services among themselves and high levels of interdependence and intimacy. The professional class did not require the same level of mutual economic co-operation and so, unsurprisingly, were more individualized and formal with each other than the farmers. The clerical and industrial workers were somewhere in between. These social divisions were reflected quite clearly in the drink system that Thornton found. The binary opposition governing the structure is that between sekt, which is the equivalent of champagne in German-speaking countries, and schnapps. All other alcoholic drinks belong more or less to one or the other of these two classes: beer and hot rum drinks belong more to the sekt class (although beer is more sektish than hot rum); cold wine beverages and hot wine drinks belong more to the schnapps class (the cold more than the hot). There can be some interchangeability between the beer and the cold wine beverages and a slightly greater amount between the hot rum drinks and the hot wine drinks. But sekt and schnapps cannot be interchanged with one another, and both indicate forms of sociality – although very different forms. Schnapps, maintains Thornton,

> is cued by a desire to promote co-operation between individuals, whereas the use of the sekt class of drinks marks culturally recognized holidays . . . Beverages belonging to the schnapps class of drinks are shared within limited networks of social co-ordination, whereas those belonging to the sekt class are exchanged in circumstances that do not imply personal commitment. (Thornton, 1987: 104–5)

It is easy to see here the same sorts of divisions as those between the farming and professional classes. Schnapps is a drink to mark intimacy; sekt is a drink to mark formal relations. Schnapps is not tied to a particular calendar but can be drunk any time intimacy needs to be marked, while sekt does follow a cultural calendar (such as national, town or personal holidays, New Year, and the like), and is thus separated from the personal and attached to occasions shared by a whole society rather than intimate groups. Thornton (1987: 108) summarizes: 'those drinks which fall into the sekt class are marketed commercially and served according to widely acknowledged conventions of taste or of season, while the class of schnapps drinks are more often prepared and served with care at home or in the community'. Non-alcoholic beverages tend not to be used to mark social occasions in the same way, and are interpreted as being mainly for quenching thirst: there is a big difference between drinking because you are thirsty (a personal thing that does not involve anybody else, at least in principle) and drinking to indicate the state of your social relations with others. The members of the farming class, who are in close and intimate dependent relations with each other, relate frequently through schnapps, while the professionals can continue to treat colleagues as strangers and not have their work suffer, and so there is no call for schnappsish relations.

Fasting and anorexia nervosa

To end this chapter, a few words on fasting. This has become familiar to us through anorexia nervosa, but the practice of starving oneself has occurred throughout European history, particularly amongst women. But why starve oneself, and why are women the main practitioners? One reason already touched upon lightly is to be found in Paul Bocuse's (1988 [1976]) comment about it being a desirable thing to leave the table feeling slightly hungry: there is a link between fasting and social prestige. The fasting person manages to overcome the low and vulgar demands of the body via a discipline exercised through restriction of food intake, and thus rises above the merely physical to attain a sort of grace that is spiritual and social at the same time. We can see versions of this in many religious practices today, such as fasting at Lent and Ramadan. When I was growing up in Catholic Ireland, a very common question just before Ash Wednesday was, 'What are you giving up for Lent?' The idea was that one would renounce a luxury during this period, so that one could attain a holier state through discipline exercised over the base desires of the body. So the concepts of control and social status may have a role to play here.

Gordon Tait (1993) considers the case of medieval fasting women. Why did they fast? A principal reason seemed to be the attaining of piety. If one asks the question, 'What does one have to do to become a saint?' one discovers that the answer differs depending upon whether one is talking about men or women. In the medieval context, writes Tait,

> The typical habitus of a male saint might include deeds such as brave missionary work, championing public morality and passionate oratory. Conversely ... there exists an alternative predominantly female model for holy conduct which features penitential asceticism, charity and mystical communication with God. With

women saints, their religious calling developed more steadily than men's, their piety was more 'body centred' than men's, and the notion of 'service and suffering' was emphasized more than men's – as exemplified in practices such as fasting. (Tait, 1993: 198)

It was also possible to attain piety by giving up one's property – but as women had little control over property during this period anyway, it was not really an option open to them. But there was an alternative: 'fasting practices became a readily available mechanism by which teenage girls could demonstrate their piety' (Tait, 1993: 198). Note this concept of a 'readily available mechanism' – here it may be used to attain holiness, but it is easy to see that it could be used to attain other goals. The only resource left to one in some situations is one's own body, and fasting is always an option that can be used in the absence of other alternatives. For Tait (1993: 198–9), the body-centredness of women in medieval times was accentuated by the oppositions that then dominated Christian thought: the male was associated with the spirit, strength, the rational and the soul, while the female was associated with the flesh, weakness, the irrational and the body. So the weak fleshly nature of women could be overcome by a disciplined approach to the body: fasting goes beyond the flesh and the body to reach the spirit and the soul, the discipline replacing irrational by rational action clearly directed towards a goal and thereby demonstrating strength rather than weakness. Holy qualities were male qualities, and women could attain such manly holiness through fasting (see Table 8.2). As Tait (1993: 199) puts it, 'the female body itself became the primary site for extravagant exhibitions of piety to be written'.

There appears to be a close link between the ascetic practices sketched above and certain functions of anorexia today. Bryan Turner summarizes some of the findings of Hilda Bruch's work:

the anorexic . . . typically regards food, eating and the body as morally or indeed spiritually degraded. Starvation and exercise represent, unconsciously or

Table 8.2   *Medieval holy women fasted because their available path to sainthood lay through body discipline*

Male	Female
Actions	*Actions*
• brave missionary work	• penitential asceticism
• championing public morality	• charity
• passionate oration	• mystical communication with God
• could renounce property	• property unavailable to renounce but body was available
Qualities already holy	*Qualities to be transcended*
• spirit	• flesh
• soul	• body
• strength	• weakness
• rationality	• irrationality

Source: based on Tait, 1993

consciously, a negation of that corruption. The anorexic avoids the shameful world of eating, while simultaneously achieving personal power and a sense of moral superiority through the emaciated body. Their attempt at disembodiment through negation becomes the symbol of their moral empowerment. (Turner, 1992: 221)

Of course the hyper-slim body also accords rather nicely with images of the contemporary female body that one finds in fashion photos and advertising. So medieval fasting women and contemporary anorexics may share the same aim of attaining moral superiority through their peculiarly disciplined approach to food and the body.

But holiness and moral superiority are not the only things that may be attained by fasting practices, for some rather more earthly goals may be attained as well. In both medieval and contemporary cases, there is evidence that the transformations wrought on the body were useful in avoiding marriage: menstruation may stop, and a very thin body will look more like that of a girl than a woman. This can be a useful form of control in situations where one feels that one has no other leverage, whether these be an arranged marriage in which one just does not want to be enmeshed or sexual relations generally. In Turner's (1992: 221) words, 'Anorexic behaviour is a personal response to the confusions and contradictions of female maturation which may be expressed in a series of dichotomies – personal autonomy/compliance, childhood security/mature independence, sexuality/neutrality.'

There is more to anorexia than can be sketched here, but it might be instructive to see the notion of control in a related context. It was suggested above that the body can be the only thing that allows one to have some power in a given situation. The same principle seems to be at work in the case of those classes of men who starve themselves – I refer, of course, to political prisoners and to those who are protesting at various other aspects of the prisoner's life (bad treatment, claiming to be innocent, or whatever). The body becomes a weapon that can be used to attain certain ends, unless the authorities resort to forced feeding. The weapon seemed to fail in the early 1980s, where over a dozen members of the Irish Republican Army starved themselves to death in prison in Northern Ireland. But normally one might expect it to obtain some sort of result in the desired direction.

Before reading this chapter, the reader may have considered food a matter of personal taste. Taste, however, appears to be another element in the articulation of social life: *à chaque société ses goûts*.

9
Tourism

Unlike the pilgrimages of medieval Europe or the aristocratic Grand Tour of the seventeenth and eighteenth centuries, tourism today is a mass activity. Tourists, as Henry James once remarked, are 'vulgar, vulgar, vulgar' (Urry, 1990: v): practically anyone can be a tourist, much to the distaste of an elite which considered that it and it alone was sufficiently educated to appreciate the joys of travel. 'I am a traveller, you are a tourist, he is a tripper' (Keith Waterhouse, quoted by Urry, 1990: v) neatly characterizes the elite view of upper-, middle- and lower-class excursionary practices.

It has been argued, however, that rigid divisions between 'high' and 'low' culture have been eaten away in contemporary societies and that more and more objects and events have become subject to the 'tourist gaze' (Urry, 1990). People of all classes, it seems, can be tourists anywhere outside home or work – town after town has become 'touristified' even for its natives. We tour ever further afield to find ever newer objects to capture with our cameras. A rich person has accumulated a lot of capital, a rich tourist has accumulated a lot of photographs. John Urry, indeed, maintains that photography was central to the development of the tourist gaze, and it is probably hardly an exaggeration to say that to tour without returning with photographs is scarcely to tour at all. Photos demand that there be things and people to photograph, and so a whole industry has grown up producing touristy things and touristy people destined to be sucked up through a lens and spread out two-dimensionally across the pages of a photo album. Almost anything can be produced for the delectation of the tourist gaze just as anything can be produced for the gaze of the consumer of art, from Warholian walls of Brillo boxes to canned *merde d'artiste* destined never to meet a tin opener.

The non-ironic tourist looks for what Dean MacCannell calls 'authenticity'; the ironic tourist – or 'post-tourist', or possibly 'postmodern tourist' – looks rather for deliberately staged inauthenticity, revelling in the play of tourist signs. MacCannell (1973, 1976) was one of the first to write about the sociology of tourism, and we consider his use of Goffman's distinctions between front and back regions in his account of tourist authenticities. Finally, we look at the rise of the 'untourist'.

Escaping through time and space: tourist literature

Let us take a look at a few tourist brochures from the New England region of Australia in order to see if we can discover anything of sociological interest. For the moment, I propose that we explore one of the simplest and most economical ways a town has of promoting itself: the headline, often a slogan, that one finds in the various promotional pieces that are available. So what do we find if we look at the 1994 edition of *The Fossicker's Way Tourist Guide* (Sweetnam, 1994), which covers the fossicking (panning for gems, gold and minerals) areas of New England and the North West Slopes of New South Wales? The results are presented in Table 9.1.

There appear to be only a small number of themes at work here: services and facilities of various types (sometimes unspecified), history, nature and culture. 'Services and facilities' refers to consumption practices generally, but 'history' is a little more specific. The use of history seems to be a convenient way of turning an otherwise uninteresting town into an object fit for the gaze of tourists and indeed, as John Urry (1990: 104–6) has suggested, history has very frequently been drawn upon in many places, not just the towns mentioned here, as a way of creating a town-for-tourists. One comes to Barraba, Uralla, Warialda or Tingha to escape not so much space as time: to tour here is to travel in time.

We are well used to the idea of tourism as travel in space, but here is a dimension the importance of which has perhaps been underrated. All towns can pretend to some sort of history, so on this level all towns may be transformed into tourist attractions. There is no need for striking sites or magnificent views: the most filthy, boring, ugly and unhealthy industrial town now also has a reason to pull in the tourists, promising an escape from present woes and troubles through the elegantly simple device of time-travel. Even a piece of waste ground can become an attraction, if a story can be attached to it. Clearly, this strategy can be used by any town at all and, hey presto, we get a tourist spot. All are citizens of Heritage Country.

The attractions of nature have more to do with travel in space and are an important legacy of the romantic view of the world: come here to see what you cannot see elsewhere, escape the artificial world of culture in which you live for the real world of nature. Towns that can provide both nature and history, of course, will be more attractive for tourists than those that can provide only one or the other: one can escape from today's everyday life in the two dimensions of time and space and, presumably, find a higher and more authentic degree of reality through such otherness, the first otherness sanctified by Father Time and the second by Mother Nature. The notion of escape, indeed, seems central to tourism: as Urry writes, 'Minimally there must be certain aspects of the place visited which distinguish it from what is conventionally encountered in everyday life. Tourism results from a basic binary division between the ordinary/everyday and the extraordinary' (1990: 11). And we can escape the ordinary and the everyday through both time and space.

History may be interpreted as lying on the side of culture, but of a culture that is elsewhere than our own and therefore just as exotic as any wonder of nature: as H. E. Bates put it, the past is another country. Aspects of culture not necessarily associated with temporal distance also appear in

Table 9.1 *Promoting place*

Services and facilities	History	Nature	Culture
Tamworth offers top facilities in every arena	Character and charm of yesteryear now lives on in streets of Barraba	Mining and fishing the big attractions [Bingara]	Mining and fishing the big attractions [Bingara]
Fine services and facilities at Manilla	Museums tell the story of Uralla's yesteryear	Warm greetings, but cold climate [Guyra]	Warm greetings but cold climate [Guyra]
Tourists well catered for in Inverell	Thriving town [Warialda] in the mid 1880s	Natural and man made attractions for visitors to see [Glen Innes]	Natural and man made attractions for visitors to see [Glen Innes]
Little town [Walcha] has plenty to offer its many guests	Nundle – a picture of nature and history	Nundle – a picture of nature and history	Armidale bursting with culture
Copeton – perfect for watersports	Tingha boasts a colourful history	Natural attractions at Tenterfield Falls and caves a must for visitors [Ashford]	

Source: Sweetnam, 1994

Table 9.1. How do these relate to nature? Bingara ('Mining and fishing the big attractions') seems to bring them together cleverly: minerals and fish are natural phenomena, but mining and fishing show how humans turn them into their own meaningful cultural activities – these are ways of being with nature but at the same time being in control of it (or at least attempting to control it), rather than giving oneself up to nature in awed amazement. Guyra suggests a balance between culture and nature: the cold climate may sound off-putting (although exotic to many Australians), but the warm greetings make up for it. Harsh nature is made liveable through human cultural practices: nature remains cold but people are warm. There is no attempt to control nature here, but neither is it presented as overwhelming humans. Glen Innes claims to have the natural and the cultural, but does not try to relate them in any way: they are equally something for tourists. Tenterfield and Ashford promise escape through nature only, while the university town of Armidale plumps for culture only, figuring perhaps that after all that fossicking around one will need to escape from nature. If to be a tourist is to escape from the ordinary everyday, then nature and history seem to be fundamental to the creation of a place for tourists. One can of course escape into another culture, although this is not prominent in the above list. In other pamphlets, though, one can find things like 'Glen Innes – Land of the Beardies', which certainly seems to promise an exotically different culture.

Let us now see how Armidale and its University of New England are promoted in a touristic manner. If we look at a recent (undated) *Visitors' Guide* to the town, we discover three different slogans: the mayor writes that 'Armidale is a City of Culture and Learning', the chair of the Armidale City Tourism Committee notes that 'Armidale has been called "A City for all Seasons" ', while the unattributed slogan on the cover is 'Armidale – City of Heritage and Beauty'. Nature, history and culture are all present here. In case we do not see how natural the City for all Seasons is, there is a photograph showing the word 'Armidale' above stylized representations of a blazing sun, an autumn leaf, a snowflake and a flower. This has the effect of creating Armidale as more natural than many places in Australia: it suggests that there are four very definitely distinguishable seasons there, and this is how nature is 'supposed to be' for people who have inherited ways of thinking about the world from north-west Europe. Leave your evergreen eucalypts and your mild winters and come where the leaves fall and there is snow on the ground. This is a real climate – rather, the slogan and photo connote the Armidale climate as the most authentically real available for those who would experience what their Anglo-Celtic ancestors did. This, oddly, is climate as cultural heritage – another escape into a past reality and countries far away.

The promotion of the historical side of the town can be seen in the tourist pamphlet *Armidale Heritage Drive*. This lists 33 places to visit, all of them accompanied by little stories and either specific dates or phrases such as 'at the turn of the century' (which occurs three times) or 'the era before mass car ownership'. Clearly, Armidale has no trouble offering history as an escape to tourists mired in the present day.

But what of the university? Could this be a tourist site? Does it too offer an escape from ordinariness? The answer is yes: it accomplishes this by placing itself in opposition to life in the big city, and we can see this if we examine a 22-page promotional brochure dating from the early 1990s. Table 9.2 is based on both the uncredited copy and from students' comments that are quoted (and pictured) in the booklet.

What does the big city look like here? It is a rat race, it is rushed, it is polluted, it is expensive, it is unfriendly, people do not accept you as you are, it is a concrete jungle, it is an impersonal degree factory. And what does Armidale look like? Very much the reverse image of the big city. Note the frequent stress on themes such as friendliness and forming part of a community: in a binary division that could come straight from the classical sociology of Ferdinand Tönnies (1964 [1887]), Armidale is constructed as the warm, cosy and friendly *Gemeinschaft* community as against the alienated, unfriendly and impersonal *Gesellschaft* of the big cities. So here is another escape: from the *Gesellschaft* relations most Australians live every day in the big cities to the *Gemeinschaft* of the small pre-industrial community where you find friendship, belonging and the person you really are. The

Table 9.2   *Promoting 'Gemeinschaft': the case of a rural university*

Advantages of city but big country town – Sydney a rat race
Better environment [than cities]
Breath of fresh air [as against the] rushed pace, pollution, cost of living in metropolitan area
Friendly country atmosphere compared with big cities
More relaxed and friendly than metropolitan centre
People more friendly and down-to-earth, accept you for what you are – more than Sydney
Trees, greenness, country – change from living in city
Walk around trees and grass [Armidale] – wander around concrete jungles [big city]
Close-knit community of scholars [Armidale] – impersonal degree factory [big city]
Easy to become part of community
Sense of community, big family, friends close
Sense of belonging
Informality and acceptance
Easy-going lifestyle
Feel very invited and safe
Friendly environment
Friendly atmosphere – [more than] other institutions
Friendly
Very friendly
People are friendly
Staff, people in college are very friendly
Friends who have shared 'the Armidale experience'
Can talk to anyone
More personalized
Personal contact
Personal 'education'
Unpolluted environment

university is saying, 'Come here for an extended holiday from the big bad city', and in this sense is operating as any tourist spot does. It also promises the *Gemeinschaft* ideal of authentic human relations, and it is precisely authenticity that, in the view of Dean MacCannell, tourists go looking for. We now turn to his 1973 article on staged authenticity, which is one of the earliest contributions to the sociology of tourism.

Staged authenticity

MacCannell implicitly draws upon the *Gemeinschaft/Gesellschaft* distinctions we have just been discussing by maintaining that individuals in societies dominated by bureaucracies and other complex organizations feel that their lives are shallow and their experiences inauthentic. It is as if all reality has been absorbed into the bureaucracy and the large corporation, leaving the individual left with nothing worthwhile, nothing real. But if a sense of reality has been stolen from people, they will nevertheless go looking for it somewhere and this, for MacCannell, is where tourism comes in. Tourism is a search for this reality that has been stolen, it is the search for a full deep life rather than a shallow one, it is the search for authentic experiences rather than the inauthenticity on offer in large, complex societies of the *Gesellschaft* type. So how does this work in the tourist setting (if, indeed, it does work)? MacCannell draws upon a famous distinction made by Goffman (1972 [1959]) in order to arrive at his account: the distinction between the front and back regions of any public performance – or, to be more theatrical about it, the front stage and the back stage. This distinction can be relevant to practically all social encounters: if you dine at a restaurant you are front stage, while the kitchen is back; we shop in the front regions of supermarkets, but all the activities that produce the front area are hidden from us. Putting this more formally in Goffman's own words:

> Given a particular performance as the point of reference, we have distinguished three crucial roles on the basis of function: those who perform; those performed to; and outsiders who neither perform in the show nor observe it . . . [T]he three crucial roles mentioned could be described on the basis of the regions to which the role-player has access: performers appear in the front and back regions; the audience appears only in the front region; and the outsiders are excluded from both regions. (Goffman, 1972 [1959]: 144)

What most characterizes the back region is the fact that it is used to hide all sorts of 'props and activities that might discredit the performance out front' (MacCannell, 1973: 590–1). If you actually knew what was going on in the restaurant kitchen, you might quickly lose your appetite.

Now this distinction between front stage and back stage has the effect of convincing people that something is being hidden from them, and because it is being hidden there is a tendency to consider the back stage as where 'real reality' can be found, as opposed to the mere show of the front stage. This is where the bodies are buried, if you will excuse the expression, this is where the casserole fell on the floor and was scooped back into the pot, to emerge triumphantly steaming on the plate of the unsuspecting guest. Putting this in more classical philosophical terms, the front stage is seen as appearance and the back stage as reality. It is only in the backstage regions that one can ever see people as they 'really are', as opposed to how they appear to be for public purposes. So if we are searching for real experiences, we will want to gain access to the back stage. If we are allowed to do this, we will have moved to a more intimate plane and will have been let in on the secrets behind the public appearance. This sharing of the back region is, for MacCannell, part of 'Being "one of them", or at one with them"' (1973: 592).

Now tourists, as part of their quest for authentic, real experiences, are out searching for back regions to share too. MacCannell writes that 'sightseers are motivated by a desire to see life as it is really lived, even to get in with the natives, and, at the same time, they are deprecated for always failing to achieve these goals' (1973: 592). The aim is to live life as the natives live it, not as tourists confined to the front stage would experience things. It might be clearer if these distinctions were rephrased in terms of the opposition between 'traveller' and 'tourist'. The traveller is supposed to be the one who mixes in with the natives, who lives with them and gains access to their back regions. By contrast, the tourist, at least viewed from the point of view of those who claim to be travellers in the above sense, remains at the frontstage level, staring at the natives from a coach and staying at upmarket hotels just like those back home. For MacCannell, though, tourists in fact aim to be travellers: they too want to get to the back stage, even if they usually fail. He is arguing here against the claims of Daniel Boorstin (1961), who maintains that the only things tourists are interested in are 'pseudo-events'. Boorstin writes that

> [tourist] 'attractions' offer an elaborately contrived indirect experience, an arti-
> ficial product to be consumed in the very places where the real thing is as free as
> air. They are ways for the traveler to remain out of contact with foreign peoples
> in the very act of 'sight-seeing' them. They keep the natives in quarantine while
> the tourist in air-conditioned comfort views them through a picture window. They
> are the cultural mirages now found at tourist oases everywhere. (Boorstin, 1961:
> 99, quoted by MacCannell, 1973: 599)

This is the eternal complaint of the traveller about the tourist, but for Mac-Cannell it is completely unfair because it fails to see that tourists too are on the quest for authentic experiences. He seems not to see the possibility that some might quite enjoy the frontstage-only aspects of the tour, having no interest at all in the authenticity of backstage regions. Neither Boorstin nor MacCannell entertains the idea that tourists may take quite an ironic stance towards what they are presented, and exult in the surface nature of it all. We return to this point below in the discussion of Urry's (1990) work.

But let us continue with his idea that the tourist searches out authentic experiences, and ask: do tourist places cater to this desire? The answer seems to be yes – but rather than actually letting the tourists gain access to true back stages, they stage the back stage. An illusion is fostered that tourists are indeed gaining access to a back stage, but the back stage they are allowed to see is really another front stage posing as a back stage. It is not a real back stage, but a simulated one. After all, access by the audience to the 'real' back stage could expose things best left hidden if the performance is not to be questioned. Special tours are put on so that people are brought in to see the inner workings of factories, banks, breweries, newspapers – even nuclear power stations producing military grade plutonium, as I recall from an advertising campaign for the Sellafield plant that appeared on British television. But the visitors have no real way of knowing if they have seen the real back stage or one assembled specifically for the tourist. At least they have the impression that they have gained access to that which is normally hidden from the public, and so have had an authentic tourist experience.

MacCannell (1973: 598) proposes a six-point model of stages in tourist settings: Stage 1 is Goffman's front region, which of course is what tourists try to get beyond, Stage 2 is 'a touristic front region that has been decorated to appear, in some of its particulars, like a back region: a seafood restaurant with a fish net hanging on the wall ... it is cosmetically decorated with reminders of back region activities: mementoes, not taken seriously, called "atmosphere" '. So this is really still a front region, with little hints of happenings beyond it. Stage 3 is 'a front region that is totally organized to look like a back region', but this often runs the risk of being seen through. A good example of this is given by Philip Pearce, who quotes the experience of an academic visiting South America:

> In Leticia, Colombia, I went on an Amazon River Tour. This tour consisting of visiting supposed authentic Indian villages was a revolting experience for me. Upon our arrival at each village, the guide would ring a bell to signal the Indians that they should disrobe and put on beads and scanty grass skirts as the tourists were coming. It appeared to me that the way of life, culture, and religion has been destroyed for these Indians. During our study the Indians listlessly attempted to sell their pathetic handcrafts which were what they thought the tourists wanted, rather than be true to their original culture. At the end of the tour, the guide left them beer and cigarettes so that they could wait in a state of stupor for the next group of tourists. (Pearce, 1982: 137)

Here we can see an example of the creation of a completely false back region, but one that did not work because the tourist saw through it and felt cheated because of it. The Indians were staging the back region the tourists expected to find, not any back region of their own. The tourist wanted to see the ordinary everydayness of an original culture where presumably the presence of the tourist would have no effect and nothing would be hidden backstage, but this rather underestimates the effect of the sightseeing tourist: those who would be looked upon can look back and start behaving specifically for tourists.

Stage 4 is 'a back region that is open to outsiders' (MacCannell, 1973: 598). Presumably this would be only one part of the 'real' back region: just enough of reality to give the tourists their authenticity fix without exposing the real back stage in a threatening way. Stage 5 is 'a back region that may be cleaned up or altered a bit because tourists are permitted an occasional glimpse in' (1973: 598). Here, the very presence of tourists makes everyone put on an acceptable front, so this area takes on the characteristics of a front region again. When the tourists leave, no doubt, people go back to placing their legs on their desks in poses unknown to polite society or bicker with their colleagues in the normal endearing manner. Stage 6 is 'Goffman's back region; the kind of social space that motivates touristic consciousness' (1973: 598). Tourists feel particularly good if they reach this stage, as in the following account from a 30-year-old Canadian management consultant quoted by Pearce:

> I was taken by my wife's uncle to a local club [Middlesbrough, England]. After only a few introductory remarks, the locals just dove in telling me about England, rugby, football, gambling, etc. – bantering, discussing and involving me, Canada and others. A great way to make a tourist a friend and to make him want to come back again. I felt wanted, an equal, not alone or an oddity (Pearce, 1982: 127).

If the uncle was a local, as is implied here, the Canadian had an unusual ticket into these regions and would have been treated differently to those with no local connections. He had a backstage pass most tourists never get.

There is perhaps another stage to which MacCannell does not refer, and that consists of regions into which tourists wander as unwanted intruders in search of illegitimate authenticity. The people who live there do not take kindly to being gazed at by tourists and deny their status as legitimate audience of any region, front or back. There was a good example of this in a report I saw on French television in the summer of 1994. There is a small tourist train that goes through various districts of one of the southern French cities. Part of the journey involves going through an ordinary working-class area so that the tourists can look at ordinary working-class people going about their ordinary everyday lives. The report showed what happened when these people got fed up with being stared at by, presumably, middle-class tourists: they went on a demonstration carrying placards with slogans like 'We are not animals in a zoo' and proceeded to pelt the visiting train-bound tourists with bags of flour. The shocked tourists finally had an authentic experience, but perhaps not the one they went in search of.

There is resistance, then, to being turned into an object for tourists: not everyone wants to play, and tourists can be an illegitimate audience. While one is a sightseeing tourist, one tends to assume that one has the right to look at anything with impunity, that everything is performed for one's visiting eyes, and it takes an exceptional event like the above to make one realize that one has been participating in the imperialism of the tourist gaze. For MacCannell, at any rate, 'The empirical action in tourist settings is mainly confined to movement between areas decorated to look like back regions, and back regions into which tourists are allowed to peek' (1973: 598). In sum, then, the tourist setting is designed in such a way that tourists do indeed get what they are searching for, but not in such a way as to threaten the real backstage regions – unless, of course, the setting has not been fully created as something for tourists.

If tourism is about experiencing the authentic, how is this actually accomplished in practice? How can tourists tell that they are really having an authentic tourist experience? This is the question explored by MacCannell in his 1976 book *The Tourist*. He draws on the idea that what passes for reality in the modern world is already discursively constructed. He would not quite put it that way, so I have translated his idea into an idiom that makes sense to me. By 'already discursively constructed' I mean that we all have some sort of idea of what to expect and how to behave when we come across certain things. If this were not so, the complex world of modern societies would risk slipping into meaninglessness. In the case of tourism this means that, even if we have never seen them in the flesh, as it were, we all have some notion of what the Eiffel Tower, Sydney Opera House, the Empire State Building, Tower Bridge, the Taj Mahal, the ruins of Angkor Wat, or whatever, is supposed to mean in modern culture. The job of the tourist, then, is to go out and actually see these things that are so important and thereby take their very own place in that culture. By being a tourist and seeing these sights, you are truly part of society as it is understood today – you make these sights your own, and in that way become a full member of the social world where these sights are granted great cultural importance.

One can see the same thing in the religious pilgrimage, which was, of course, the first example of large-scale tourism: here, your job is to seek out for yourself the sacred sites that are so important to your religion. It is only if you do this that you will be fully a part of it, for you will have made them part of your being. You say: 'so *that's* it', and bring the memory home in your mind, on a photograph, postcard, or whatever. So you are not a tourist simply for yourself: as MacCannell notes, 'An authentic touristic experience involves not merely connecting a marker to a sight [by, for example, saying 'so *that's* it' or 'it's more magnificent than I thought'], but a participation in a collective ritual, in connecting one's own marker to a sight already marked by others' (MacCannell, 1976: 137). This is what guidebooks allow us to do: they show us what the sacred secular sights are, and invite us to see for ourselves, to participate in the collective ritual. Note that one does not have to be in a group to participate in the collective. The collective here is society in general as it recognizes certain sights as especially meaningful, not a particular tour group, and one can perfectly well accomplish tourism in this sense while travelling alone. If one takes the Armidale Heritage Drive, for example, one is actively claiming to assimilate in some degree the past history and personalities of the town – a collective act, even if carried out individually.

But just getting to the sight is not really enough – having made the journey, there must be something about the sight that rewards us with a special shiver of authenticity: MacCannell calls these 'truth markers'. He gives the example of a guide at Independence Hall in Philadelphia: 'It is commonly believed that the Liberty Bell cracked because it was rung too hard celebrating American Independence. Actually [this is the truth marker] the Bell was not manufactured properly at the factory where it was made in England' (MacCannell, 1976: 138). But what is the function of truth markers? MacCannell again: 'Truth markers function to cement the bond of tourist and attraction by elevating the information possessed by the tourist to privileged status' (1976: 137–8). The tourist does not just see the sight, but gets some special insight into it as a reward for having made the journey. It hardly matters if the truth marker is true in any historical or scientific sense, of course, for it merely functions as something that proposes privileged insights. Thus, MacCannell maintains, tourist and sight are bonded together in a special way denied to those who have not been there.

This essential lack of any truth that would not be merely a discursive effect suggests something else about tourism: here it is intrinsically post-modern in the sense that the marker of truth does not have to be true in any real sense – we are in the realm of playful signs.

The tourist gaze

MacCannell's account of tourism placed great store on the notion of auth-enticity as central to the tourist experience. John Urry, however, maintains that it is not really authenticity that is at stake. Instead, he suggests that 'one key feature would seem to be that there is a difference between one's normal place of residence/work and the object of the tourist gaze' (1990: 11), a point we already touched upon in the notion of tourism as an escape. The tourist is looking for the contrast with everyday experiences, and is perhaps not so naïve as to believe that an experience of authenticity is poss-ible. Urry's tourists are a bit more sophisticated than MacCannell's, perhaps, driven to look for signs of tourism rather than anything else: these would be the 'post-tourists', who know that the whole thing is a game of simulations anyway. What do tourists look at? 'The tourist gaze is directed to features of landscape and townscape which separate them off from every-day experience. Such aspects are viewed because they are taken to be in some sense out of the ordinary' (Urry, 1990: 3). This gaze is not something given in nature, but is constructed. Urry sees this construction as taking place through signs, and he sees tourism as the collection of signs:

> When tourists see two people kissing in Paris what they capture in the gaze is 'timeless romantic Paris'. As Culler [1981: 127] argues: 'the tourist is interested in everything as a sign of itself . . . All over the world the unsung armies of semioti-cians, the tourists, are fanning out in search of the signs of Frenchness, typical Italian behaviour, exemplary Oriental scenes, typical American thruways, tra-ditional English pubs'. (Urry, 1990: 3)

Tourists in this perspective are not searching for the real but for signs of the real, which they recognize and collect in their photo albums or on their videotapes. The tourist professionals recognize this, of course, and try to organize matters so that the tourists will find the right signs.

Urry lists a number of ways in which the 'division between the ordinary and the extraordinary' which is so important to tourism 'can be established and sustained' (1990: 12), only some of which will be mentioned here. Firstly there is the unique object, the sacred cultural site/sight: there is only one in the world and you have seen it. It is easy to see how one might experience authenticity here, for one is faced with the one and only, the original. Secondly, one can look for particular signs of typicality, as mentioned above: 'the typical English village ... the typical German beer-garden', and so forth. Here one looks for the pre-established signs of tourism. Perhaps we could call this 'typicality-spotting'. It already pushes us away from a real to be experienced authentically and towards signs to be read. Thirdly, we can see 'unfamiliar aspects of what had previously been thought of as familiar' (Urry, 1990: 12) such as, for example, museum exhibitions of the lives of ordinary people. Ordinary life is made extraordinary by being subjected to all the complex discourses that museums weave about objects. Fourthly, there is the reverse: 'ordinary aspects of social life being undertaken by people in unusual contexts. Some tourism in China has been of this sort. Visitors have found it particularly interesting to gaze upon the carrying out of domestic tasks in a "communist" country' (Urry, 1990: 12).

The tourist gaze has not always been with us in its present form. Urry suggests that it is part of a new form of visual perception that grew up in the great nineteenth-century cities, and he takes Paris as an instance of this. The city was transformed from a medieval chaos of small, narrow streets to a much more open city of wide boulevards and great avenues by the work of Baron Haussmann. Not only were these fairly handy for troop movements in the days when popular uprisings were a distinct possibility, but they also completely transformed what could be seen and how it could be seen. In the narrow streets one could see little other than what was near at hand, but the new organization of urban space created sights that could not be seen in the old Paris:

> Haussmann's plan entailed the building of markets, bridges, parks, the Opera and other cultural palaces, with many located at the end of the various boulevards. Such boulevards came to structure the gaze, both of Parisians and later of visitors. For the first time in a major city people could see well into the distance and indeed see where they were going and where they had come from. Great sweeping vistas were designed so that each walk led to a dramatic climax. (Urry, 1990: 136–7)

In this way the city became a site of things to be seen in a way that simply did not exist before. But the sights of the city were not just the buildings: the great boulevards were also the places where large numbers of people circulated, and the people too became sights of the city. If one could contemplate marvels of architecture simply by looking up and down the boulevards, one could contemplate the marvels of people by staring at the passing throng from the terrace of the café, or circulate slowly among them oneself: everybody gazed at everyone else as they strolled about the great metropolis which had become a feast for the eyes. Indeed, there was a special name for the male street stroller: he was the *flâneur*, a 'modern hero, able to travel, to arrive, to gaze, to move on, to be anonymous, to be in a liminal zone' (Urry, 1990: 138). The public space for women, as we saw in Chapter 4, was the department store rather than the street and so the *flâneur* was male.

The *flâneur* can be seen as the forerunner of the modern tourist and in particular, as Urry remarks, 'of *the* activity which has in a way become emblematic of the tourist: the democratised taking of photographs – of being seen and recorded and seeing others and recording them' (Urry, 1990: 138). Susan Sontag (1979: 55) is quite explicit about the link between the *flâneur* and the photographer: photography 'first comes into its own as an extension of the eye of the middle-class *flâneur* . . . The photographer is an armed version of the solitary walker reconnoitring, stalking, cruising the urban inferno, the voyeuristic stroller who discovers the city as a landscape of voluptuous extremes' (quoted by Urry: ibid.). So if the changes in cityscapes produce sights to be seen and strollers to see them, the camera makes it possible to capture these sights for one's own private collection. One now sees through the eye of one's camera, and the figure of the tourist, camera slung around the neck or hanging off the wrist, becomes a common sight. Travel comes to be punctuated by photo-stops and the tourist is driven by the search for things to capture with the camera, which leads Urry to remark that 'travel is a strategy for the accumulation of photographs' (Urry, 1990: 139). Travel is particularly a search for sites/sights that have been pre-constructed as notable by the travel books and television travel series, and it is primarily these that one goes searching for in order to return with photographic evidence of the existence of that of which one had already seen a photograph before going away. But the *flâneur* still lives too, without a camera: when we stroll about the shopping malls that seem to have grown up everywhere in large cities we also gaze at sights, objects and people. The mall allows us to act as tourists even in our own home towns, consuming images of space or actual commodities depending upon our finances.

Wine-soaked maps versus garish promotions: the 'untourist'

The environmental movement in Australia seems to have given a new lease of life to the old tourist/traveller dichotomy, reformulating it as a tourist/untourist opposition through the appearance of the UnTourist Network in the 1990s. Synonyms for 'untourist' include 'eco tourists, green tourists, cultural tourists, alternative tourists, educational tourists' (Huie, 1994: 2). In this section, we analyse Jaqueline Huie's 'An Introduction to Untourism' (1994). Huie is a founding director of the UnTourist Co. Pty. Ltd.

Untourists are hardly post-tourists, for their main categories are the traditional ones of romantic reactions to industrial societies dressed in slightly updated vocabulary:

we sought out all the most discerning, untouristy people we knew – the insiders, the writers, the foodies, the fishermen, the sailors, the farmers, the culture buffs, the historians and the savvy locals – they helped to hunt out the best of everything the destination could offer in things to do, see, eat, buy, and in places to stay. (Huie, 1994: 4)

Many of these pre-industrial categories of person – fishermen, sailors and farmers – represent traditional manual occupations while writers and historians appear as examples of intellectual strata that would also have existed in older societies. Foodies and culture buffs are more recent terms, but of an intellectualized type. Insiders and savvy locals clearly promise to bring the untourist to the back region which, as we know from MacCannell, is what all tourists are after anyway. Pre-industrial manual occupations, traditional intellectual strata, modern intellectual strata with new middle-class preoccupations, and guides to the back region: most of the social categories that are implicated in *industrial* societies are absent.

Again unlike the post-tourist who plays with signs, the untourist does not exist in ironic mode but is out to track down authenticity. Untourists do not seem to be aware of post-tourists, for they explicitly understand themselves to be in opposition to the categories of traditional mass tourism:

Mass tourism is about infrastructure (big hotels, souvenir shops, garish promotions and the fast buck) whereas untourism is about caring for people, maintaining unspoiled environments, authenticity and value-for-money . . . If untourists won't go to places created solely to soak up the tourist dollar, preferring to see and do what the locals do . . . there will be less and less room to spoil what is natural, authentic and/or special about a place. (Huie, 1994: 3)

Untourists 'trek through the wilderness carrying biscuits, cheese and wine-soaked maps in preference to relaxing in the comfort of an air-conditioned tour bus' (Huie, 1994: 2). Trekking through wilderness is associated by Urry with the service class and by Bourdieu with 'intellectuals' (Urry, 1990: 89), and indeed we can see a certain middle-classness if we simply substitute 'wine-soaked maps' with 'beer-stained maps' in the preceding sentence. 'Wine' and 'beer' are simple indicators of social class in Australia (see Chapter 8), 'wine' signalling rather higher cultural capital, to use Bourdieu's term. But the untourist is also quite explicitly high in economic capital: 'value-for-money . . . does not mean cheap . . . the untourist is a free spender when it comes to getting exactly what he or she wants . . . untourists prefer simple personal style rather than overt luxury – regardless of cost' (Huie, 1994: 3–4). So not only are untourists well-off, they have the cultural capital to know how to use money in a culturally sophisticated way – they reject 'overt luxury' for what is presumably a more subtle kind. Untourists, then, are high in both cultural and economic capital, but rather low in ironic capital (if I may add a third dimension to the Bourdieu model).

It seems likely that post-tourists and untourists will be the elite tourist categories of the future, the former representing the postmodern strand of culture discussed in Urry (1990: 83ff.) and the latter growing out of the environmental strand. Ironic players with appearance and earnest seekers after 'authentic' reality: the two poles of philosophical approaches to the world hardly ever seem to change. Perhaps the 'traveller' is an uncertain mixture of both, while mass tourism will continue to serve those with lower levels of the various types of capital.

10
The Body

It is only relatively recently that the body has become a topic for sociology. Before the mid-1980s, most sociologists seemed to look right through the fleshly substantiality of the body and fix their interrogative gazes upon the shimmering immaterialities of the knowing, reflective, philosophical human subject. The latter phenomenon appeared to transcend such mundanities as birthing, mutilation, imprisonment, illness, the experiences of adolescents as their bodies seem to run out of control, bleeding, wearing 13-centimetre spiked heels, or having a facelift – the 'real subject' was somehow behind or beyond all these. Certainly, the sociology of vomiting practices still awaits its Marx, Weber and Durkheim. But why did sociology fail to face the flesh for so long? Writers such as Turner (1992) see part of the explanation in the mind/body split associated with Cartesian philosophy. Descartes's motto was 'I think, therefore I am' – not 'I eat, drink, sleep and have sex, therefore I am'. The human subject was to be found not in the body, but in the mind. One important consequence of this split was that the body was seen to belong to the domain of the natural sciences, and the mind to the realm of the humanities. As Turner (1992) points out, this is perhaps most clearly evident in the German term for the humanities: *Geisteswissenschaften* – the sciences of the mind. The body therefore seemed to have no legitimate place in sociology, a discipline steeped in the humanities.

Perhaps a second reason for the sociological neglect of corporal reality lies in the victory of the European hygiene movements in the last century. Here, religion and medicine seem to meet: cleanliness is next to godliness and therefore makes one a more spiritual (and less material) person, but it also slows the spread of the diseases that threatened to ravage the large populations thrown together in the rapidly expanding towns of early industrialization. The cleaner the body, the less it can betray itself as something made of flesh by giving off odour or leaving bits of its waste products about the place as evidence of its passage. The body that points to its own material existence as such disappears, and becomes the canvas on which can be read messages about status, class and gender. The new body gives off impressions, not smells. Not only, then, did sociology have philosophical reasons for neglecting the body, but the body itself began to disappear as something that forced itself upon olfactory consciousness. Turner puts this in terms of foundationalist and anti-foundationalist approaches: for the first, the body is lived experience, while for the second, the body has become discourse – a system of symbols. In consumer culture, the latter version of the body predominates. The body in its physicality becomes a machine to be kept in good order, so that the body as appearance can be maintained as a marketable commodity. The consequences of these developments are explored in this chapter.

The body in sociological theory

One of the more curious aspects of sociology, at least until recently, is the relative absence of the body from its considerations. There may be social actors with identities, but the impression one would retain from much sociology is that these actors exist in some unfleshly world, mere carriers of disembodied meanings and ideals. But why should this be? Bryan Turner argues that it springs from the legacy of the philosophy of René Descartes, for whom the split between mind and body was fundamental: 'I think, therefore I am' suggests that my being would appear to be somehow disembodied. It was assumed that there was no significant interaction between the two parts of the Cartesian dualism, and so, as Turner writes, 'these two realms or topics can be addressed by separate and distinctive disciplines. The body became the subject of the natural sciences including medicine, whereas the mind or *Geist* was the topic of the humanities' (1992: 32). So we end up with splits like nature–body–environment on the one hand and society–mind–culture on the other (Turner, 1992: 33).

The sides of this split tended to remain isolated from each other, and those that worked on one side paid little attention to what was happening on the other. Sociology, with its interest in the meanings of social action that grew out of Weber's approach in particular, lined up on the society–mind–culture side, and so the body as such became invisible to the sociological gaze. The social actor was understood in terms of consciousness, knowledge and meaning – not embodiment. Even though the body is a major way in which we actually recognize social actors, it seems to have been rather like a transparent balloon to sociologists. It contained a bunch of things like consciousness, knowledge and meaning, but was itself not worthy of further investigation – one looked through it and saw only these other things. As Turner remarks, 'Who I am rests crucially on having a specific body which I do not share with other social agents' (1992: 37), but the implications of this have not been explored in sociology until quite recently. Can we replace 'I think, therefore I am' with 'I embody, therefore I am'? Let us approach this question through an examination of the various ways in which the body has come to be an object.

Machines, diets and discipline: the body becomes an object

The body has had many different statuses, but let me mention only a few. It is an aesthetic object of complex social significance to be painted, clothed, plucked, shaved, pierced, tattooed and corseted; a political object to be trained, disciplined, tortured, mutilated and locked away; an economic object to be exploited, fed and reproduced; and a sexual object to seduce and be seduced. But the main status that interests us for the purposes of this section is the notion of the body as a machine. This appears to be quite a modern way of looking at the body, and hardly existed before the eighteenth century. Two examples may serve to illustrate the 'machinization' of the body: the advent of chronological time and the shift to the detailed division of labour.

How was time measured before chronology? E.P. Thompson writes:

> in seventeenth-century Chile time was often measured in 'credos': an earthquake was described in 1647 as lasting for the period of two credos; while the cooking-time of an egg could be judged by an Ave Maria said aloud. In Burma in recent times monks rose at daybreak 'when there is light enough to see the veins in the hand'. The *Oxford English Dictionary* gives us English examples – 'pater noster whyle', 'miserere whyle' (1450), and (in the *New English Dictionary* but not the *Oxford English Dictionary*) 'pissing while' – a somewhat arbitrary measurement. (Thompson, 1967: 58)

The important point to note here is that time had to do with certain forms of activity that had their basis in the body: the saying of a prayer, the visibility of a hand, or the process of urination. In other words, the sense of time came from the body and the world was encompassed in these terms. Similarly, in the British war film *Ill-Met by Moonlight* the Greek partisan character measured time in terms of the number of cigarettes he could smoke during the period in question: 'how far away is it?' – 'twenty cigarettes'. So here, the body makes sense of the temporality of the world.

With the advent of chronology, the relationship between the body and the world is reversed: instead of the body being a subject which measures the world, chronological time with its clocks and watches turns the body into an object of measurement. It then becomes possible to co-ordinate bodies to the same 'objective' chronological time, something that was clearly useful in the organization of factory production. The objectively co-ordinated body can then be matched to the objectively co-ordinated machine – machine time takes over from body time; or rather, the latter is subordinated to the former.

The second point refers to the detailed division of labour. It will be recalled from elementary sociology courses that one striking difference introduced by capitalist industrialization was the breaking up of a given task into its component parts. In Adam Smith's well-known example (1977 [1776]: 4–5), one person was no longer responsible for the 18 separate operations that were involved in the manufacture of a pin. Instead, 18 persons were each responsible for carrying out just one of these operations. This has numerous implications, but let us merely note that the shift to a detailed division of labour also leads to a shift in the status of the body. If you can and do perform all the operations, then the pin-making process can be seen as the product of your body as a controlling subject – but if you do only the one operation, then your body becomes just an objective part of the pin-making process: you do not co-ordinate the overall process, you are merely as much part of it as the tools you use. Here, your body has become part of the overall machinery involved in the production of a pin: it is now a simple mechanical element. But it is not only that the body becomes part of the machinery of production: the body also begins to be seen as a machine in its own right. We can see this in the case of diet.

The dieting body

For Bryan Turner, 'the growth of theories of diet appears to be closely connected with the development of the idea that the body is a machine, the input and output requirements of which can be precisely quantified mathematically' (1992: 182). Turner gives the example of George Cheyne, who wrote several books on diet in the early eighteenth century. What did the body look like to Cheyne? Turner writes:

> Following the inspiration of Harvey's experimental approach to the circulation of blood, Cheyne declared that 'An animal Body is nothing but a Compages or contexture of pipes, an Hydraulic Machin, fill'd with a Liquor of such a Nature as was transfus'd into it by its Parents'. This complex system of pumps, pipes and canals can only be satisfactorily maintained by the correct input of food and liquid, appropriate exercise and careful evacuation . . . In general, the body as a machine requires surveillance under appropriate 'Diaetetick Management'. (Turner, 1992: 184–5)

We can see how this can fit into Foucauldian approaches that stress the ways in which human populations were surveyed and hence controlled through new practices, disciplined in detail and in depth (see, for example, Foucault, 1977 [1975]). Here the surveillance and discipline ('Watch your weight!') closes in on the body as an object in itself: the person occupying it begins their slow historical exit, bleeding away from the body until the latter is just a piece of matter to be kept functioning in good condition.

The extremely widespread practice of dieting is a contemporary inheritance of the machine metaphor: we may diet for all sorts of reasons, but in the end we seem to want our machine to be in impressive condition. We are probably so used to thinking of the body as a machine that we do not realize that the metaphor is a relatively recent one. The practice of aerobics is permitted by the machine metaphor. Elite sport is perhaps another good example, with athletes wired into all sorts of contraptions, their bodily indicators – a phrase itself machine-like – measured and evaluated, their diets closely controlled. Shilling, indeed, remarks that 'Radical critics of sport have noted that the vocabulary of the machine *dominates* the language of sport' (1993: 37, my emphasis).

Turner introduces three different orientations to the body that might be worth pondering upon: having a body, doing a body, and being a body. The first of these appears to indicate those times when there seems to be some sort of disjunction between the body and our sense of self. The body seems to be carrying on its own existence beyond our control or at the very least imposes a resistance. This is particularly apparent in illness; cancer, where we cannot stop our cells reproducing themselves at a dangerous rate, is a good example. The body here may appear as something outside of ourselves, and indeed is also often created in this way by conventional medicine. The body becomes alienated from us, and can seem either to have a life of its own or to belong to someone else, such as the physician or the medical profession generally. Indeed, the notion of having (rather than, say, being) a body may be what permits external intervention in the body in the first place as a thing separate from the person. It is then possible for medicine to treat the body as separate object, which is why some people feel that they have been treated as pieces of meat by agents of the medical profession. The idea of having a body, then, appears to have certain kinds of implications.

Being a body seems to mean that the body does not pose any sort of troubling resistance to us: we do not have to issue the special order 'walk!' and watch the body obey us. As Turner remarks, in this case the body is phenomenologically absent – we do not really notice it. One may wonder, however, if this is not an exceptional case. Every morning, we do various things to our body in order to present it as an acceptable body for those we will meet throughout the day: we wash, comb our hair, perhaps use various cosmetics. The point here is that even if we 'are' a body, we are often a body for someone else as much as, or more than, ourselves: for very particular persons or even for complete strangers who may see us on the street. In a sense, then, our bodies belong to the social world, and it is our duty to present *proper* bodies to this world through various sorts of body practices. We are more or less obliged to consider our bodies as objects for ourselves and for others, but here as *objects of representation*. This seems to be what Turner means by 'doing a body': 'the body appears as a collection of practices over which we might have a certain mastery or sovereignty. Through childhood socialization, all of us acquire certain basic body techniques for presenting and maintaining and reproducing bodies in time and space' (Turner, 1992: 40–1). The social aspects of such elementary body acts as walking were demonstrated by the French anthropologist Marcel Mauss (1979 [1936]) in his essay 'Body Techniques': one might imagine that the way one walks, for example, is a highly personal thing to do with the peculiarities of one's very own body, but Mauss (1979 [1936]: 99–100) showed that there were different national styles of marching. The way we walk is determined culturally as well as physically. He also shows that different genders and age groups engage in different body techniques, and I think one could add class to this.

So the body appears to be a rather two-sided thing: it is ours and not ours, it can be experienced subjectively or objectively, it is natural and cultural at the same time. This double-sidedness, for Turner, is best expressed in German, which has different terms for each: when we are talking about the lived body as we experience it, German uses *der Leib*, while when we are referring to the body as something outside ourselves, something objective and exterior, that language says *der Körper*. Sociology with its Cartesian inheritance has tended to see the body, when it has seen it at all, only as *Körper* – as something exterior, objective and impersonal. For phenomenologists, however, our perception is grounded in our lived body, and this includes not only senses of taste and smell but also the so-called 'higher' perceptions, such as mental functions. If this is so, then sociology cannot treat the body as mere *Körper* – it must be able to tackle the double-sidedness of the body.

Turner puts much the same point slightly differently when he makes the distinction between foundationalist and anti-foundationalist approaches to the body. The foundationalist tends to treat the body as *Leib*, as lived experience, where the anti-foundationalist sees the body as a discourse about the nature of social relations, as a thing on which are inscribed the signs of power and knowledge in society. The foundationalist sees the body as existing as something separate to and prior to various social discourses, the anti-foundationalist sees it as a canvas upon which are painted the signs of society: for the latter, the body does not exist in any important way 'before' or prior to social discourses, it is rather the 'effect' of such discourses. It should be clear that the latter approach is prevalent in the literature of consumption. In order to sell commodities such as fashionable clothing, cosmetics, and the like, the body must be seen as something that floats about the world signifying things about the status of its 'owner'. What matters about the body here is its capacity to act as a sign, as an element in a language: the body here is representation, rather than lived reality.

But what about all these things that are promoted as diets, or even as food that is good for us? They may appear to target the body as lived experience, and indeed they do depend on this in order to get us to buy the items. But such advertising usually promotes a specific ideal body shape or type, and in this way says that the real point of the product is, yet again, to give one a body that will signal the right sorts of things in a particular society. In order to sell food and diets, the body must be addressed initially in terms of its lived experience, its foundational nature (feel good about yourself), but this is then subordinated to the task of producing a body acceptable to the canons of beauty of the world in which we find ourselves. So the end product is again a signifying object rather than lived experience: we find both foundationalist and anti-foundationalist approaches here, the first functioning as a mode of address to the consumer that allows the second initial entry and subsequent domination. My argument here is of course a starting point, and one would need to examine a corpus of, say, advertisements or diet books in order to see how far it might work out. Anthropologists have long tended to view the body anti-foundationally, as a discourse carrying the major markers of social relations – Michel Foucault (1977 [1975]) sees the body as an effect of discourses and knowledges acting upon it, producing it as the body we know.

The disciplined body

The Foucauldian body is very much a body to be disciplined by and for others, and a clear instance of this can be found in the following French advertisement from 1860:

> Martin and Gelbké. Compassionate Surgical Appliances Against Onanism. These appliances, never before seen, have both a moral and a hygienic purpose: they form an unbreachable barrier against the solitary habits stigmatized by religion and society. All doctors know from experience that these habits inevitably lead to idiocy, wasting away, depression, and often death. Prescribe them in urgent cases, and find a new way of helping society. These appliances have no metal fittings and so are very comfortable to wear indeed. They have won two first class silver medals from the Society of Arts and Sciences and the Academy of Universal Sciences in Paris, judged by the reports presented by commissions composed of medical doctors and manufacturers of surgical appliances. Lack of space prevents us from giving you a copy of these reports. When properly used, these appliances are designed to morally and physically regenerate the human species and to avoid familial deceptions and disappointments (*Report of the Academy of Universal Sciences*). We therefore recommend them to the medical profession, children's homes, fathers of families and to everyone with responsibility for the protection of good morals. Two institutions have tried them, and rushed to put them into wider practice. They realize that these appliances are the means of stopping in its tracks a disease that can spread like wildfire, and so advise their purchase by the parents of incorrigible children. We believe that this measure will be taken up by parents who know that the future depends on health, morals and instruction. We have prices to suit every pocket: 25, 40, 60, 80 and 500 francs. (Reprinted in Tissot, 1980 [1760]: 171, my translation)

This is an excellent example of the sort of power that Foucault writes about. Let us examine this advertisement in detail. First, we may note an explicit link between the most private of practices and the wider world, for these habits are stigmatized by both religion and society. In the epoch of sovereign power that preceded the age of disciplinary power, neither society nor religion would have been interested in this (Bauman, 1982: 40). Here, by contrast, the individual never escapes being subject to society and religion. Social and religious discourses make it their business to regulate private behaviour.

The advertisement proposes to enable this social and religious control by way of a second point we may find interesting: the medicalizing of a private practice provides the practical instruments of control. Saying that this problem for society and religion can be translated into a problem for medicine offers a concrete way of controlling it through the surgical appliances that medical technology can provide. This is only one example of the general principle that bodies are much easier to control once they have become the objects of a medical discourse. We are so used to this situation that sometimes we find it hard to imagine that the body has only recently come under the control of medicine as understood in the West. Putting this another way, it is only relatively recently that humans have lost control over their bodies to medical practitioners. I exaggerate slightly here to make the point. I am not saying that there is no longer any resistance to medical claims to control (far from it, indeed), I am merely trying to show that there is nothing natural or inevitable about medical claims over the body: it is a form of disciplinary power that had to be achieved.

Linked with the medicalization and technologicization of the body is the third point of interest, namely the increasing division of the world into experts on the one hand, who possess knowledge and the right to use it, and non-experts on the other, who are now subject to the legitimate control of the experts – legitimate, because professions have managed to gain some sort of monopoly of what is considered 'proper' use of power. 'Expert knowledge' pushes 'everyday knowledge' out of the frame of legitimacy, and new expertise can of course do the same thing to old expertise. Use of power by those not accredited as experts becomes illegitimate power. This did not take place without a struggle, a good example being the fight between midwives and medical doctors for the right to exert 'expert' knowledge and control (Murphy-Lawless, 1992 [1988]).

We find several sorts of expert in the advertisement. First there are the medical doctors who collaborate with the second group, the manufacturers of surgical appliances, to make up commissions that report to the most institutionalized forms of knowledge: learned societies like the Society of Arts and Sciences or the Academy of Universal Sciences. The fact that these bodies exist also shows that expertise is something held not so much by a person as by social institutions that lend supra-individual legitimacy to the individual 'expert'. The 'expert' not only possesses knowledge, but is supported in this by a whole social apparatus. A third group are those who run children's homes: instead of a give-and-take between these people and the children, there is a one-way relationship. Expertise here is borrowed from medical authority through the use of medical/surgical technology, so these would be sub-experts rather than experts.

This is one of the things that the advertisement is trying to do: set up a hierarchy of powers from the medical doctors and surgical appliance manufacturers giving out first-class silver medals, to those who run children's homes, then the next group, fathers of families, and finally the vague category of everyone responsible for the protection of good morals. These sub-experts, by doing what the advertisement says, become the agents of medical/surgical disciplinary power; and children seem to be the main category targeted here as subject to this power. Note that this attempts to displace the traditional powers of fathers and people in charge of such homes: the latter might traditionally be considered to hold their own powers by virtue of their positions and not need any outside authority to tell them how to run their ship. In the old model, the Father was the Sovereign of the household and his word was Law. Here, though, these traditional – almost arbitrary and absolute – powers are replaced by disciplinary powers originating in outside bodies. Old forms of control based on old fashioned tyranny are replaced by the new forms of control based on cool, rational, scientific expertise. A sort of generalized bureaucratization of power takes place.

Our fourth interesting point concerns the claims made for the social and personal benefits that the use of these appliances is said to provide. If we are left on our own we will engage in habits that lead to idiocy, wasting away, depression and death – but Martin and Gelbké's surgical appliances can lead us away from such a path. Here, of course, is another attempt to replace the discourse of the lonely practitioner with that of the medical expert: 'all doctors know from experience'. Our solitary friend may think that the habits have nothing to do with idiocy, wasting away, depression and death, but this is silenced by the expert discourse. All that we are allowed to hear is the voice of the expert. The solitary individual act is then linked to the much larger issue of the moral and physical regeneration of the human species, which would seem a rather large claim for an advertisement. This both affirms individuality and denies it: it denies it by showing that the individual is part of the human species, that is, a member of a general category, and affirms it by claiming that an individual act when committed alone can affect the more general category of the human species. It is this double quality that allows the advertisement to make the claims that it does: by intervening on the individual, it also intervenes on the whole. Indeed it would appear to be this double quality that allows expert intervention generally. If there was no link between the individual and the whole, then expert medical discourse intervening on individuals would have no social impact and therefore be devoid of social power. Individual bodies are constructed as both discrete entities and conductors of the social – as metal conducts electricity, the body conducts the social.

We can see this oddly expressed point more clearly where the advertisement states that 'these appliances are the means of stopping in its tracks a disease that can spread like wildfire'. The individual body is a conductor of the 'disease', much to the dis-ease of the advertisers. Perhaps more accurately, each body induces the solitary habit in another. The electrical analogy holds up quite well here: electric current can flow from one body to another by direct connection (think of sexually transmitted diseases) or by proximity rather than direct connection (a current flowing through a coil will induce current in another coil wound around it but not actually directly connected to it). This seems to be a form of imitation, if we may translate it into social terms, and that appears to be what the advert is targeting here. The central point, then, is that bodies are both discrete and social, and expert discourse needs to intervene on individual bodies in order to save the human species as a whole. Indeed, expert knowledge has the right to do this precisely because of the link with the whole. The individual may be a good cell or a bad cell of the social body, and the rapid reproduction of bad cells, as in our wildfire-like 'disease', clearly calls for intervention.

Not the least important line is the very last one: 'We have prices to suit every pocket'. The new discipline was not to be confined to any particular social group or category: everybody is involved in the formational disciplinary society – rich or poor, you can still become an agent of disciplinary power. Interventions at such intimate levels as we see in this advertisement would not have occurred in earlier times.

An intimate connection between the individual body and the social body becomes visible through the above analysis. Here framed in terms of the disciplining of onanistic practices, the connection can also be seen in all disciplined corporeal practices (dieting, dressing, cosmetics, sports training, and so on) that have become so important in consumer society.

The body in consumer culture

Turner (1992: 58) draws a distinction between the internal and the external body. The internal body is concerned with the restraint and control of desire and passion in the interests of social stability, and this is associated with asceticism. We may remember from the discussion of Colin Campbell in Chapter 1, however, that control of this sort can eventually be used to control the expression of emotion in a hedonistic way, so perhaps we could add this in to Turner's model. The external body refers to 'the representations of the bodies in social spaces and their regulation and control' (Turner, 1992: 58). On the level of populations, the external problem has to do with social regulation through the use of such things as surveillance broadly understood, through institutions such as prisons, schools and factories as explored in the work of Foucault. The external body on the individual level is characterized by representational and commodified aspects particularly relevant to consumption, as they allow the body to fit into society as something needing the aid of various commodities in order properly to be.

Mike Featherstone (1991b [1982]) pays most attention to the external body, interpreting the internal body as having merely the role of something that needs to be maintained in good health in order the better to promote the external body as desirable appearance. In a culture dominated by appearance and image, our bodies are on display whether we like it or not. Featherstone takes drinking as an example: 'the traditional intimate "local" pub has been gradually replaced by the large through-lounge pub, which incorporates a different organisation of social space with much greater opportunities for surveillance and display' (Featherstone, 1991b [1982]: 173). This has been quite a striking development in the UK and Ireland: snug intimacy with known persons recedes in importance compared with the passing display – or rather displayed passing – of many unknowns. The interior of the pub becomes a place for bodily display through appearance, and it is the change in the internal layout of the pub that promotes this shift. This sounds very like the changes we discussed in Chapter 9, when we saw how the medieval layout of Paris was changed to the broad sweeps of the new boulevards which created sights to be seen, out of both buildings and people. The pub becomes one more victim of the specular society.

If our bodies are to hold on to their marketable value in the world where appearances rule, they must be maintained, and the various body maintenance industries are quite vocal in reminding us of this fact. Image becomes quite crucial in this perspective, and Featherstone has some interesting comments on the role of photography and cinema in this respect. The photograph allows us to compare the appearances of our body over time, and this is likely to make us very conscious indeed of any changes we may undergo as we age. Without our collections of photographs, we would have no real way of doing this. Now we can make our very own before-and-after comparisons. And, of course, we have the cinema and television. Featherstone notes that the theoretician of film, Bela Balázs,

> speculated in the early 1920s that film was transforming the emotional life of twentieth-century man by directing him away from words towards movement and gesture. A culture dominated by words tends to be intangible and abstract, and reduces the human body to a basic biological organism, whereas the new emphasis upon visual images drew attention to the appearance of the body, the clothing, demeanour and gesture. (Featherstone, 1991b [1982]: 179)

So new images of the body began to spread throughout the world along with the Hollywood film, and these bodies were presented as attractive and ideal. Now everywhere there was a cinema in village, town or city, or even a projector and screen set up temporarily in the outback, there was a representation of what people ought to look like. In Chapter 4 we encountered the effects of the shift from headless and shapeless shop dummies to the use of those with heads and a definite shape, and here we see a similar effect but on a grand, almost global, scale, with definite models for both women and men parading about on the screen. There was an ironing out of regional and local differences, and a great gathering of the appearance of human bodies under the global totem of the Hollywood body. Featherstone quotes the English writer J.B. Priestley (1977 [1934]) who, in 1933, observed from his position drinking tea in a rural café that

> the girls of the nearby tables had carefully modelled their appearance on their favourite film stars: 'Even twenty years ago girls of this kind would have looked quite different even from girls in the nearest large town; they would have had an unmistakable small town rustic air; but now they are almost indistinguishable from girls in a dozen different capitals, for they all have the same models, from Hollywood'. (Featherstone, 1991b [1982]: 180)

Marcel Mauss makes a similar point about the influence of Hollywood: he was in hospital in New York, and was surprised at the ways the nurses walked. Finally he realized that he had seen this style of walking in the cinema. Back in Paris, he noticed that this American way of walking was also being copied by young French women (Mauss, 1979 [1936]: 100). So Hollywood seems to have had an effect on something as elementary as the very way in which people walk. Keeping up these appearances, of course, involves hard work and demands body maintenance practices of various sorts. The body, indeed, becomes living evidence of the care (or lack of it) lavished upon it: we judge at a glance if someone has or has not maintained their body through the 'proper' diet, fitness practices, cosmetics, or whatever – these have become moral imperatives if we want to have the 'proper' body that will pass the never-ending tests of the gazing society. An improperly styled body becomes evidence of moral laxity, of laziness – the body of the worthy person displays evidence of proper maintenance practices, and so the body that fails to present the right evidence is deemed unworthy: a moral failure (Featherstone, 1991b [1982]: 183, 186).

In consumer culture, suggests Featherstone, the version of the self that predominates is that of the performing self, which 'places greater emphasis upon appearance, display and the management of impressions' (Featherstone, 1991b [1982]: 187). One can perhaps see the change that has occurred more clearly if one contrasts the ideal of the self promoted in the nineteenth century with that promoted in the twentieth. Featherstone takes the example of self-help manuals: in the nineteenth century, these

> emphasised the Protestant virtues – industry, thrift, temperance, not just as means but as valid ends in their own right . . . Achievement was measured not against others but against abstract ideals of discipline and self-denial. With the bureaucratisation of the corporate career these virtues gave way to an emphasis upon competition with one's peers, salesmanship, 'boosterism' and the development of 'personal magnetism'. (Featherstone, 1991b [1982]: 188)

Putting this another way, we find a distinction between nineteenth-century *character* and twentieth-century *personality*. Character was associated with 'citizenship, democracy, duty, work, honour, reputation, morals, integrity and manhood'. Personality was supposedly 'fascinating, stunning, attractive, magnetic, glowing, masterful, creative, dominant, forceful' (ibid.). These are not so much abstract ideals as effects that can be obtained by performing in front of others in such a way as to convince them that one is indeed stunning, fascinating, and all the rest. Featherstone comments that 'The new personality handbooks stressed voice control, public speaking, exercise, sound catering habits, a good complexion and grooming and beauty aids – they showed little interest in morals' (ibid.). We express our 'self' through such things. A good complexion may not have counted for much when duty, work and moral integrity were at stake, but it can be central to the self that performs: we have been turned into actors on stage all the time. We measure our success by portraying the right image to others, whereas our nineteenth-century ancestors would have measured their success by how far they matched abstract, internalized ideals. Cosmetic surgery becomes a rational, thinkable option.

The body as appearance to be interpreted

From the above, one might imagine that the body only became of importance as appearance in the consumer culture of the twentieth century. This, however, is rather misleading. For many centuries, attempts have been made to see how an individual's observable physical features were related to that individual's character and personality. I refer, of course, to physiognomy. Joanne Finkelstein writes that:

Generally, physiognomy has dealt with the uncovering of personality traits through the study of facial features, body structure and overall physical appearance. It has been assumed that there was an immanent and univocal essence in humans which was reflected through identifiable body parts ... physiognomists claimed that character could be read from specific features of human appearance, especially those which were immobile [such as] the chin and forehead. (Finkelstein, 1991: 20–1)

This approach reached its greatest degree of systematization in the eighteenth-century work of Johann Caspar Lavater, who produced a four-volume treatise on 'how physical characteristics corresponded with moral traits' (Finkelstein, 1991: 22). Finkelstein provides the details in her first chapter, but in order to convince the reader that physiognomy is not confined to earlier centuries I want to give some examples of this sort of reasoning from a book that appeared as recently as 1950: *Character Reading from the Face: The Science of Physiognomy*, by Grace Rees. This seems to have been meant for popular consumption, as it was published in a series that included such titles as *Ride a Horse, Become a Golfer, How Others Get On* and *Pig Keeping and Breeding*. The publisher's medical reader summarizes the physiognomist's stance by writing that 'It has always been my view that a judgement on sight, by one experienced in the art, is more likely to be right than all the intelligence or other tests devised' (Rees, 1950: 8).

Let us consider the case of the nose. The shape and size of the nose is supposed to be an index of the sort of person who carries it. A large nose combined with a low, sloping or concave forehead 'denotes the erratic disposition of a faddist or fanatic, due to inadequate reasoning ability' (Rees, 1950: 36). A Roman nose with a thin-lipped mouth signifies 'Domination, drive, imperious will', while one with fuller lips denotes 'a more sympathetic nature. A fine leader, who, being more considerate, obtains loyalty' (Rees, 1950: 37). The Grecian nose indicates 'Exquisite refinement and good taste. The nose of the artist, poet and sculptor. Creative power predominates' (Rees, 1950: 39). The holder of the hooked nose has 'driving force, enterprise and money-making ability' (Rees, 1950: 41), while those gifted with the celestial tip-tilted nose have an 'Attractive, hasty, impulsive, inquisitive nature. If the mental power is well-developed, a versatile and talented subject' (Rees, 1950: 42). But woe betide the unfortunate snub-nosed person:

It is pathetic to find this small, snub, undeveloped nose on the face of an adult. It signifies an undeveloped intellect as stunted as the nose. Fortunately it is rarely seen except where the person has a mind fit only for menial, repetitive, routine work. As a rule it is found only where there has been very little, if any, education. The character will be unassuming, unpretentious, insignificant – the mind mediocre and commonplace. The nature may be primitive, even coarse, according to the upbringing. (Rees, 1950: 42–3)

Similar sorts of analysis were made of the other features of the face. It could be argued that consumer culture may simply be the finest flowering of what Finkelstein (1991) calls physiognomic reasoning: such reasoning has been extended from the face to the rest of the body and has perhaps finally drowned out alternative approaches to the interpretation of the body. It is consumer culture that universalizes physiognomic reasoning and helps it become the main way in which we look at the world of appearing bodies today – it is this reasoning, allied with the notion of the body as a commodity, that encourages such practices as the facelift. But even this is not really new, nor confined to consumer culture, for many societies have manipulated the body in various ways. The point here is to turn the body into an acceptably social object rather than an unacceptably natural one, and it has to be worked on for this to happen. The nineteenth-century ideal types that Featherstone (1991b [1982]) evokes may merely be odd deviations from the normal human practice of taking the body as meaningful social appearance and manipulating it so that it becomes properly expressive within a given social context. Consumer culture, then, may simply be returning us to normal relations with our bodies. I embody, therefore I am.

11
Clothing and Fashion

Richard Sennett (1978 [1976]) understands clothing as an important means of indicating social standing, but notes that what is expressed has changed over time. In eighteenth-century London and Paris it was easy to tell social status from street clothes because these were very highly codified and deliberately indicated the *public* status of an individual, for example their occupation. The individual as expressive personality was confined between the walls of the home, while only social masks stalked the city streets. But industrialization and the rise of bourgeois culture brought with them the new individual, and so instead of clothing indicating the *public* character of the wearer it began to be interpreted as indicating the *personal* character-istics of its carrier. As a result, people started to dress in a very uniform and unindividual way, fearing that an unusual button on a cuff would betray them as deeply flawed and deviant creatures to eyes ever on the alert for clues to the inner person. Twentieth-century consumer culture, with its cre-ation of the 'individual' lifestyle, appears to have transformed this fear into a pleasure.

For Veblen (1975 [1899]), dress was an expression of the pecuniary culture. To put this in rather more straightforward terms: clothing provides an excellent way of showing off how wealthy we are to all and sundry. Apparel is more suited to this style of display than any other object, because we carry it on our backs wherever we go and so even complete strangers can tell at a glance how rich we are (or are not: 'A cheap coat makes a cheap man': Veblen, 1975 [1899]: 169). From this perspective, clothing was not worn to protect one from the elements, and indeed many went cold just to appear well dressed. Prestige was enhanced if one's clothing indicated that one could not possibly be engaged in manual labour of any sort, that is, that one consumed without producing. Davis (1989) considers how Veblenian invidious distinctions work in the case of that apparently most democratic and working class of garments: blue jeans.

In 1883, Lady Paget remarked that 'The reason why fashions change so rapidly now is because they at once spread through every stratum of society, and become deteriorated and common' (Paget, 1883: 463). This is perhaps the earliest statement of one of the classical sociological theories of fashion change in commodity society: emulation of the dress of a higher class, fol-lowed by a change once the lower class appears to have caught up with the higher – in other words, fashion change results from class competition on the level of appearances. Georg Simmel (1957 [1904]) established this approach in the discipline of sociology and his ideas are explored in the present chapter. Sometimes referred to as 'trickle-down theory', this has its highest explanatory power when there is general agreement on the fact that a higher social class ought to be imitated. McCracken (1988) points out that 'chase and flight' would be a more appropriate phrase to apply than 'trickle-down', as the lower classes are actively chasing after the upper and hence the dynamic is in an upward rather than a downward direction.

Although many writers have noted that clothing can function as a means of expression, it is only relatively recently that dress has been treated as a language and its semiotic structure explored. Sahlins (1976) attempts to show how dress as a semiotic system can be seen as a map of the cultural universe in which we live. McCracken (1988), however, challenges the view that apparel may usefully be understood as a language, arguing that a lack of combinatorial freedom in dress renders the analogy inadequate in a crucial way.

From social status to personal states

We often imagine that the primary purpose of clothing is to express our personality, and indeed this is how psychology generally looks at dress. Such an idea is quite recent, and we can see the shift towards this way of interpreting apparel in Richard Sennett's (1978 [1976]) comparison of the way people dressed in the eighteenth and nineteenth centuries. The eighteenth-century wearer of clothing seemed to act as if dress was very much something that indicated not personal states but social status:

> Appearances on the streets of London and Paris two centuries ago were manipulated so as to be more precise indicators of social standing [than today]. Servants were easily distinguishable from laborers. The kind of labor performed could be read from the peculiar clothes adopted by each trade, as could the status of a laborer in his craft by glancing at certain ribbons and buttons he wore. In the middle ranks of society, barristers, accountants, and merchants each wore distinctive decorations, wigs, or ribbons. The upper ranks of society appeared on the street in costumes which not merely set them apart from the lower orders but dominated the street. (Sennett, 1978 [1976]: 65)

It was almost as if people went about wearing labels telling the world of their status in very explicit terms. Here was a highly formal and ceremonial theatre where the audience could instantly grasp the sort of person the actor was portraying. Roland Barthes's remark on theatrical costume may be applied to eighteenth-century street dress: '*the costume must be an argument* . . . costume had a powerful semantic value, it was not there only to be seen, it was also there to be *read*, it communicated ideas, information or sentiments . . . Powerful, popular and civic theatres have always utilized a precise vestimentary code' (Barthes, 1967 [1964]: 94, italics in original). So the one in the white hat is always the good guy. Social order was perfectly visible in the appearances that paraded about the street.

But as the eighteenth century wore on and capitalist industrialization exerted increasing influence, there was a growing gap between the street and the home in terms of what they meant and how people dressed. The public world remained formal, but the world of the home began to appear less so: if in public the body was hidden behind highly conventional clothing indicating social status, at home looser dress permitted the body to emerge from behind the formal façade. The body began to be seen as a natural thing to be expressed. This can be seen very clearly in the philosopher Diderot's 1769 essay on his old dressing gown. He remarks that:

> It was made for me and I was made for it. It closely fitted all the bends of my arms and legs without obstructing me. The new one is stiff and starched, and turns me into a mannequin . . . I was the absolute master of my old dressing gown, I have become the slave of the new one. (Diderot, 1971 [1769]: 7–8, my translation)

The shift here is from the body as ruling clothes to clothes as ruling the body, which is actually the reverse of the historical tendency over the last couple of centuries – nevertheless, it makes the point clearly. Sennett (1978 [1976]: 67–8) writes that 'At home, one's clothes suited one's body and its needs [like Diderot's old dressing gown]; on the street, one stepped into clothes whose purpose was to make it possible for other people to act as if they knew who you were.' It was not until the nineteenth century that this idea of the body as something natural to be expressed really took off in the public sphere as well. Indeed, for some writers things eventually went so far that clothing began to be seen not as a mask for the body but as an extension of it – our bodies began to invest our garments with their own significances. The writer I have in mind is the now fairly obscure Hermann Lotze, whose book *Microcosmus* appeared in English in 1885. His general principle was as follows:

> Wherever, in fact, we bring a foreign body into relationship with the surface of our body . . . the consciousness of our personal existence is prolonged into the extremities and surfaces of this foreign body, and the consequence is feelings now of an expansion of our proper self, now of the acquisition of a kind and amount of motion foreign to our natural organs, now of an unusual degree of vigour, power of resistance, or steadiness in our bearing. (Lotze, 1885: 592)

In relation to the things we wear, he remarks that,

> the earrings, the floating, hanging ribbons and sash-ends of our maidens, the light lace, the heavier knots and tassels of uniforms, massive chains and crosses, plumes, watch-appendages, waving veils and mantles, all these means are applied by ingenious fancy in order not merely to expand our existence on all sides, but to create the pleasing delusion that it is ourselves that float and wave and sway in all these appendages, rising and falling in rhythmic cadences. And where there actually is no sensation it even supplies this lack, and in the delicate tissue of hanging lace makes us think we hang and take part in its swaying motion. (Lotze, 1885: 594)

This is a much more body-centred view of dress than one finds in the eighteenth century: clothing and accessories now seem to be the very carriers of our body and our self – our personality, if you prefer that word.

If in the eighteenth century social status stood out clearly on the street, in the nineteenth everything became more blurred as people began to dress in such a way as to blend into an anonymous crowd. Drabness was in. Sennett suggests that this was because people wanted to protect themselves from the upheavals in the city: if the eighteenth century was the century of social order, the nineteenth was more like the century of social disorder, with a rapidly growing working class concentrating in the cities and many uprisings and revolutions. The spread of mass manufacture and the sewing machine made it possible for everyone to dress more or less like everyone else. This characteristic seems to have given rise to one of the earlier socio-logical theories on the importance of clothing, Gabriel Tarde's rather neglected work *Les Lois de l'imitation* (The Laws of Imitation). For him, the social being was in essence imitative, and society therefore *was* imi-tation. The spread of fashion was seen as one form of imitation, and Tarde saw the logical consequence of this as the creation of a single society, with uniform appearances. As he put it, 'the extraordinary progress of fashion as applied to clothing, food, dwellings, needs, ideas, institutions and arts is on its way in Europe to turning out the same sort of person in editions of hun-dreds of thousands of copies' (Tarde, 1900: 17, my translation). This is the theoretical version of a fantasy about a harmonious social order where everyone will be like everyone else, an arrangement very dissimilar to the eighteenth-century model of order springing from the ways in which people were different but knew their place.

For Sennett (1978 [1976]: 161ff.), one result of the increasing sameness of appearance was a shift away from reading social status from clothing and a shift towards reading details of personality. It is easy to see why: when dress indicates social status and there are many differently apparelled bodies on the street, then all one can see is the social mask – the person themselves is eclipsed by the sign that is their dress. But when bodies are very similarly apparelled one is more likely to be able to pay attention to the person, because that is where the site of difference is now to be found. This seems to have been an unintended consequence of the new tendency to incon-spicuous dressing: one may be less conspicuous socially, but one becomes more conspicuous personally. So people began scrutinizing each other in order to gather clues about their personalities, and such scrutiny took place at an almost microscopic level. This is not surprising, for if the overall impression is sameness then it is only in the details that one will find differ-ence. Two areas in particular obsessed the middle-class nineteenth-century observer of dress: whether someone had become a gentleman, and sexual status.

Sennett gives a rather delightful example of the extremely subtle interpretations now possible when he quotes a story to the effect that 'one could always recognize gentlemanly dress because the buttons on the sleeves of a gentleman's coat actually buttoned and unbuttoned, while one recognized gentlemanly behaviour in his keeping the buttons scrupulously fastened, so that his sleeves never called attention to this fact' (Sennett, 1978 [1976]: 166). Women had to worry about being perceived as 'loose', and again this needed only the tiniest of signs – perhaps the cut of fingernails or a neckline one millimetre lower than the norm promised frissons of bliss to the passing stranger. The nineteenth century, then, made details tell for the middle classes at least. No doubt broader class differences were perfectly evident in the cut and quality of clothing. Even if the same model of appearance is a shared aspiration, as Sennett seems to suggest, a hierarchy of quality still directly translates class differences. *Occupational* differences may have blurred and simplified into *class* differences, which means that the eighteenth-century social street theatre did not simply disappear as Sennett would have it, but was transformed from an occupational theatre with many different roles to a class theatre with fewer, broader roles.

Veblen's pecuniary theory of dress

For Veblen, dress expresses one particular aspect of the social structure: wealth. We already know, of course, that this is how he looks upon all consumer goods in the era of conspicuous consumption, but he finds dress an extremely good example of this general tendency:

> expenditure on dress has this advantage over most other methods, that our apparel is always in evidence and affords an indication of our pecuniary standing to all observers at the first glance. It is also true that admitted expenditure for display is more obviously present, and is, perhaps, more universally practised in the matter of dress than in any other line of consumption. (Veblen, 1975 [1899]: 167)

Dress does not exist just to keep us warm. We are so little interested in the protective aspects of apparel, indeed, that we are prepared 'in an inclement climate ... to go ill clad in order to appear well-dressed' (Veblen, 1975 [1899]: 168). Things are perhaps not quite so sweeping today, for there is evidence that this depends on the age of the persons being considered. Here are some brief extracts from interviews on clothing that I carried out in Dublin. I asked a 58-year-old woman 'Do you think people in Ireland dress according to the weather, generally?' She replied:

> I think the older people do, but. I'm not so sure, I don't think the younger ones do, I think they dress according to what they're going to. If they're going to a party or, out for an evening and even if the snow is on the ground, and they have a nice pink dress, they'll wear that. I have seen people going out shivering at bus stops heh. But I think older people do all right. They don't mind the image, as long as they're [voice trails off]

Either social occasion or weather can dominate dress, with social occasion the deciding factor for younger persons' dress practices and the weather with older. This reasoning would appear not to be confined to 58-year-olds, as we can see from the comments of a 20-year-old woman I interviewed as part of the same project. She provides a very similar answer, situating herself as young person and substituting fashion for social occasion:

> I think young people wouldn't be too fussy, I know myself, well I mean if it's very bad now the weather I'll tuck up yih know, but I mean normally I don't go out

and buy with the intention of, oh God, the weather, but ehm I'd say older people *would* now, they dress for the warmth. Ehm. Well they say they feel the cold, maybe they do when yih get older yih *do* feel the cold more so, than when you're young. Or maybe when yih're young yih're willin to risk, gettin out in, cold things just for the sake of the fashion or whatever.

So it appears, if I may generalize from a very small sample, that the protective aspects of clothing become more important as one ages, but other considerations, such as social occasion or the demands of fashion, predominate among younger age groups. The body seems important to both groups: one for display, the other to be protected.

But to return to Veblen. Merely to indicate wealth is not the only service clothing can render us. The reader may recall from Chapter 2 that an important way of distinguishing oneself in the Veblenian world was to indicate that one took part in no form of productive labour, which is why, to repeat the example given earlier, it makes a lot more sense to learn dead languages rather than living: the more useless the better, to avoid the taint of work. Clothing, too, can be used to indicate that one has not sunk to the shameful level of productive labour. How does it do this? Veblen writes:

> Much of the charm that invests the patent-leather shoe, the stainless linen, the lustrous cylindrical hat, and the walking-stick, which so greatly enhance the native dignity of a gentleman, comes of their pointedly suggesting that the wearer cannot when so attired bear a hand in any employment that is directly and immediately of any human use. (Veblen, 1975 [1899]: 170–1)

Women's apparel was seen as still more likely to prevent productive labour due to its even greater range of restrictions. It is easy to see why the corset was so important in this perspective: it contributed still more to the proudly unproductive image of the wearer. This fits very well with the discussion in Chapter 2 of vicarious leisure and vicarious consumption, where the job of wives and liveried servants was to set off the ability of the husband/master to pay – her clothing should show that the woman does not work, and thereby show that the husband can afford to keep her in this state. Veblen explains the peculiarities of women's dress as a result of the dominance of patriarchal relations of property (the woman as chattel).

The Veblen perspective also allows one to understand why the already-noted shift to drabness and the subtlety of details took place. The growth of wealthy classes in the nineteenth century led to the existence of a large enough number of the wealthy, and a sufficient rate of meeting with each other, to justify no longer paying attention to what the lower classes thought. There were now enough wealthy people about to form the principal audience for one's appearance. Only those who were not of this class dressed in a loud manner, and were seen as vulgar for addressing untrained tastes. The rich had the time and the leisure to train their tastes in the Kantian manner we discussed before, and so fine details invisible to the untrained counted for much (like the gentleman's sleeve buttons quoted above). Veblen writes that 'As the community advances in wealth and culture, the ability to pay is put in evidence by means which require a

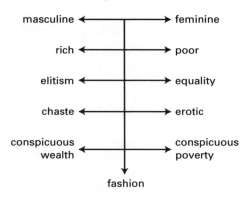

Figure 11.1   *Fashion as the result of tensions between oppo-sitions, 1 (Davis, 1989, 1992)*

progressively nicer discrimination in the beholder. This nicer discrimination between advertising media is in fact a very large element of the higher pecuniary culture' (Veblen, 1975 [1899]: 187). By the end of the nineteenth century, people seemed to be looking to clothing for details betraying both wealth and personality, and we have seen how these two aspects are linked to the general tendency to dress in a more drab and subtle manner (in the case of men especially).

Blue jeans, social similarity and social differentiation

For Fred Davis (1989, 1992), fashion in clothing springs from a series of ambivalences and tensions between a number of oppositions: for example, masculine versus feminine, elitism versus democracy, haves versus have-nots, the erotic versus the chaste, and so forth (see Figure 11.1). This is more complex than Veblen, but we will look at just one example here that relates to the tensions over social status: the curious case of blue jeans. From a Veblenian viewpoint, one would assume that blue jeans function as a way of indicating the relative poverty of their possessors, and the better-off would never wear them. The function of indicating economic standing can be translated into the function of indicating political views, and so rich versus poor becomes elitist versus democratic (the translation is not as simple and direct as that, of course, but let us assume that this is not a problem for the purposes of this chapter).

Where do blue jeans fit in here? Davis quotes Charles Reich from 1971: 'The new clothes (jeans) express profoundly democratic values. There are no distinctions of wealth or status, no elitism; people confront one another shorn of these distinctions' (Davis, 1989: 347). So here, jeans seem to lie entirely on the side of the democratic – they do away with all the dis-tinctions that the theorists of consumption tell us are so vital to an understanding of the world. However, Davis also reproduces this quote from a copy of the *Los Angeles Times Magazine* dating from 1987: 'Karl Lagerfeld for Chanel shapes a classic suit from blue and white denim, $960, with denim bustier, $360 . . . and a denim hat, $400. All at Chanel Boutique, Beverly Hills' (Davis, 1989: 347).

Social distinction of the Veblenian type comes rushing back in here. It is simply impossible to say that jeans are no more than the symbol of democracy and equality. They are caught up in the ever-present tension between elitism and equality, becoming the instrument through which this tension is played out. They are also caught up in the tension between fashion and anti-fashion: sometimes thought of as an anti-fashion item, they nevertheless make it into Chanel boutiques. What might appear the garment of equality embraced by everyone is actually differentiated in all sorts of ways so that social distinctions may still be expressed. On the one hand one finds jeans used to indicate conspicuous poverty through fading and fringing and a consequent contempt for those whose jeans are merely new (the latter lack patina, the functions of which were discussed in Chapter 1), while on the other we find designer jeans signed Yves Saint Laurent or Gloria Vanderbilt used to indicate conspicuous wealth. The reaction to that of course is for some groups to remain hyper-faithful, as Davis says, to the original blue jean – but then those who are really fashionable take this over again. There is no escape, it seems. Items of clothing are the sites at which the various tensions and ambivalences noted by Davis are played out. Veblen talked of only one side of this (indication of wealth), but his contribution to the understanding of at least one important function of dress remains fundamental.

Waste, beauty, ugliness and fashion

Veblen distinguishes between societies in which clothing hardly ever alters and those, such as our own, where dress undergoes quite rapid changes in fashion. He explains this in terms that should be familiar by now: where wealth is indicated through the practices of conspicuous leisure, there will be a tendency for clothing to remain stable. Where wealth is indicated through conspicuous consumption, on the other hand, fashion becomes dominant. Since it is conspicuously wasteful to change one's clothing long before it becomes worn out in any physical sense, rapid change is a clear indicator of one's social standing. Oddly, Veblen seems reluctant to leave matters at that level – oddly, because this approach seems simple, elegant, and with a certain explanatory power. He pulls the notion of aesthetic beauty out of his hat, and sees a curious tension at work between the law of conspicuous waste and the idea of beauty. It is as if we are always searching for the truly beautiful in dress, but never reach it because the law of conspicuous waste demands that we keep changing in order to indicate our wealth. As he writes, 'the norm of conspicuous waste is incompatible with the requirement that dress should be beautiful or becoming. And this antagonism offers an explanation of that restless change in fashion which neither the canon of expensiveness nor that of beauty alone can account for' (Veblen, 1975 [1899]: 176). Veblen's own aesthetic seems to be based on the fact that what is purposeless and wasteful in dress is intrinsically ugly, and that we always eventually see the useless and wasteful aspects of fashionable dress, become aesthetically disgusted, and change fashion – only for the same process to be repeated again and again. He admits that 'The prevailing fashion is felt to be beautiful' (Veblen, 1975 [1899]: 177), but claims that this feeling does not rest on aesthetic grounds. Instead, we find something beautiful because it is expensive and/or wasteful. He posits a native aesthetic sense above and beyond this which eventually gains the upper hand and sees what was once beautiful as now ugly. His dislike of fashion societies is plain in these comments:

> The presumption ... is that the farther the community, especially the wealthy classes of the community, develop in wealth and mobility and in the range of their human contact, the more imperatively will the law of conspicuous waste assert itself in matters of dress, the more will the sense of beauty tend to fall into abeyance or be overborne by the canon of pecuniary reputability, the more rapidly will fashions shift and change, and the more grotesque and intolerable will be the varying styles that successively come into vogue. (Veblen, 1975 [1899]: 178)

There are two sorts of social actors for Veblen: those who believe that something is beautiful because it is wasteful, and those (like himself) who think it is ugly because it is wasteful. Both hold economic theories of aesthetics, but merely with reversed signs. Veblen also thinks that there is an aesthetics somewhere beyond economics, an autonomous 'native aesthetics' that comes into force occasionally. Unfortunately, he seems to have no way of accounting for this, and it is perhaps at this stage that the moralist takes over from the sociologist.

Simmel: dualism and trickle-down theory

Georg Simmel's essay on fashion appeared in 1904, and was an early articulation of what later became known as the 'trickle-down' theory of fashion diffusion. Simmel sees society in general, and not only fashion in particular, in a dualistic way. There is a tension between a principle of generalization and a principle of specialization. As Simmel writes:

> The essential forms of life in the history of our race invariably show the effectiveness of the two antagonistic principles. Each in its sphere attempts to combine the interest in duration, unity, and similarity with that in change, specialization, and peculiarity. It becomes self-evident that there is no institution, no law, no estate of life, which can uniformly satisfy the full demands of the two opposing principles. The only realization of this condition possible for humanity finds expression in constantly changing approximations, in ever retracted attempts and ever revived hopes. (Simmel, 1957 [1904]: 542)

So change arises from the constant tension between the two opposing principles, a tension which is never resolved and never in final balance. Simmel then maps the opposing forces onto two different types of individual. The first type corresponds to the principle of generalization and is incarnated in the imitating individual. He comments that 'Whenever we imitate, we transfer not only the demand for creative activity, but also the responsibility for the action from ourselves to another. Thus the individual is freed from the worry of choosing and appears simply as a creature of the group, as a vessel of the social contents' (Simmel, 1957 [1904]: 542–3). It will be recalled that Tarde made a similar point when he wrote of fashion 'turning out the same sort of person in editions of hundreds of thousands of copies' (Tarde, 1900: 17). So the imitator straight away appears to be a proper member of the group, without having to think too much about it. The opposite to the imitator, and the one who corresponds to the principle of specialization, is called by Simmel the teleological individual. By this he means someone who 'is ever experimenting, always restlessly striving, and [reliant] on his own personal convictions' (Simmel, 1957 [1904]: 543).

It will not surprise the reader to discover that Simmel sees in fashion an excellent example of the result of the tension between these two opposed principles. As he puts it:

> Fashion is the imitation of a given example and satisfies the demand for social adaptation; it leads the individual upon the road which all travel, it furnishes a general condition, which resolves the conduct of every individual into a mere example. At the same time it satisfies in no less degree the need of differentiation, the tendency towards dissimilarity, the desire for change and contrast, on the one hand by a constant change of contents, which gives the fashion of today an individual stamp as opposed to that of yesterday and of to-morrow, on the other hand because fashions differ for different classes – the fashions of the upper stratum of society are never identical with those of the lower; in fact, they are abandoned by the former as soon as the latter prepares to appropriate them. Thus fashion represents nothing more than one of the many forms of life by the aid of which we seek to combine in uniform spheres of activity the tendency towards social equalization with the desire for individual differentiation and change. (Simmel, 1957 [1904]: 543)

Figure 11.2 provides a graphical summary of Simmel's account of fashion.

If we accept that there are fashions for different classes, then we can see that fashion can fulfil the dual function of inclusion and exclusion at exactly the same time: it brings together all those who have adopted the fashion of a particular class or group, and excludes those who have not. Thus fashion produces similarity, union and solidarity within the group and the simultaneous segregation and exclusion of everyone else.

The idea of class is central to Simmel's account of fashion change. If everyone successfully imitated everyone else, then there would be no fashion because we would have a society of uniform appearances. If no one imitated anyone else, then there would be no fashion because we would have a society of unrelated individual appearances. Add class to the equation and we end up with groups trying to look internally the same but

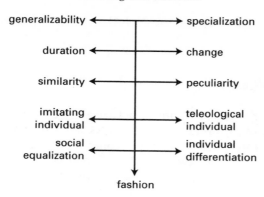

Figure 11.2   *Fashion as the result of tensions between oppositions, 2 (Simmel, 1957 [1904])*

different to other groups. However, this does not necessarily lead to fashion either, for groups may be perfectly happy to display difference and have no interest in looking like other groups. But if groups do want to look like groups above them in a class hierarchy, then we get fashion change in the Simmel sense: 'Just as soon as the lower classes begin to copy their style . . . the upper classes turn away from this style and adopt a new one, which in turn differentiates them from the masses; and thus the game goes merrily on' (Simmel, 1957 [1904]: 545). This of course assumes a society that accepts the legitimacy of the hierarchy and believes that one can ascend that hierarchy in at least some senses by imitating superior classes.

Grant McCracken (1988: 94) points out that the term 'trickle-down' that is often applied to the above theory is really not suitable – if anything, it gives exactly the wrong impression. It is not that fashions trickle down to passively receiving lower groups, it is rather that the latter actively search out and imitate the superior groups, forcing them to change. McCracken suggests that 'chase and flight' might be a more suitable term.

Fred Davis certainly agrees that the trickle-down theory no longer applies to class imitation, for we do not now have 'a hierarchically organized, symbolically consensual prestige structure in society, one in which all groups, classes, and coteries looked . . . in the same direction for cues for what was to be thought beautiful, acceptable, and fashionable . . . students of fashion diffusion in today's world claim that a condition of polycentrism prevails' (Davis, 1992: 108). Society is much more fragmented into groups, and the fragmentation is not only along class lines – there is no consensual view of the way things are supposed to be done, and hence Simmel would appear to have limited use. Davis further criticizes the Simmel approach for paying no attention whatsoever to the various agencies that shape the fashion process: 'competition among designers and fashion centers . . . the fashion choices of buyers for big . . . department stores . . . the fashion press' (Davis, 1992: 114) and so on. Davis considers some of these agencies in his book

Fashion, Culture and Identity, to which the reader is referred for further details.

Clothing as a language

One of the major twentieth-century approaches to clothing has been to see it as a language of its own, organized in a formal way and using a definite grammar and syntax. The first major contribution here came from the Russian folklorist Petr Bogatyrev, who attempted to examine 'the total structural interrelationship of the functions which the individual costume serves' (Bogatyrev, 1971 [1937]: 34). He recognizes four basic costume types in his example of Moravian Slovakia: everyday, holiday, ceremonial and ritual costumes. Each of these possesses a number of functions: practical, aesthetic, regionalistic, ceremonial, holiday, ritual and nationalistic, and they are ordered in a different hierarchy of importance according to the basic costume type. Everyday costume, for example, has practicality as the most important function, followed by social status or class identification, then aesthetic and then regionalistic functions. At the other extreme we find the ritual costume, which has a ranking order of ritual, holiday, aesthetic, nationalistic or regionalistic, social status or class identification and, bringing up the rear, the practical function. Social status includes occupation, age, religious affiliation and marital status. Costume indicates each of these through a combination of particular elements: 'one item may have different functions, depending on which other items are combined with it' (Bogatyrev, 1971 [1937]: 42). For example, 'the *vonica* (an elaborate type of nosegay) ... serves to designate either a bridegroom or an army recruit' (Bogatyrev, 1971 [1937]: 41) depending upon the trousers worn with it.

Bogatyrev is the first to break down costume into a number of different elements, and to understand the way in which costume communicates socially through certain combinations of these elements. That is, he proposes the existence of a sort of grammar of costume.

Werner Enninger (1984) builds directly on Bogatyrev in his work on Old Order Amish costume. He maps particular combinations of above-the-waist male dress onto bio-social status (his terminology) and social events (Figure 11.3). He distinguishes lower, middle and upper layers of clothing as initial units, and shows that the first of these can be filled by two alternative elements (different types of shirt), the second – which can be unfilled – also by two (waistcoats [vests] of different colours), and the third by five (differently coloured jackets and coats) – it, too, can remain unfilled. Specific combinations of elements and layers indicate gender, age, minister/non-minister *and* social event: everyday, travel/shopping, visiting, on way to service, at church service. So dress, through quite a precise combination of elements, can indicate all the main characteristics and moments of Amish society.

Sahlins applies some very similar ideas in his sketch of the American clothing system:

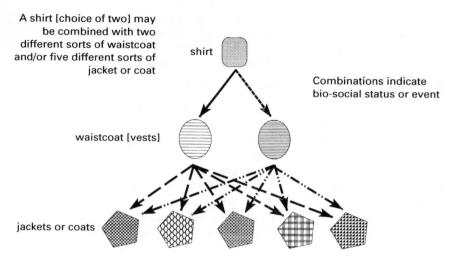

A shirt [choice of two] may be combined with two different sorts of waistcoat and/or five different sorts of jacket or coat

shirt

Combinations indicate bio-social status or event

waistcoat [vests]

jackets or coats

Note: Colours have been replaced by patterns for black and white reproduction

Figure 11.3   *Amish male dress – a semiotic analysis* *(Enninger, 1984)*

The outfit as a whole makes a statement, developed out of the particular arrange-ment of garment parts and by contrast to other total outfits. Again there is a logic of the parts, whose meanings are developed differentially by comparison at this level, in a Saussurean way: as, for example, the value of women's slacks is simul-taneously determined by opposition to other garments of that locus, such as skirts or men's pants, as well as by contrast to other examples of the same class (slacks) that differ in color, pattern, or whatever. (Sahlins, 1976: 179–80)

So contrast and difference are essential to the meaning of dress, just as they are to the meaning of language. At a greater level of detail, Sahlins tries to discover the constituent units composing the discourse of dress, that is, how elementary physical contrasts relate to social meanings. Blue collar indicat-ing manual labour and white collar indicating bureaucratic labour is one rather idealized instance. If we take the case of gender differences, we see that sleeves can be mapped onto one or the other gender depending upon whether they are more tailored and full length (masculine) or looser and three-quarter length or less (feminine), and a jacket displays gender through buttoning along the right- or left-hand side.

The difference between work and leisure is matched with differences between various sorts of clothing, and Sahlins suggests that the elementary contrast operating here is between Veblen's terms of ceremonial (leisure) and workmanship (work). For example, if we divide work into bureaucratic and manual, the more ceremonial dress will be on the side of the bureau-cratic and the more work-style dress will be on the side of the manual. If we look at bureaucratic dress as a class, we again find the distinction at work, and a new differentiation between executive (more ceremonial) and white collar (work dress) takes place within the overall category 'bureaucratic', which itself is of course a ceremonial category when compared with manual work (Sahlins, 1976: 187–8). In sum, clothing for Sahlins is something that can be read in a systematic way to reveal the important social differentiations of a given society – it is a sort of language, complete with elementary constituent units and rules of combination.

Grant McCracken (1988: 62–6) argues *against* the usefulness of the idea of clothing as a language. Putting it simply, his reasoning is based on the idea that language proper allows a great deal of combinatorial freedom, a freedom that produces discourses that can flow on and on. We may have to follow very rigid rules of grammar when writing clauses or sentences, but we become much freer when we start putting sentences together. At the highest level, we can use language to say what we like, although at the lowest level we are still bound by relatively inflexible rules. But there is not the same combinatorial freedom with clothing. McCracken carried out a number of interviews with people and asked them to interpret the meaning of various outfits. He discovered that once the wearers began to combine things with the same freedom as language allows, they produced not discourse but confusion. His informants could not figure out what the outfits meant: they worked with pre-set meanings, and new combinations were just puzzles. Where clothing tends to be linked to relatively fixed meanings, language can generate all sorts of new ones as it goes along – if language is an open code, clothing is a closed one. So although we may still say that clothing communicates, for McCracken it does not communicate in quite the same way as language.

The increase in interpretative uncertainties

We know that clothes can 'make' class, gender, age, occupation, and so on. It has been argued, however, that matters are not as straightforward as that. Writing from Belgium, Devleeshouwer (1977: 173, 175) maintains that appearances have become less precise and more confusing since the First World War: if one considers a working-class crowd of the immediate pre-war years one can spot almost immediately the profession of each of its members, whereas a post-war crowd indicates only the general status of membership of the working class.

By the 1970s, it became difficult to tell class from class due to a much more subtle organization of difference. Featherstone (1991a: 17) maintains that the 'ever-changing flow of commodities mak[es] the problem of reading the status or rank of the bearer of the commodities more complex' and that the 'oversupply and rapid circulation of symbolic goods and consumer commodities have the danger of threatening the readability of goods used as signs of social status' (1991a: 19). Davis (1985: 17) writes that clothing in

Western society is 'much more given to "undercoding" than to precision and explicitness'. Furthermore, 'what some combination of clothes or a certain style emphasis "means" will vary tremendously depending upon the identity of the wearer, the occasion, the place, the company, and even something as vague and transient as the wearer's and the viewer's moods' (Davis, 1985: 17). The code of Western clothing is certainly 'more ambiguous and semantically indeterminate' (Davis, 1989: 338) than that of language. Now this would seem to promise – or threaten – a confusing proliferation of clothing discourses: a postmodern world where signifier is detached from signified and icons are meaningless (Evans and Thornton, 1989: 75), and society would no longer contain fixed status groups recognizable by their choice of symbolic goods such as dress (Featherstone, 1991a: 83). Some limits to this profusion may nevertheless be traced through a consideration of work that has used photographs to provoke interpretations of clothing.

In her sample, Duflos-Priot (1981) found that the presumed occupation of the photographed person was massively predominant in interpretation, considerably outweighing all other factors. Social class took on meaning only in association with this. A definite system seemed to underlie interpretations, with individuals often read in terms of closeness to or distance from a particular type such as 'manager' or 'worker'. However, this system tended to break down at one point: interpretations of young people. Social classes or occupations were here not distinguished; instead simply a generation was seen. Views of the young themselves do not appear to have been canvassed in this piece of research.

Herpin (1984) showed four photos each of a man and a woman to a sample of 83. His analysis of the responses delimits three separate vocabularies used to account for dress: social status, daily activities, and style and personal taste. The first is used to refer to occupation and economic standing; the second indicates the activity about to be undertaken, such as clothing for 'pottering about' or for 'relaxing'; and the third depicts clothing in terms of specific styles, such as 'classical' or 'sporty', or more diffusely as, for example, 'elegant', 'distinguished', 'not bad', 'tasteless'. Social status was not predominant in the interpretations: the second and, especially, the third vocabularies were more frequently drawn upon by the sample. Nevertheless, this suggests that there is not an unlimited proliferation of interpretations: occupation and/or class is still drawn upon more or less insistently, age is an equally perennial interest, while Herpin's second vocabulary could perhaps be understood as the extension of occupational dress – which is a form of dressing for a specific activity – into the areas of home and leisure. His third may refer to an individual's competence, or lack of it, in dressing appropriately for a social world composed of occupations, classes, ages, activities and bodies.

Whether clothing is undercoded or not, interpretations are still made – although these will vary in confidence depending on the level of coding as seen from the viewpoint on the interpreter. Take the case of the incapacity of Duflos-Priot's (1981) sample to see anything more informative than an indication of age group in young people's clothing. Clothing here would appear to be both undercoded and 'overcoded' at the same time: under-coded because of the lack of trustworthy fine discriminations such as class or occupational distinctions, yet overcoded because unambiguously indi-cating age group. Work on young people suggests that, unsurprisingly, they see their own clothing in quite a heavily coded way. Although they may be 'opaque to the dominant culture' (Evans and Thornton, 1989: 75), Willis (1990: 88) remarks that 'Young people are very adept at the symbolic work of developing their own styles and also at "reading off" and decoding the dress styles of others and relating them to musical, political and social orien-tations.'

If clothing is heavily coded, it will be possible to make trustworthy, fine distinctions among all the relevant categories. If lightly coded, this will not be possible. In practice, interpretation of clothing is mixed: some social attributes appear overcoded and some undercoded, and this will vary according to the circumstances mentioned above by Davis (1985: 17). The more social discriminations can be coded trustworthily in clothing, the closer the latter comes to being society's visible account of itself: 'our costume' in Bogatyrev's phrase (1971 [1937]: 95–8).

Perhaps more than any other element of consumer culture, clothing is the most efficient at announcing one's status to the world. At a broad level, anyone will be able to read some useful social information from dress. At a narrower level, others will be able to read more complex messages from the same items. The street theatre of dress has not one audience, but many.

12
Conclusion

Goods, continuity and change

Grant McCracken (1988: 131) points out that Western society is an 'ethnographic oddity' in the sense that it is undergoing continual change while traditional societies were relatively stable. But does not continual change and transformation threaten to make everything fall apart? Where is the continuity in such permanent transformation? McCracken suggests that consumer goods play a large role in both change and in surviving that change. Goods in this perspective are agents *both* of continuity and of change. Let us begin by taking the case of goods as an instrument of continuity.

The reader may recall from Chapter 2 that Douglas and Isherwood (1979) maintained that one of the chief functions of goods was to stop the drift of meanings – to pin down meaning for a time, and allow us to see how the social world was ordered in an at least temporarily stable manner. Goods, then, can be seen as a more or less reliable map of social reality. The basic cultural categories of a society are made visible in concrete ways. For Sahlins (1976), for example, the differences between women and men were stabilized through the particular cut, line, material or texture of a garment, while Goffman's account of advertisements showed how particular body postures and placings marked gender belonging. Much of the research on class distinction also works on the premise that class status can be indicated through consumer goods, even if there is a class struggle going on that makes certain goods only temporary refuges of fixed meaning. Bourdieu's work (1984 [1979]) is a good example of this. McCracken suggests that goods do not merely indicate the categories of culture in a given society – they also act to persuade us that this is the way things naturally are.

Perhaps an instance of this was Adrian Forty's (1986) comparison of the maps of the London underground. The old one showed the stations in their correct geographical locations, and so it was possible to make realistic estimates of the time it would take to travel from A to B, but the new maps were schematic, and replaced geography with an abstract model: London escaped from its geography, and was turned into the plan of a system, where distance was abolished and only interconnections counted as real. This new map produced quite a different mental picture of the city, persuading Londoners and visitors that this was what London was really like. Now the map can stand in as a perfectly persuasive account of 'London', even though it is quite fictitious and downright misleading when one is thinking in geographical terms. The Bon Marché map of monuments showing Paris as represented by the department store is another example of the power of a good – here, a map – to persuade us of important categories. The suit worn by many men may also serve to persuade us of the apparently natural authority held by them, whereas if we saw the same bodies in casual dress we might not be at all persuaded. It is perhaps not too much to assert that authority lies in a particular piece of cloth here. In this sense, goods can work in a very conservative way – they hold things in place. They may also recuperate protest, and transform the potentially destabilizing into one more piece of evidence of continuity. Every time someone launches an attack on art or literature or fashion, we may be sure that art, literature or fashion will soon embrace these attacks, assimilate them, and turn them out as yet more glorious examples of art or literature or fashion.

But goods for McCracken are not just agents of continuity. They are also vehicles of change in two different capacities. The first capacity refers to the novel and innovative uses of cultural categories: one experiments with existing categories and produces something new. For example, a group may want to create a new definition for itself 'and a revision of the cultural category to which it belongs . . . Goods are a means with which the group can rethink itself' (McCracken, G., 1988: 135). A common pattern is for a group to throw over the old goods with which it is associated and then begin to take over the goods of other groups. Trickle-down theory, when understood as 'chase and flight', is one possible example of this. His example is that of radical feminism in the 1960s, which dissociated itself from conventional female clothing and its message of conventional gender roles, and looked around for something more suitable, which it discovered in working-class male attire. The second capacity can be seen as a way of publicizing the change – the bulletin board and the billboard of goods, to use McCracken's terms. Members of a group indicate first to each other what the appropriate goods are for the particular status they are claiming. Clearly, this is especially necessary in the early stages of group definition, when one knows that distinctive goods are needed but is not sure which goods are the most appropriate. Once some sort of consensus grows up, the goods act as a billboard to proclaim group identity and ideas to the general public: now the group is known by its goods, and the general public will react in various ways, thus reinforcing the definition of the group (especially if the reactions are negative). In the end, then,

> the object-code serves as a means by which a society both encourages and endures change. It helps social groups establish alternative ways of seeing themselves that are outside of and contrary to existing cultural definitions. But it also serves to help a society incorporate these changes into the existing cultural framework and to diffuse their destabilizing potential. (McCracken, G., 1988: 137)

The confusing categories of postmodernism

It has been argued that the present state of society is describable as postmodernist. This is relevant to the sociology of consumption, for it suggests that there has been a fundamental shift in the ways in which goods are used symbolically. Under modernism, there was a relatively fixed relationship between class belonging and the consumer goods used to indicate this belonging. Under postmodernism, this fixity has become loosened, and indication of class has been replaced by a more individualistic indication of lifestyle, or even by temporary groupings of people beyond individualism – what Maffesoli (1996 [1988]) calls 'tribes'. Goods have to some extent been freed from their symbolic moorings and have begun to drift about the world of signs, ready to be used by various groups in various ways. Instead of the coherent collection of cultural practices that characterized modernism, we get a more eclectic grouping – goods and practices become things to be played with for a while, then ditched as we move to something else. They are no longer reliable badges of our social status. The old modernist distinction between high and low culture, which certainly served to keep classes in their places, is frittered away as universities give courses on the *œuvre* of a popular singer or a best-selling author, while discs by classical tenors, Gregorian chanters and hitherto little-known Polish composers make it onto the popular hit lists. The intellectual classes (the masculine part anyway) no longer lose caste by displaying an interest in working-class games such as soccer or rugby league, and some even stoop so low as to run courses on the sociology of consumption. Clearly a sign of the end of modernist civilization.

For Mike Featherstone (1991a), the postmodern world is very much one where culture, broadly understood, plays the major role. Instead of consuming the goods themselves, we consume the meanings of goods as constructed through advertising and display (although I think we have been doing that ever since the department store). Instead of going to the museum to receive instruction in high culture, we go to touch, to see, and to experience. If in the old museum the instruction was 'Do Not Touch', the new museum encourages hands-on experiences. This demystifies the temples of culture into places where child-like desires are given full rein: the old Kantian aesthetic is overturned in its sacred sites and is replaced by an anti-Kantian aesthetic. Anyone who has had lunch at Sydney's Powerhouse Museum since about the middle of 1994 will know that the restaurant has been completely redecorated – walls and ceiling included – by Ken Done and his associates. This seems to be a good example of the anti-Kantian aesthetic of the immediately sensual, appreciable by relatively untutored eyes – it is probably very popular with children, who would form a large part of the Powerhouse market anyway.

For Featherstone, very many galleries and museums are moving in this more populist direction, where austere instruction in the mysteries of high culture is replaced by, in his words, 'the spectacular, the popular, the pleasurable and the immediately accessible' (Featherstone, 1991a: 97). The discipline and difficulty of *discursive* culture is replaced by the immediacy of *spectacular and sensual* culture, a development understood by Maffesoli (1996 [1988]: 31) as 'the passage from the proletariat as an active historical subject to the masses freed of responsibility for the future'. Here, the loss of a future project means that there is no reason to defer anything in the interests of a greater aim lying somewhere (far) down the road, nor is there any need to learn the complex discursive culture that is essential for future planning. Time loses the notion of the future to an immediate present, and consequently the past also loses its old bourgeois-Marxian character as progress. This makes it possible to play indiscriminately with past styles, as the past shorn of forward direction also falls into the realm of the present. Hence we have 'that often playful and ironic jumbling and fusing of traditions, that many take as typical of postmodernism in general' (Kumar, 1995: 106). The past is sucked into the present, which then lays out what was once diachronically separated on a single synchronic plane.

Furthermore, discursive culture demands a long and relatively difficult apprenticeship, while spectacular and sensual culture is much easier to apprehend immediately and is more difficult to restrict to elite classes. It becomes more and more difficult to draw boundaries between art and everyday life, so we can plausibly begin to claim that everyday life *is* art, and that we are artists of life. This stance clearly legitimizes the great use of and experimentation with all sorts of consumer goods – instead of doing something boring like indicating our wealth, they indicate our artistic sensibilities. Of course, we need to be relatively well-off in order to think and perform like this in the first place, so wealth indication is by no means as unimportant as one might wish to make out. After all, it is sometimes said that only the rich can truly afford the luxury of saying that money does not matter.

But is it really the case that everyone in consumer societies lives postmodernistically? Featherstone reminds us that 'we need to ask the stark sociological questions about not only where the postmodern lifestyles take place; but how many people from which range of groups participate and for how long' (1991a: 105). We always need to be on guard against a tendency to assume that what seems most characteristic of an era is the same as what most people think, experience or do – very frequently, it is only a tiny minority who engage in practices that end up being interpreted as 'typical' of the time or place. There may have been very few hippies, punks or Vietnam protesters, but looking back we think that everyone must have been a hippie, a punk or a Vietnam protester – a tendency gratefully exploited by those who would like to give the impression that they were indeed daring members of those categories in the past. In post-Second World War France many became retrospective members of the Resistance, and almost nobody admits to having supported a recently overthrown leader. Some measure of scepticism comes in useful in sociological analyses. Featherstone sees postmodern lifestyle as the plaything of the new middle class and of those cities that have managed to build up a large reserve of cultural capital (like Paris or London) or have managed to repackage themselves for the tourist gaze (which seems to be almost everywhere at this stage).

Deindustrialization and consequent gentrification of inner city areas in Europe and America brings back wealth, display and consumption to the streets of the centre, while the poor who used to live there are pushed out to other areas. Those who are not fully up to the game of play and display are shoved out of sight – and consequently out of the mind of cultural commentators. The people who move into the old areas are precisely the ones who value display as a way of life and who have the financial means to indulge in it (even if they lack traditional high cultural capital – rather, it is because of this lack that they play with appearances: it is all they can handle).

Featherstone comments that:

> This process of increased segregation as the middle classes move back into the central areas is also symbolized in the postmodern architecture with towers, moats and drawbridges which create defensible privatized spaces free from the unemployed, the poor, rebellious youth, and other residues of the 'dangerous classes'. It creates what David Harvey has called 'voodoo cities' in which the postmodern facade of cultural redevelopment can be seen as a carnival mask which covers the decline of everything else. (Featherstone, 1991a: 107)

Shopping centres and malls are similar: both Chaney (1990: 49) and Langman (1992: 48) remark upon the highly controlled nature of such enclosed spaces, and Shields (1992: 5) writes of the 'new marginals being created from those denied access, based on the flimsiest of judgements and reasoning, by security guards (private armies who ensure retailers conform and shoppers "behave")'. In such ways is contemporary urban space made safe for postmodernism. Classification and hierarchy are by no means abolished – they are merely made to disappear discreetly out of sight.

But perhaps the era of shopping centres and malls is already passé, taking the sociologist-*flâneur* with it. Whether one sees such places as overwhelmingly lower middle class (Chaney, 1994: 175, writing on Britain) or as patronized by a wide cross-section of society (Shields, 1992: 5, writing on North America), they are at least actually-existing spaces where people may gather as family, friends, Maffesolian 'tribes' or simply as anonymous crowds. The future may hold something else, to judge by the following advertisement dating from August 1996:

> The MEGAMALL Lifestyle Browser™ is Australia's first Virtual Reality Shopping Centre on CD ROM for Windows, Windows 95 and Macintosh.
> Shopping in MEGAMALL™ is just like a trip to your local department store – without all the parking hassles.
> See the latest ranges from retailers such as David Jones, Katies, Innovations and many more. If you see anything you like – have it delivered to your home. Try your luck in the Casino playing Black Jack, Pokies and Roulette. Hear the latest music, see the latest video's [*sic*] – all from the comfort of your own home.

At a (key)stroke, the shift from an actually-existing to a virtually-existing space abolishes the potentially exciting and troublesome public gatherings of the strolling consumer, renders unnecessary the building of centres and malls (thus saving retail, infrastructural and security costs), and keeps people safely chained to their computer terminals. The virtual mall promises almost all that the real mall can deliver, and at far lower costs to the purveyors of goods and services: the latest from major retailers, spaces for play, the thrill of gambling, opportunities to hear and see the most recent products of the music and video industries. Missing, of course, is the social dimension of the public spaces in which embodied consumers actually, if temporarily, dwell. Shopping places have been sites where people met one another ever since the first market, and many more things happened than buying and selling. Indeed, Gottdiener (1995: 83) suggests that, given the dangers of less regulated public spaces, the mall may have become the principal site of social communion for many people living in the metropolitan areas of the United States. One could easily spend hours in a mall or shopping centre without actually purchasing anything at all, one French study reporting that 'one-third of people exiting from suburban Paris shopping malls had made no purchase' (Shields, 1992: 10). The virtual mall promises an end to all this, although the non-shopping elements of shopping may yet turn virtual malls into actual white elephants. The mall-strolling sociologist may not be out of a job just yet.

The usefulness of consumer goods in indicating continuity and change, as McCracken sees it, suggests that they will be with us for a long time, as will the symbolic struggles that take place around such goods. Saunders (1986: 347) argues that consumption is so important because it, and not production, is the area that allows people to extend control over their lives. Enormous parts of the economy depend upon consumerism, and capitalism has thus far been very successful both in extending its reach and in continually reinventing itself and overcoming its crises, but there can be no way of telling how long this will last. Consumers are the perfect creatures of capitalism, and consumer movements provide some of the checks and balances that such an anarchic system needs. Leisure services may become more important than goods in the system, as they may be more expandable than goods. This reverses the position of the early part of the twentieth century when, according to Cross (1993: 5), 'consumer culture emerged in the often unacknowledged social decision to direct industrial innovation toward producing unlimited quantities of goods rather than leisure'. The leisure industry as such was barely developed then, but that is no longer the case. Perhaps trade in cultural goods and information may eventually supply the dynamic, as capitalism lurches into yet another stage. But futurology is the most inexact of sciences.

References

Allport, Floyd Henry (1924) *Social Psychology*. Boston: Houghton Mifflin. Quoted in Ewen (1976).

Althusser, Louis (1971 [1970]) 'Ideology and Ideological State Apparatuses', in *Lenin and Philosophy and Other Essays*, translated by Ben Brewster. London: New Left Books. pp. 121–73.

Australian Customs Service (1992) *Customs Information for Travellers*. No place of publication indicated.

Australian Home Beautiful/Your Garden 1996 Annual (1995). Melbourne: Pacific Publications.

Australian Women's Weekly (1993). Sydney: Australian Consolidated Press. May.

Ballaster, Ros, Beetham, Margaret, Frazer, Elizabeth and Hebron, Sandra (1991) *Women's Worlds. Ideology, Femininity and the Woman's Magazine*. Basingstoke: Macmillan.

Barth, G. (1980) *City People*. New York and Oxford: Oxford University Press. Quoted in Laermans (1993).

Barthes, Roland (1967 [1964]) 'The Diseases of Costume', *Partisan Review*, 34, October: 89–97.

Barthes, Roland (1989 [1957]) *Mythologies*. London: Paladin.

Baudrillard, Jean (1988 [1970]) 'Consumer Society', in *Selected Writings*, edited by Mark Poster. Cambridge: Polity Press. pp. 29–56.

Baudrillard, Jean (1990 [1968]) 'Subjective Discourse or the Non-Functional System of Objects', in *Revenge of the Crystal. Selected Writings on the Modern Object and its Destiny, 1968–1983*, edited and translated by Paul Foss and Julian Pefanis. London: Pluto Press. pp. 35–61.

Bauman, Zygmunt (1982) *Memories of Class. The Pre-History and After-Life of Class*. London: Routledge & Kegan Paul.

Bocuse, Paul (1988 [1976]) *The Cuisine of Paul Bocuse*, translated by Colette Rossant and Lorraine Davis. London: Grafton Books.

Bogatyrev, Petr (1971 [1937]) *The Functions of Folk Costume in Moravian Slovakia*, translated by Richard G. Crum. The Hague: Mouton.

Bohannon, Paul (1959) 'The Impact of Money on an African Subsistence Economy', *Journal of Economic History*, 19: 491–503. Quoted in Kopytoff (1986).

Bonney, Bill and Wilson, Helen (1983) *Australia's Commercial Media*. South Melbourne: Macmillan.

Boorstin, Daniel (1961) *The Image: A Guide to Pseudo-Events in America*. New York: Harper & Row. Quoted in MacCannell (1973).

Bourdieu, Pierre (1984 [1979]) *Distinction. A Social Critique of the Judgement of Taste*, translated by Richard Nice. London: Routledge & Kegan Paul.

Braun, Friederike (1988) *Terms of Address. Problems of Patterns and Usage in Various Languages and Cultures*. Berlin, New York, Amsterdam: Mouton de Gruyter.

Brown, Roger and Gilman, Albert (1960) 'The Pronouns of Power and Solidarity', in Thomas A. Sebeok (ed.) *Style in Language*. Cambridge, Mass.: MIT Press. pp. 253–76.

Campbell, Colin (1983) 'Romanticism and The Consumer Ethic: Intimations of a Weber-style Thesis', *Sociological Analysis*, 44(4): 279–96.

Campbell, Colin (1987) *The Romantic Ethic and the Spirit of Modern Consumerism*. Oxford: Basil Blackwell.

Castles, Ian (1992) *Social Indicators Australia 5*. Canberra: Australian Bureau of Statistics.

Chaney, David (1983) 'The Department Store as a Cultural Form', *Theory, Culture & Society*, 1(3): 22–31.

Chaney, David (1990) 'Subtopia in Gateshead: The Metro-Centre as a Cultural Form', *Theory, Culture & Society*, 7(4): 49–68.

184   *The Sociology of Consumption*

Chaney, David (1994) *The Cultural Turn. Scene-setting Essays on Contemporary Cultural History*. London: Routledge.

Charles, Nicola and Kerr, Marion (1987) 'Just the Way It Is: Gender and Age Differences in Family Food Consumption', in Julia Brannen and Gail Wilson (eds), *Give and Take in Families. Studies in Resource Distribution*. London: Allen & Unwin. pp. 155–74.

Corbin, Alain (1994 [1982]) *The Foul and the Fragrant. Odour and the Social Imagination*. London: Picador.

Corrigan, Peter (1989) 'Gender and the Gift: The Case of the Family Clothing Economy', *Sociology*, 23(4): 513–34.

Cross, Gary (1993) *Time and Money. The Making of Consumer Culture*. London: Routledge.

Csikszentmihalyi, Mihaly and Rochberg-Halton, Eugene (1981) *The Meaning of Things. Domestic Symbols and the Self*. Cambridge: Cambridge University Press.

Culler, Jonathan (1981) 'Semiotics of Tourism', *American Journal of Semiotics*, 1: 127–40. Quoted in Urry (1990).

Davis, Fred (1985) 'Clothing and Fashion as Communication', in Michael R. Solomon (ed.) *The Psychology of Fashion*. Lexington, Mass.: D.C. Heath. pp. 15–27.

Davis, Fred (1989) 'Of Maids' Uniforms and Blue Jeans: The Drama of Status Ambivalences in Clothing and Fashion', *Qualitative Sociology*, 12(4): 337–55.

Davis, Fred (1992) *Fashion, Culture and Identity*. Chicago: University of Chicago Press.

Devleeshouwer, Robert (1977) 'Costume et société', *Revue de l'Institut de Sociologie*, 2: 167–85.

Diderot, Denis (1971 [1769]) 'Regrets sur ma vieille robe de chambre', in *Oeuvres Complètes*. Volume VIII. Paris: le Club Français du Livre. pp. 7–13.

Douglas, Mary and Isherwood, Baron (1979) *The World of Goods. Towards an Anthropology of Consumption*. London: Allen Lane.

Duflos-Priot, Marie-Thérèse (1981) 'L'Apparence individuelle et la représentation de la réalité humaine et des classes sociales', *Cahiers Internationaux de Sociologie*, 70: 63–84.

Durkheim, Emile (1984 [1893]) *The Division of Labour in Society*, translated by W.D. Halls. Basingstoke: Macmillan.

Dyer, Gillian (1988 [1982]) *Advertising as Communication*. London: Routledge.

Elias, Norbert (1994 [1939]) *The Civilizing Process*, translated by Edmund Jephcott. Oxford: Blackwell.

Enninger, Werner (1984) 'Inferencing Social Structure and Social Processes from Nonverbal Behavior', *American Journal of Semiotics*, 3(2): 77–96.

Ervin-Tripp, Susan (1986 [1972]) 'On Sociolinguistic Rules: Alternation and Co-Occurrence', in John J. Gumperz and Dell Hymes (eds) *Directions in Sociolinguistics. The Ethnography of Communication*. New edition with corrections and additions. Oxford: Basil Blackwell. pp. 213–50.

Evans, Caroline and Thornton, Minna (1989) *Women and Fashion*. London: Quartet Books.

Evans-Pritchard, E.E. (1940) 'The Nuer', in *The Political Institutions of a Nilotic People*. Oxford: Clarendon Press. Quoted in Douglas and Isherwood (1979). pp. 17–19.

Ewen, Stuart (1976) *Captains of Consciousness. Advertising and the Social Roots of the Consumer Culture*. New York: McGraw-Hill.

Falk, Pasi (1994) *The Consuming Body*. London: Sage.

Featherstone, Mike (1991a) *Consumer Culture & Postmodernism*. London: Sage.

Featherstone, Mike (1991b [1982]) 'The Body in Consumer Culture', in Mike Featherstone, Mike Hepworth and Bryan S. Turner (eds) *The Body. Social Process and Cultural Theory*. London: Sage. pp. 170–96.

Federal Bureau of Consumer Affairs (1993) *Consumer Power. A Guide to Consumer Affairs in Australia*. Canberra: Australian Government Publishing Service.

Fiddes, Nick (1991) *Meat. A Natural Symbol*. London: Routledge.

Finkelstein, Joanne (1991) *The Fashioned Self*. Cambridge and Oxford: Polity Press in association with Basil Blackwell.

Forty, Adrian (1986) *Objects of Desire. Design and Society since 1750*. London: Thames & Hudson.

Foucault, Michel (1977 [1975]) *Discipline and Punish: The Birth of the Prison*, translated by Alan Sheridan. Harmondsworth: Penguin.

Frazer, Elizabeth (1987) 'Teenage Girls Reading *Jackie*', *Media, Culture & Society*, 9(4): 407–25.

Goffman, Erving (1972 [1959]) *The Presentation of Self in Everyday Life*. Harmondsworth: Penguin.

Goffman, Erving (1979 [1976]) *Gender Advertisements*. London: Macmillan.

Goldman, Robert (1987) 'Marketing Fragrances: Advertising and the Production of Commodity Signs', *Theory, Culture & Society*, 4(4): 691–725.

Goldman, Robert (1992) *Reading Ads Socially*. London: Routledge.

Gottdiener, M. (1995) *Postmodern Semiotics. Material Culture and the Forms of Postmodern Life*. Oxford: Blackwell.

Hermes, Joke (1995) *Reading Women's Magazines. An Analysis of Everyday Media Use*. Cambridge and Oxford: Polity Press in association with Basil Blackwell.

Herpin, Nicolas (1984) 'Comment les gens qualifient-ils les tenues vestimentaires?', *Economie et Statistique*, 168: 37–44.

Home Decorator (1966) No. 4, Summer. Alexandria, NSW: Federal Publishing Company.

Homes and Living Renovations (1996). Perth, WA: HB Management.

Huie, Jaqueline (1994) 'An Introduction to Untourism', in Suzanne Baker, *The UnTourist Guide to Tasmania*. Balmain, NSW: The UnTourist Company Pty Ltd. pp. 2–4.

Kingston, Beverley (1994) *Basket, Bag and Trolley. A History of Shopping in Australia*. Melbourne: Oxford University Press.

Kitchens and Bathrooms Quarterly (n.d.) Vol. 2 No. 3. North Ryde, NSW: Universal Magazines.

Kopytoff, Igor (1986) 'The Cultural Biography of Things: Commoditization as Process', in Arjun Appadurai (ed.) *The Social Life of Things. Commodities in Cultural Perspective*. Cambridge: Cambridge University Press. pp. 64–91.

Kumar, Krishan (1995) *From Post-Industrial to Post-Modern Society. New Theories of the Contemporary World*. Oxford: Basil Blackwell.

Laermans, Rudi (1993) 'Learning to Consume: Early Department Stores and the Shaping of the Modern Consumer Culture (1860–1914)', *Theory, Culture & Society*, 10(4): 79–102.

Langman, Lauren (1992) 'Neon Cages. Shopping for Subjectivity', in Rob Shields (ed.) *Lifestyle Shopping. The Subject of Consumption*. London: Routledge. pp. 40–82.

Lee, David and Newby, Howard (1983) *The Problem of Sociology. An Introduction to the Discipline*. London: Hutchinson.

Lifestyle Yearbook (1996). Alexandria, NSW: Federal Publishing Company.

Löfgren, Orvar (1994) 'Consuming Interests', in Jonathan Friedman (ed.) *Consumption and Identity*. Chur, Switzerland: Harwood Academic Publishers. pp. 47–70.

Loftie, W.J. (1879) *A Plea for Art in the Home*, London. Quoted in Forty (1986).

Lotze, Hermann (1885) *Microcosmus. An Essay Concerning Man and his Relation to the World*, Volume I, translated by Elizabeth Hamilton and E.E. Constance Jones. Edinburgh: T. & T. Clark.

MacCannell, Dean (1973) 'Staged Authenticity: Arrangements of Social Space in Tourist Settings', *American Journal of Sociology*, 79(3): 589–603.

MacCannell, Dean (1976) *The Tourist. A New Theory of the Leisure Class*. New York: Schocken Books.

McClintock, H.F. (1943) *Old Irish and Highland Dress, with Notes on that of the Isle of Man*. Dundalk: Dundalgan Press.

McCracken, Ellen (1993) *Decoding Women's Magazines. From 'Mademoiselle' to 'Ms.'*. Basingstoke: Macmillan.

McCracken, Grant (1988) *Culture and Consumption. New Approaches to the Symbolic Character of Consumer Goods and Activities*. Bloomington: Indiana University Press.

McKendrick, Neil, Brewer, John and Plumb, J.H. (1982) *The Birth of a Consumer Society. The Commercialization of Eighteenth-century England*. London: Europa Publications.

Maffesoli, Michel (1996 [1988]) *The Time of the Tribes. The Decline of Individualism in Mass Society*, translated by Don Smith. London: Sage.

Mandrou, R. (1961) *Introduction to Modern France, 1500–1600.* London: Arnold. Quoted in Mennell (1987).

Marchand, Roland (1985) *Advertising the American Dream. Making Way for Modernity, 1920-1940.* Berkeley: University of California Press.

Marx, Karl (1974 [1867]) *Capital. A Critical Analysis of Capitalist Production*, Volume I, translated from the third German edition by Samuel Moore and Edward Aveling and edited by Frederick Engels. London: Lawrence & Wishart.

Marx, Karl (1975 [1844]) 'Economic and Philosophical Manuscripts', in *Early Writings*, translated by Rodney Livingstone and Gregor Benton. Harmondsworth: Penguin in association with *New Left Review*. pp. 279–400.

Mauss, Marcel (1979 [1936]) 'Body Techniques', in *Sociology and Psychology*, translated by Ben Brewster. London: Routledge & Kegan Paul. pp. 95–123.

Mennell, Stephen (1985) *All Manners of Food. Eating and Taste in England and France from the Middle Ages to the Present.* Oxford: Basil Blackwell.

Mennell, Stephen (1987) 'On The Civilizing of Appetite', *Theory, Culture & Society*, 4(2–3): 373–403.

Miller, Daniel (1987) *Material Culture and Mass Consumption.* Oxford: Basil Blackwell.

Miller, Michael B. (1981) *The Bon Marché. Bourgeois Culture and the Department Store, 1869–1920.* London: Allen & Unwin.

Mills, C. Wright (1956 [1951]) *White Collar. The American Middle Classes.* New York: Oxford University Press.

Murphy-Lawless, Jo (1992 [1988]) 'The Obstetric View of Feminine Identity: A Nineteenth Century Case History of the Use of Forceps in Ireland', in Ailbhe Smith (ed.) *The Abortion Papers: Ireland.* Dublin: Attic Press. pp. 66–84.

Ovid (1955 [8 AD]) *Metamorphoses*, translated by Mary M. Innes. Harmondsworth: Penguin.

Paget, Lady W. (1883) 'Common Sense in Dress and Fashion', *The Nineteenth Century*, 13, March: 458–64.

Parmentier, Richard (1994) *Signs in Society. Studies in Semiotic Anthropology.* Bloomington and Indianapolis: Indiana University Press.

Pearce, Philip L. (1982) *The Social Psychology of Tourist Behaviour.* Oxford: Pergamon Press.

Priestley, J.B. (1977 [1934]) *English Journey.* Harmondsworth: Penguin. Quoted in Featherstone (1991b [1982]).

Propp, Vladimir (1973 [1928]) *Morphologie du conte*, translated by Marguerite Derrida, Tzvetan Todorov and Claude Kahn. Paris: Seuil.

Recreations of a Country Parson (1861). London. Quoted in Forty (1986).

Reekie, Gail (1992) 'Changes in the Adamless Eden. The Spatial and Sexual Transformation of a Brisbane Department Store 1930–90', in Rob Shields (ed.) *Lifestyle Shopping. The Subject of Consumption.* London: Routledge. pp. 170–94.

Reekie, Gail (1993) *Temptations: Sex, Selling and the Department Store.* St. Leonards: Allen & Unwin.

Rees, Grace A. (1950) *Character Reading from the Face. The Science of Physiognomy.* Kingswood, Surrey: Andrew George Elliot.

Reich, Charles (1971) *The Greening of America.* New York: Bantam Books. Quoted in Davis (1989).

Richards, Lyn (1990) *Nobody's Home. Dreams and Realities in a New Suburb.* Melbourne: Oxford University Press.

Sahlins, Marshall (1976) *Culture and Practical Reason.* Chicago: University of Chicago Press.

Saunders, Peter (1986) *Social Theory and the Urban Question*, 2nd edition. London: Unwin Hyman.

Saussure, Ferdinand de (1974 [1916]) *Course in General Linguistics*, translated by Wade Baskin. London: Fontana/Collins.

Sennett, Richard (1978 [1976]) *The Fall of Public Man. On the Social Psychology of Capitalism.* New York: Vintage Books.

Shields, Rob (1992) 'Spaces for the Subject of Consumption', in Rob Shields (ed.) *Lifestyle Shopping. The Subject of Consumption.* London: Routledge. pp. 1–20.

Shilling, Chris (1993) *The Body and Social Theory*. London: Sage.

Simmel, Georg (1957 [1904]) 'Fashion', *American Journal of Sociology*, 62(6): 541–58.

Smith, Adam (1977 [1776]) *The Wealth of Nations*. London and Toronto: Dent.

Sontag, Susan (1979) *On Photography*. Harmondsworth: Penguin. Quoted in Urry (1990).

Sweetnam, Kim (ed.) (1994) *The Fossicker's Way Tourist Guide*. Inverell, NSW: The Inverell Times.

Tait, Gordon (1993) ' "Anorexia Nervosa": Asceticism, Differentiation, Government Resistance', *Australian and New Zealand Journal of Sociology*, 29(2): 194–208.

Tarde, Gabriel (1900) *Les Lois de l'imitation*, 3rd edition. Paris: Felix Alcan.

Thompson, E.P. (1967) 'Time, Work-Discipline, and Industrial Capitalism', *Past and Present*, 38, December: 56–97.

Thornton, Mary Anna (1987) '*Sekt* versus *Schnapps* in an Austrian Village', in Mary Douglas (ed.) *Constructive Drinking. Perspectives on Drink from Anthropology*. Cambridge: Cambridge University Press. pp. 102–12.

Tissot, Samuel Auguste David (1980 [1760]) *L'Onanisme. Dissertation sur les maladies produites par la masturbation*. Paris: Le Sycomore.

Tönnies, Ferdinand (1964 [1887]) *Community and Society*, translated and edited by Charles P. Loomis. East Lansing: Michigan State University Press.

Troubridge, Laura (1931 [1926]) *The Book of Etiquette*. Kingswood, Surrey: The World's Work.

Turner, Bryan S. (1992) *Regulating Bodies. Essays in Medical Sociology*. London: Routledge.

Urry, John (1990) *The Tourist Gaze. Leisure and Travel in Contemporary Societies*. London: Sage.

Veblen, Thorstein (1975 [1899]) *The Theory of the Leisure Class*. New York: Augustus M. Kelly.

Vialles, Noëlie (1994 [1987]) *Animal to Edible*, translated by J.A. Underwood. Cambridge: Cambridge University Press; Paris: La Maison des Sciences de l'Homme.

Vigarello, Georges (1987 [1985]) *Le Propre et le sale. L'hygiène du corps depuis le Moyen Âge*. Paris: Seuil, Collection Points Histoire.

Walker, Joseph Cooper (1788) *An Historical Essay on the Dress of the Ancient and Modern Irish*. Dublin: George Grierson.

Weber, Max (1948) 'Class, Status, Party', in H.H. Gerth and C. Wright Mills (eds) *From Max Weber: Essays in Sociology*. London: Routledge & Kegan Paul. pp. 180–95.

Weber, Max (1976 [1904]) *The Protestant Ethic and the Spirit of Capitalism*, translated by Talcott Parsons, 2nd edition. London: Allen & Unwin.

Weekend Australian (1996) Sydney: Nationwide News, 23–24 March.

Williamson, Judith (1978) *Decoding Advertisements. Ideology and Meaning in Advertising*. London: Marion Boyars.

Willis, Paul [with Simon Jones, Joyce Canaan and Geoff Hurd] (1990) *Common Culture*. Milton Keynes: Open University Press.

Windschuttle, Keith (1988) *The Media. A New Analysis of the Press, Television, Radio and Advertising in Australia*, 3rd edition. Ringwood: Penguin.

Winship, Janice (1987) *Inside Women's Magazines*. London: Pandora Press.

Index